MARKETING GEOGRAPHY

with special reference to retailing

MARKETING GEOGRAPHY

with special reference to retailing

Ross L. Davies

Department of Geography
University of Newcastle upon Tyne

Methuen & Co Ltd
London

First published in 1976
by Retailing and Planning Associates
Corbridge, Northumberland

First published as a University Paperback in 1977
by Methuen & Co Ltd, 11 New Fetter Lane
London EC4P 4EE

© 1976 Ross L. Davies

Printed in Great Britain by
Richard Clay (The Chaucer Press) Ltd
Bungay, Suffolk

ISBN 0 416 70700 9

Acknowledgements

Few academic books are written these days without the help and co-operation of a large number of people. My thanks are due to the following: Professor Peter Hall, who initially urged me to write the book; Professor Richard Lawton, who carefully guided me through the whole exercise and spent considerable time on editing the manuscript; Mr. Eric Quenet and Miss Christine Jeans who drew the maps and diagrams; Mrs. Doreen Shanks, who photographically reduced all the illustrative material; Mr. John Knipe, who supervised the cartographic and photographic procedures; Miss Jane Potts, Miss Yvonne Lambord, Mrs. Pat Bass, and my wife who collectively dealt with the typing involved. I hope there will be at least sufficient merit in this work to justify the support and encouragement that all these people have given me.

Acknowledgements are also due to the various authors and publishers who gave me permission to reproduce or adapt a large number of maps and diagrams from their own sources. These persons and firms are cited in the figure captions.

Contents

List of Illustrations

List of Tables

1 The Scope of Marketing Geography

Relatively little use has been made in Britain of the title 'marketing geography' to describe that aspect of geography which is concerned with tertiary economic activities and particularly the distributive trades. This is curious because there has been a traditional interest in the history of the market place in towns as the genesis of modern commercial practices and numerous, recent, theoretical investigations into the part played by market forces in shaping the locational patterns of different types of firms. There has been much more reference to marketing geography as a distinct field of enquiry in the USA, but mainly only in connection with certain specific studies on retailing. This book does not seek to establish the precise boundaries of the field and to provide a definitive treatise of its overall content. It attempts more modestly to draw together some selected work with common underlying themes.

Marketing, in a general business sense, is concerned with the identification of the demand for various goods and services and with the arrangements for the supply of these through an efficient distribution network. It is essentially that function of management that oversees the buying and selling of a firm's commodities. The strategies and policies involved in marketing are inevitably manifest in some spatial form. It is the areal expression which is given to the sources of demand and the areal structure of the systems of supply that provide the foundations for a geographic study of marketing.

The spatial context of marketing activities may be examined from two completely different scale perspectives, however.[1] On the one hand, it is possible to interpret marketing geography in broad, global terms as being mainly concerned with the inter-

1

national aspects of commerce and trade; in which case, attention might be focused on general patterns of overseas demand and the locations of major production centres of supply. This could involve, for example, the study of competing industrial operations within the European Common Market. On the other hand, it is possible to interpret marketing geography in much more narrow, local terms with an emphasis on those daily trading practices conducted by small business firms. In this case, the core focus of attention will be the distributive trades of retailing and related wholesaling and service activities, considered primarily from the standpoint of their consumer catchment areas and the business centres within which they are located. It is with this smaller-scale approach that the bulk of the work most appropriately labelled as marketing geography has been associated in recent years and with which this book is exclusively concerned.

THE SPECIFIC AMERICAN CONNOTATION OF MARKETING GEOGRAPHY

William Applebaum is widely regarded as the chief architect of marketing geography as a separate field of study in the United States. He defined the subject as being 'concerned with the de-limitation and measurement of markets and with the channels of distribution through which goods move from producer to consumer'.[2] By channels of distribution are meant the organisational systems of stores and centres utilised by the distributive trades; by markets are meant the catchment or trade areas for these stores and centres, which may range in size from small rural communities, through metropolitan spheres of influence, to entire national territories.

Applebaum has also emphasised that marketing geography should be viewed essentially as an applied, rather than a purely academic, subject. In his own work he has been concerned particularly with linking broad geographical insights to the decision-making functions of marketing in practice. Specifically, his work has focused on the contributions which marketing geography can make to store location research and forecasts about the business performance of individual firms. This has involved a close collaboration with mainly retailing companies and the development of research methodologies outside the academic environment. Applebaum considers 'the best place to develop the field of marketing geography is in business itself. The marketing geographer should either work for business full-time or should seek to conduct research for business on a part-time consultant basis.'[3] Applebaum, indeed, campaigned for the subject as a visiting lecturer to the Harvard Graduate School of Business Studies, rather than establishing himself within a geography department, and devised a teaching programme based on case-study methods of actual business decisions[4] rather than the extensive literature surrounding geographical theories of location.

This special relationship with practical work has been consolidated by other leading American marketing geographers, such as Saul Cohen, Howard Green and Bart Epstein. When Raymond Murphey introduced a special edition of the journal *Economic Geography* in 1961 under the title 'Marketing Geography Comes of Age'[5] he presented a range of mainly shopping studies exclusively concerned with actual business problems. More recently, Brian Berry, a leading protagonist of theoretical enquiry into marketing systems, has stated that 'marketing geography carries the retail interests of the geographer into practice within metropolitan areas, in the service of private business enterprise'.[6] The most clear-cut expression of the marketing geographer in practice in the USA is in the career of store location analysis.[7] This gained considerable momentum as a field of employment during the enormous changes in the pattern of retail distribution in the 1950s and 1960s that followed the widespread suburbanisation of American cities.

There has been relatively little development of this particular kind of marketing geography in Britain, however. In part, this is because there have been fewer entrenched linkages between academics and business concerns and the opportunities for consultancy work have been consequently more limited. A recent exception to this has been the creation of the Retail Outlets Research Unit at the University of Manchester under the directorship of David Thorpe. This establishment has undertaken a wide range of sponsored studies into new and future forms of retailing and also wholesaling activities.[8] More important than the lack of interchange between geographers and market practitioners in Britain, nevertheless, has been the fact that when changes in methods of business operations have taken place, the spatial implications of these have been severely governed by town and country planning regulations. The applied studies which have been made in marketing geography have therefore been much more conspicuously related to public planning problems than those of a private, business kind.

THE IMPORTANCE OF PLANNING CONTROL IN BRITAIN

The major changes in retail and related business methods of the last two decades (mainly in the development of chain groups of 'self-service' operations) have had a relatively limited spatial impact in Britain because the new stores have been usually forced by planning legislation to occupy sites in existing types of centres. There has been no widespread decentralisation of shopping facilities on the scale seen in the USA but rather a continued concentration of activities in the traditional main centres (or central areas) of towns as part of a national emphasis on re-development schemes. Whereas the overall business pattern in the USA is therefore effectively the result of speculative private enterprise, the business pattern in Britain is increasingly an expression of public planning controls, although a considerable legacy of unplanned Victorian distributions remains. This is not to deny that there have been increasing planning interventions in the USA, but their effect has been of an altogether much weaker (or alternatively, more flexible) kind.

The relevance of this strict British planning control for studies in marketing geography is twofold. First, many geographers have worked directly within the planning profession itself, just as many American geographers have worked in business companies, and have made substantive contributions to understanding and dealing with problems of a general marketing geography kind. The best-known practitioner is probably William Carruthers in his work for the former Ministry of Housing and also Greater London Council.[9] In addition, many geographers have worked in consultancy positions in planning, as for example Derek Diamond in forecasting the shopping capacities of New Towns,[10] Ronald Jones in classifying the distribution of suburban centres in Edinburgh,[11] and also this author in conducting consumer behaviour surveys to identify the functional use of shopping centres in Coventry.[12] Secondly, those engaged in marketing geography in Britain have generally been much more concerned with studies of the overall systems of supply and demand, mainly in studies of the broad pattern of city-wide shopping centres and the broad structure of consumer behaviour, when the Applebaum school of marketing geographers have been primarily interested in individual store locations and localised or particular customer demands.

Similar kinds of relationships between geography and planning have been increasingly fostered in the USA, however, and particularly by those concerned with the development and application of spatial theories of marketing. Foremost among these is Brian Berry whose work in central place theory has been extensively utilised for planning purposes in Chicago[13] and elsewhere. T. R. Lakshmanan and W. G. Hansen have also jointly contributed a major case study application from general interaction theory in their assessments of the growth capacities of new shopping centres in Baltimore.[14]

THE THEORETICAL BASES TO MARKETING GEOGRAPHY

Central place theory and general interaction theory provide the major frameworks for macro studies in marketing geography since they may be used to describe and explain aspects both of the structural system for the supply of goods and services and the spatial character of consumer demand. There are few branches of geography, in fact, which can claim such comprehensive theoretical terms of reference, and within which there has been as much exhaustive empirical research. Significantly, however, these theories have been less utilised in those applied studies most closely linked to marketing practice than those which are related to planning. Partly, this is because the studies geared to marketing practice take a more micro approach and are more heavily dependent on special policies within an individual firm; partly, it is because they reflect a different methodological perspective in the minds of the researchers. Berry has pointedly criticised the Applebaum school for their disregard of the potential utilities of employing theoretical frameworks. Specifically, he argues that 'the practice of marketing geography is to produce the basic figures required in central place theory'.[15]

Central place theory and also general interaction theory have been particularly important in a planning context in Britain. Central place theory has been used primarily as a rationale for determining the sizes and spacing standards of new shopping centres at both an urban and regional scale and also for evaluating the efficiencies of existing arrangements. The Distributive Trades Committee of the National Economic Development Office has recently recommended that the concept of the hierarchy, which lies at the root of this theory, remains the most suitable organisational basis for guiding the implementation of development controls.[16] General interaction theory, with its family of mathematical formulae called gravity models, has provided a more flexible avenue for specific forecasting purposes and especially in terms of trade area estimation and predicting the size capacities of shopping centres. Gravity models are currently the most commonly used techniques in this country for tracing the impact of changes within the retail system and testing the consequences of alternative future strategy designs.

It should be stressed, however, that neither of these theories has a universal relevance or application to the sum total of marketing activities. Central place theory provides little explanation for the main locational features of wholesaling trade;[17] general interaction theory offers little scope for simulating the major patterns of commercial as opposed to shopping movements. Even with respect to retailing activities, the two theories need careful qualification. The viewpoint expressed throughout this book is that the theories are primarily useful as reference frameworks which then need to be expanded and modified in the light of particular situations.

There are several additional theories which may be used in connection with certain specific aspects of marketing geography. It is sufficient at this stage to mention just two of these appropriate much more to a micro-scale level of enquiry. First, there is rent theory which is applicable to the evaluation of individual store sites and the internal land use characteristics of business centres.[18] Secondly, there is a loose collection of behavioural theories, many of which are linked to perception research and characterised as a 'cognitive-behavioural' approach,[19] and these have a special relevance to understanding the nature of individual consumer behaviour and store patronisation. These two particular theoretical avenues are important not only in furnishing a better insight into the complexities of small-scale activities but also in relating much more fully to those theoretical developments which have taken place in land economics and the business sciences.

In general, there has been a shift in emphasis in the theoretical interests of marketing geographers during the last two decades which closely parallels the changing emphasis in geography as a whole. Much of the early work in the so-called quantitative revolution was bound up with evaluations of central place theory and studies of retail structure. In the 1960s, much more attention was given to the concept of the 'distance-decay' function in geography and this involved considerable testing of gravity models, with considerable applications to the broader patterns of shopping movements. More lately, the general interests in behavioural studies and also social policy-oriented research within the discipline have been mirrored by numerous enquiries into individual consumer attitudes and preferences and the problems of dealing with minority tastes and demands.

THE MAIN THEMES

The emphasis in this book is on the spatial characteristics of retailing activities rather than the full spectrum of the distributive trades, not only because retailing is the dominant land use, but also because there has been much less geographical research into wholesaling and related service activities. The distributive trades will often be collectively referred to as business activities, however, particularly in the context of large centres where the term business or commercial complex is often more appropriate to use than that of shopping centre.

The first two chapters provide contrasting accounts of the theoretical bases to marketing geography and the factual setting of the distributive trades. These are then wedded together in succeeding chapters which deal with more specific topics and problems essentially linked around two complementary themes. The first deals mainly with the organisational structure of business supply. The relationship between the theoretical and empirical approaches to marketing geography is strongest in those studies with a traditional concern for describing the sizes and locations of business centres. This work is examined both in the context of national and regional systems of centres and of those at the urban scale. Special attention is given to the main centre or central area of the city where most business activities continue to be concentrated. These broadly descriptive chapters are then followed by a discussion of changes in the urban business pattern and the ways in which planners and business firms have dealt with the problems of renovating the old parts of the city and providing new types of facilities in the suburbs. The second theme is predominantly concerned with the spatial expression of consumer demand. Broad patterns of trade areas are initially examined and in the context of those theories which help to explain them. The major features of shopping behaviour are identified, as are emerging trends in consumer tastes and preferences. These have clear implications for the future organisation of shopping provision which is then discussed in relation to forecasting techniques that can be used in planning. More detailed aspects of individual consumer behaviour are treated separately and in relation to the problems involved in store location research. The final chapter of the book focuses on those major developments which are likely to occur in the future, both in terms of consumer demand and in terms of business supply.

REFERENCES

1. For a broad definition of the scope of marketing geography, see Dawson, J. A., 'Marketing Geography' in Dawson, J. A. and Doornkamp, J. C. (eds.), *Evaluating the Human Environment: Essays in Applied Geography* (Edward Arnold, 1973).
2. Applebaum, W., 'Marketing Geography' in James, P. E. and

Jones, C. F. (eds.), *American Geography: Inventory and Prospect* (Syracuse University Press, 1954).

3. Applebaum, W. *ibid.*

4. Applebaum, W., 'Teaching Marketing Geography by the Case Method', *Economic Geography*, **37** (1961), 48–60.

5. Murphey, R. (ed.), Special Issue of *Economic Geography*, **37** (1961).

6. Berry, B. J. L., *Geography of Market Centres and Retail Distribution* (Prentice-Hall, 1967).

7. For examples of this work, see the papers by Applebaum and others in Kornblau, C. (ed.), *Guide to Store Location Research: With Emphasis on Supermarkets* (Addison-Wesley, 1968).

8. See, for example Thorpe, D., 'The Density of Cash and Carry Wholesaling', *Manchester University Business School, Retail Outlets Research Unit, Report No. 2* (1971); Thorpe, D. and Kivell, P. T., 'Woolco: Thornaby—A Study of an Out-of-Town Shopping Centre', *Manchester University Business School, Retail Outlets Research Unit, Report No. 3* (1971).

Several sponsored studies have also been undertaken in the Geography Department at the University of Newcastle. See, for example, Davies, R. L., 'Evaluation of Retail Store Attributes and Sales Performance', *European Journal of Marketing*, **7** (1973), 89–102.

9. Carruthers undertook a study for the Royal Commission on Local Government in Greater London (1957–60). The results are contained in Carruthers, W. I., 'Service Centres in Greater London', *Town Planning Review*, **33** (1962), 5–31.

10. Diamond, D. and Gibb, E. B., 'Development of New Shopping Centres: Area Estimation', *Scottish Journal of Political Economy*, **9** (1962), 130–46; 'Shopping Provision' in *The Lothians Regional Survey and Plan*, **1** (1966).

11. Jones, R., 'Retail Facilities in the City of Edinburgh', University of Edinburgh, Dept. of Geography (1963); Edinburgh Planning Department, *Shopping Report, 1968* (Edinburgh Royal Burgh Corporation, 1968).

12. Davies, R. L., 'Patterns and Profiles of Consumer Behaviour', *University of Newcastle, Dept. of Geography, Research Series 10* (1973); Coventry Planning Department, *Corporate Planning Survey Report, 1972, vol. 7, The Promotion of Commercial and Industrial Development* (Coventry Corporation, 1972).

13. Berry, B. J. L., 'Commercial Structure and Commercial Blight', *University of Chicago, Dept. of Geography, Research Paper 85* (1963).

14. Lakshmanan, T. R. and Hansen, W. G., 'A Retail Market Potential Model', *Journal of the American Institute of Planners*, **31** (1965), 134–43.

15. Berry, B. J. L., *Geography of Market Centres and Retail Distribution* (Prentice-Hall, 1967).

16. National Economic Development Office, Committee for the Distributive Trades, *Urban Models in Shopping Studies* (1970).

17. A separate theory to explain the evolution of wholesaling is proposed in Vance, J. E., *The Merchant's World: The Geography of Wholesaling* (Prentice-Hall, 1970).

18. The importance and contributions of rent theory to marketing geography are demonstrated in Scott, P., *Geography and Retailing* (Hutchinson, 1970).

19. For a definition of this approach, see Garner, B. J., 'Towards a Better Understanding of Shopping Patterns' in *Geographical Essays in Honour of K. C. Edwards* (Nottingham University, 1970).

2 Traditional and Theoretical Frameworks of Study

Most of the conceptual work in marketing geography has focused on the relationships between business centres and their surrounding trade areas. These relationships have been considered at both a regional and urban scale of enquiry, and in terms of a full range of business activities or alternatively a particular activity such as retailing. In addition, they have been examined both from detailed field, empirical research and from the point of view of theoretical abstractions.

More important than these differences in scale, content and methodology, however, is a fundamental distinction in the conceptual literature concerning the purpose of these studies. On the one hand, many studies have been undertaken to serve as case examples of very broad issues in urban and economic geography, such as the general interaction which takes place between town and country. On the other hand, other studies have been much more firmly rooted to actual marketing problems, dealing with the specific interaction between business firms and their customers. Sometimes, of course, the precise objectives of a study are not made clear and there is a considerable blurring between the two sets of aims.

The essential difference between the general and specific studies may be seen in the traditional empirical literature in the following way. From the 1930s until the early 1950s there was considerable interest within geography as a whole in defining the notion of the functional region (in contradistinction to the formal region), and especially in terms of the city-region. Many case studies were undertaken using map plots of shopping movements, retail deliveries, and wholesale shipments as general indicators of the extent of city regions. Over the same period,

11

a growing awareness for the spatial complexity of business activities led to more in-depth studies of the distributive trades for their own sake. Some of this work remained primarily descriptive of the main patterns to be observed; other work became much more distinctly applied to practical problems confronting the marketing and planning professions.

A parallel is to be found in the more recent theoretical literature. Central place theory and general interaction theory, for example, have been used both in connection with studies of broad settlement patterns and general population movements, and in more detailed descriptions and specifications about the locations and sizes of certain types of shopping centres. Even those models based on rent theory and perception research which relate more to the micro-scale levels of marketing activity represent analogous extensions from more general kinds of studies treating a wide mix of land uses in rural as well as urban environments.

TRADITIONAL STUDIES OF CENTRES AND TRADE AREAS

We have suggested that in the past the core interest of marketing geography has been determination of the relative business importance or status of centres and the delimitation of the boundaries of their trade areas and that this has led to two different but complementary types of studies. First, a number of studies have applied the terms 'centres' and 'trade areas' to entire urban places and the broad spheres of influence which they exert over the countryside. These have primarily been concerned with assessing the external relationships of towns and cities. Secondly, a number of alternative studies have applied the terms 'centres' and 'trade areas' more precisely to particular kinds of business complexes (usually shopping centres) and the specific territories from which their customers are drawn. These have mainly, although not exclusively, been concerned with the internal relationships of towns and cities.

Studies of External Relationships

The majority of studies made before and just after the Second World War focused on the extent to which different settlements act as market centres, or service centres or central places. This involved a ranking of their overall business importance using selected criteria. The main methods employed consisted of either counting the numbers of establishments for certain activities, such as shops, wholesaling depots and offices, or recording the presence and absence of particular types of functions and firms. These were then compared against the population sizes of the settlements to see whether an excess or deficiency of business provisions occurred. In some cases, it was possible to use more precise data, as in Dickinson's ranking of market centres in East Anglia according to the volume of livestock sales recorded.[1] In other cases, a wide range of social as well as economic indicators were brought together, as in Smailes' ranking of all the major towns and cities in Britain, using such criteria as the number of secondary schools and hospitals, as well as the incidence of banks and cinemas and newspapers.[2] Usually, these studies drew on documentary information rather than on detailed land use surveys.

A similar reliance on broad indicators or proxy variables characterised those studies aimed at delimiting the boundaries of urban spheres of influence, which have been variously called hinterlands, umlands and urban fields. Several separate boundary lines for different movement criteria were compared on maps and then a compromise or best-fit general approximation to these subjectively derived. Smailes used the range of retail deliveries, wholesale shipments and newspaper circulations to ascertain the 'urban field' of Middlesbrough.[3] Howard Green combined a wide range of flow data about transport services, newspaper circulations and telephone calls with land-use studies of agriculture, manufacturing and recreation to measure the precise break in metropolitan spheres of influence of New York and Boston.[4] Many geographers, and particularly F. H. W. Green, made use of data on bus service provisions between towns in an age when public transit systems were by far the greatest means of general population movements[5] (Figure 2.1).

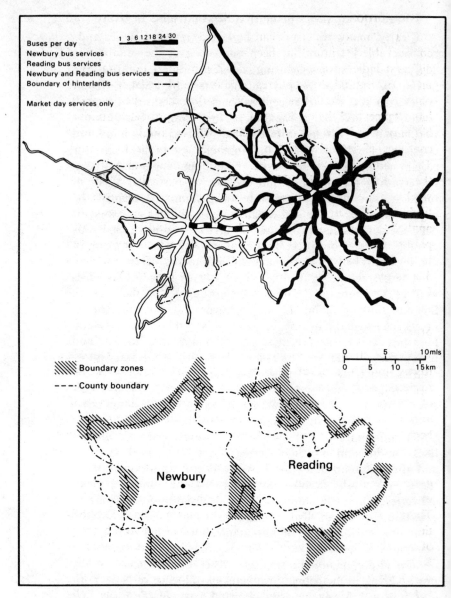

FIG. 2.1 *Former trade areas of Reading and Newbury based on the frequency and direction of radiating bus services.* (After Green, F. H. W., 'Urban Hinterlands in England and Wales: An Analysis of Bus Services', *The Geographical Journal*, **66**, 1950, 64–81)

Clearly, many criticisms can be levied at these studies and a considerable literature has been built up over the suitability of different indices for measuring both the business importance of urban places and their spheres of influence. A number of more objective ratio methods have been developed to index business importance; and the tradition of a single, compromise boundary has tended to be replaced by a graded series of lines representing contours of intensity in the functional use made of centres. These are discussed later in connection with more recent theoretical case studies. Nevertheless, much of the traditional work provided useful 'rules-of-thumb' for comparing centres and trade areas at a regional level, and these were subsequently applied to many marketing and planning problems.[6] Two major publications which reflect these methods and which have proved to be important practical manuals are Geographia Limited's *Marketing Areas Handbook*[7] of Britain and Rand McNally's *Commercial Atlas and Marketing Guide*[8] of the USA.

Studies of Internal Relationships

The early studies of business centres and trade areas inside towns and cities differed from the regional enquiries in two respects: more interest was shown in classifying different types of centres as well as distinguishing between their size levels in importance; there was also more common use of field surveys, both land-use inventories and consumer questionnaires, especially in relation to studies of individual centres or trade areas.

Amongst the first full classifications of the urban business pattern were Applebaum's study of Cincinnati[9] and Rolph's study of Baltimore,[10] both conducted at the beginning of the 1930s. These not only examined variations in the functional compositions of centres, but also clearly distinguished between a range of different locations and forms. The typologies recognised by Rolph, in particular, influenced a number of subsequent studies which were later linked to theoretical concepts to become the basis for most of the modern American classifications. His main distinction lay between a series of centres proper, described as the central shopping district, neighbourhood centres and sub-centres, and a set of non-concentrated developments and string-streets. Other studies gave special attention to the competition between the central area and suburban centres, particularly in the late 1940s and early 1950s.[11] These were also paralleled by numerous enquiries into consumer attitudes towards traditional 'downtown' shopping provisions versus the newly expanding suburban opportunities.[12]

Many special techniques for conducting in-depth field surveys were developed within the marketing and planning professions. Much more detail about the physical characteristics of particular centres and the socio-economic characteristics of their customers was required for store location research purposes and for dealing with growth problems. Thus assessments of the relative attractiveness of particular centres paid considerable attention to such variables as floorspace, car parking provision and bus-staging points, the layout of shops, and the number and mix of business activities found. Similarly, various kinds of trade area boundaries were mapped according to population income differences and for different shopping trip purposes, such as those for convenience goods versus durable goods or specialty goods. Once again Applebaum pioneered much of the scope and content of these studies which remain important features of the present-day marketing and planning literature.[13]

Most of the land-use survey methods used to distinguish between types of business activities have been based on the categorisations of the distributive trades listed in the American Census of Business and the British Census of Distribution. These classificatory procedures have been linked with a variety of mapping and visual appraisal techniques to determine the form as well as the functions of any centre. The delimitation of trade areas from consumer questionnaire surveys has mainly been accomplished in two ways: either by 'pavement' or 'store-based' types of interviews, where the investigator stands at some focal position within a centre or inside a shop and solicits passers-by as to where they have come from; or, alternatively, by 'home' interviews, where the investigator visits people in their residences and asks them which centre or stores they most frequently go to. The 'pavement' type surveys have generally been preferred in trade area studies since they allow larger samples to be collected more quickly and cheaply. However, 'home' interview procedures permit more in-depth studies of consumer behaviour and have been extensively used in broader shopping enquiries. An important refinement of this technique is the 'diary' type of survey, in which consumers keep actual records of the details of their trips over several days. A 'diary' survey undertaken for the city planning department in Cedar Rapids, Iowa, in 1947,[14] subsequently became a major data source for testing various central place theory postulates in America for more than two decades.[15]

CENTRAL PLACE THEORY

Central place theory was originally formulated by the German economist and geographer, Walter Christaller, in the early 1930s[16] but its most extensive examination and utilisation in the English-speaking world has occurred in relatively recent times. In general terms, the theory seeks to explain an apparent order in the spatial distribution of urban settlements. This order is most conspicuous in the sizes and spacing of those settlements particularly important for providing goods and services to surrounding populations, and described as central places. The theory, however, does not account for urban growth characteristics arising from industrial or other productive forces. It is concerned much more specifically with explaining regularities in the locations of tertiary activities as these are manifest in business centres. It was considered by Christaller as complementary to Weber's theory of industrial location[17] and von Thunen's theory of agricultural location.[18] The basic postulates depend on a similar set of assumptions involving isotropic conditions, namely a featureless plain with equal densities in rural population and uniform levels of purchasing power.

The Classical Model

It is possible to understand the mechanism of the theory both in terms of a set of economic constraints operating on individual firms and by examining the geometrical relationships of complexes of firms or centres in the idealised landscape.[19] The former approach is useful for tracing the growth processes involved in the emergence of an optimum business or settlement pattern; the latter approach gives greater clarification to the structural regularities that are found.

1. There are two main economic constraints which control the potential locations of individual firms. First, there must always be some minimum level of consumer demand or lower limit of trade area support for any particular firm to make a profit and become established. Secondly, the effective size of this demand or trade area support will be circumscribed to an upper limit, defined as the maximum distance consumers will be prepared to journey to that firm before going elsewhere. The combined result of these constraints is that firms engaged in the convenience trades become densely distributed over the landscape, since they can survive from the frequent visits of a small local population; firms engaged in more specialised trades become much more widely dispersed, since they can exist from the occasional visits of a larger, non-local population. When a further constraint is introduced, that no firms are allowed to make excess profits, and hence all trade areas for a common type of good become equivalent in size, it will be seen that the firms engaged in the same line of trade become spaced at equal distances apart, as shown in Figure 2.2. In a more realistic situation, the individual firms collect together as business complexes, but it is only certain of these which then grow in status and size. It is the business complexes most highly centralised with respect to the whole region which attract the most specialised and greatest number of activities and emerge as the dominant centres and central places. They continue to perform all the same functions as smaller centres besides offering goods unique to themselves.

2. The precise locations of the largest centres in relation to the smaller ones may be found when the trade areas for these are depicted as being hexagonally shaped. Hexagons represent the nearest geometrical equivalents to circles and when superimposed on the idealised plain allow for every parcel of territory, and thus every rural dweller, to be aligned with specific centres.

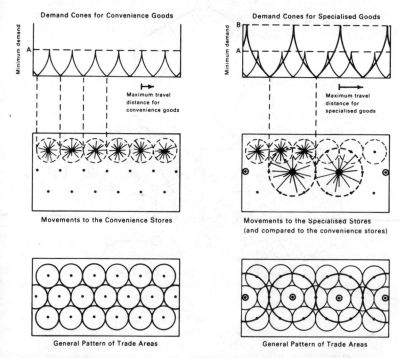

FIG. 2.2   *The process involved in the development of equi-distant business firms and their trade areas.* It is assumed that there is perfect competition within the idealised landscape and each of the two types of stores shown conduct similar lines of trade. The relationship between the level of demand for convenience versus specialised goods and the distances consumers are prepared to travel for them dictates the relative locations of firms and the overall sizes of their trade areas.

(A network of circles would leave either unaffiliated intersticial areas if tangentially arranged or provide some rural customers with a choice in centres to visit if overlapped with one another.) Assuming that the locations of the single most dominant centres are known, then the locations of the next largest centres will occur exactly at the midpoints between three of these, or at the apexes of their hexagonal trade areas. Figure 2.3 indicates that the hexagons of these next largest centres will be equal in size to those trade areas for the same type of 'lower order' goods in

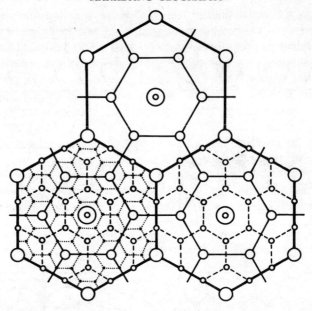

Fig. 2.3 *The arrangement of centres and trade areas according to Christaller's classical (marketing) model.* The diagram shows how the locations of successively smaller-sized centres and trade areas may be worked out in relation to the largest ones to produce a complicated honeycomb effect.

the most important centres. For successively smaller levels of centres, further locations will be determined at the midpoints between three larger centres or the apexes of their hexagonal trade areas. It will then be seen that any one centre is always surrounded by six lesser important centres.

The regularities observed in these geometrical locational relationships and also the growth processes behind them lead to specific rules about the frequencies in occurrence of different sizes of centres and trade areas. In the case of centres, there is a progression from one single largest centre to two at the next size level, then 6, 18, 54 and so on (in multiplicities of three). This may be understood in relation to Diagram A in Figure 2.4. Although for the largest centre shown there appears to be six next smaller centres, these are located on the boundary of the highest order trade area and only part of them, equivalent to one third of each (or two whole centres), actually lend support to the largest centre. At the next level, that of the smallest centres, however, six of these are entirely enclosed within the main trade area and hence direct all of their support to the largest centre. The frequency progression for trade areas, on the other hand, follows immediately with multiplicities of three, so that for one single largest trade area, there will be three at the next size level, then 9, 27, 81 and so on. In reference to the diagram again, it will be seen that the largest trade area is made up from six third-parts of the trade areas of second-level centres plus the trade area of the largest centre for

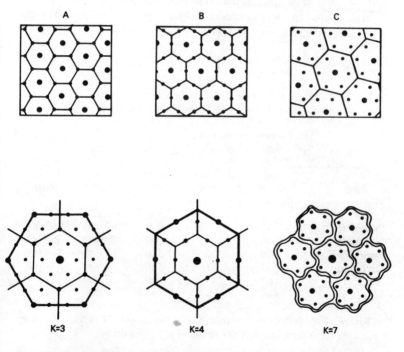

FIG. 2.4 *A comparison of the main features of Christaller's alternative trade area arrangements.* A. The perfect marketing case; B. Where there have been transportation influences; C. Where there have been administrative boundary effects.

second-order goods. This consistent progression by three in the case of trade area size relationships has come to be known as the K proportionality factor.

Although Christaller provided detailed specifications about the frequencies in occurrence of centres and trade areas, he gave no formal indication of the precise sizes of different centres or trade areas; since the number of people and activities to be found will always depend on any initial assumptions made about the density of rural dwellers or purchasing power within the original landscape. The only rules that apply to size relationships, therefore, are that centres will become organised into discrete size levels or tier groups as a *hierarchy* of centres; trade areas will become organised into a network of interlocking hexagons as a *nested* pattern arrangement. Some rough estimates to illustrate the characteristics of these in predominantly agricultural regions were provided by Christaller and are reproduced in Table 2.1.

TABLE 2.1

Christaller's Examples of Size Characteristics for Centres and Trade Areas in Agricultural Regions (c. 1930)

Type	Theoretical Number of Centres	Theoretical Number of Trade Areas	No. of Types of Goods Offered	Typical Population of Centres	Typical Population of Trade Areas
Landstadt	1	1	2,000	500,000	3,500,000
Provinzstadt	2	3	1,000	100,000	1,000,000
Gaustadt	6	9	600	30,000	350,000
Bezirkstadt	18	27	330	10,000	100,000
Kreisstadt	54	81	180	4,000	35,000
Amtsort	162	243	90	2,000	11,000
Marktort	486	729	40	1,000	3,500

Source: Christaller, W. (translated by Baskin, C.), *Central Places in Southern Germany* (Prentice-Hall, 1966).

Extensions to the Theory

There have been three principal ways in which the classical

'marketing' model has been developed and modified in theoretical terms. First, Christaller himself sought to improve the realism of the model by tracing the impact of certain major distorting influences.[20] Secondly, Lösch showed how a whole series of different types of central place systems could be derived through various geometrical manipulations.[21] Thirdly, Berry and Garrison re-formulated the basic tenets of the theory in much more flexible terms than had previously been the case and extended the model to include the internal characteristics of urban areas as well as their external relationships with the rural environment.[22]

1. Christaller's Modifications

Christaller considered the problem of what would happen to the locational relationships of centres and trade areas if consumers in the idealised landscape were influenced in their movements by either the provision of a transport network or the super-imposition of a series of administrative boundary lines. In the original model, all consumers have complete freedom of move-ment in any direction. The implication is that consumers would either have improved access to certain centres rather than others because of the availability of channels of communication, or alternatively they would be constrained to visit certain centres rather than others because of political enactments.

The conditional response to these influences on the pattern of locational relationships is shown in Diagrams B and C of Figure 2.4. It is assumed that the transportation network is an optimum one connecting all centres and that the administrative network divides up the landscape into equal political units. The effect in the transportation case is that smaller centres, instead of locating at the midpoints of the three larger centres, position themselves exactly halfway along the major communica-tion lines between pairs of larger centres. This produces a re-alignment in the arrangement of trade areas whereby centres become located on the sides of hexagons rather than at their apexes. The K proportionality factor then becomes four and frequency specifications for centres and trade areas are respec-tively 1, 3, 12, 48, 192 etc. and 1, 4, 16, 64, 256 etc. By contrast, the effect of administrative division is that smaller centres become allocated to the political territories of larger centres and wholly enclosed within their hexagons. The minimum most efficient arrangement is for six smaller centres to be subsumed in this way. The K proportionality factor thus becomes seven and frequency specifications for centres and trade areas are respectively 1, 6, 42, 294 etc. and 1, 7, 49, 343 etc.

2. Lösch's Modifications

Lösch examined the geometry of hexagonal-shaped trade areas in much greater detail than Christaller and initially from the point of view of individual goods supplied by individual firms rather than the relationships between whole centres. He demonstrated that a wide range of different sizes and alignments of trade areas

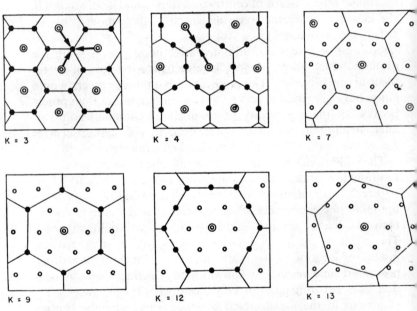

Fig. 2.5 *Further trade area arrangements according to Lösch's geometrical manipulations.* These are mainly the result of enlarging the sizes of trade areas and changing their directional alignment. (After Haggett, P., *Locational Analysis in Human Geography*, Edward Arnold, 1965)

would be required to support the varying lines of trade offered and that these would then dictate the locations actually occupied by firms. Several of these alternative trade area possibilities are shown in Figure 2.5. Since settlements comprise complexes of activities, however, a single optimum pattern for these should be determined from the average of all the conceivable trade area arrangements or the most common incidence in positions of the firms providing the goods. To find the optimum pattern, in fact, Lösch had to geometrically tilt and swivel the entire range of different trade area networks about a base set of smallest centres until a maximum coincidence in location was achieved. This resulted in an extremely complicated solution, part of which is shown in Figure 2.6.

There are three particularly significant features in the final pattern. First, there are certain areas in the landscape which contain a dense distribution of centres and others with a relative sparseness. These are conspicuous in six separate sectors. Secondly, when the size relationships of the total number of centres are plotted in profile, the distinctive stepped-like hierarchy postulated by Christaller becomes blurred and the centres form much more of a size-continuum. Thirdly, the functional structures of the centres are such that those of similar size will not necessarily offer the same types of goods as each other; likewise, larger centres will not necessarily provide the complete range of goods to be found collectively in smaller centres.

3. Berry and Garrison's Modifications

The contribution of Berry and Garrison to central place theory is much more distinctive than the others in being firmly rooted to empirical research. From extensive case study applications in the USA[23] they found that the structural regularities of the hierarchy proposed by Christaller seemed to occur in reality despite the absence of those isotropic conditions originally postulated in the theory. In other words, hierarchies could be observed in areas of unequal population density and unequal purchasing power. Typically these take the form of a five-tier structure: the hamlet, village, town, city and metropolis (or regional capital). However,

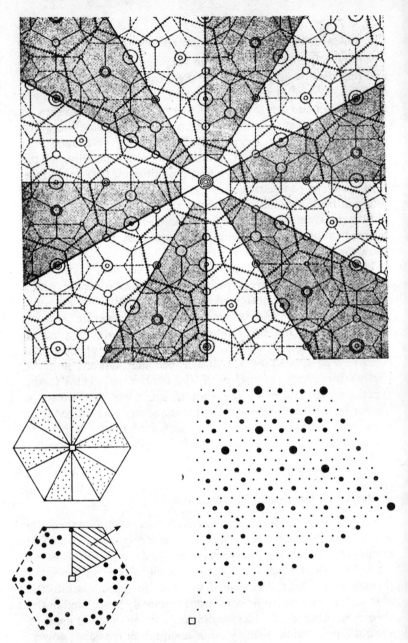

FIG. 2.6 Part of the Löschian complex landscape with extracts of the main features involved. A. The city-rich and city-poor sectors; B. The distribution of the larger cities; C. The distribution of all types of centres to be found within one sector. (After Isard, W., *Location and Space Economy*, M.I.T., 1956)

the same studies gave less clear evidence of there being distinct nested patterns of trade areas within real world landscapes.

Berry and Garrison also showed that hierarchies of centres may be observed inside individual urban areas, particularly metropolitan areas, as well as within the settlement system as a whole. These urban hierarchies essentially comprise a set of compact or nucleated shopping centres, and the following five-tier structure has been described: isolated corner stores, neighbourhood shopping centres, community (or district) shopping centres, regional shopping centres and the central business district. This extension of the hierarchy principle for explaining the internal characteristics of urban areas led Berry and Garrison to designating central-place theory as part of a wider theory of tertiary activity.[24]

The theory of tertiary activity is based on two concepts: the notion of *threshold* (which constitutes the minimum level of demand necessary to support a business activity, or the conditions of market entry) and the *range of a good* (which reflects the maximum distance consumers will be prepared to travel to a firm, or the spatial extent of its trade area). The interrelationships between these are sufficiently regular to lead to a hierarchical differentiation of centres though not to a formal arrangement to hexagonal trade areas. This lack of order in the patterns of trade areas arises primarily because certain centres may now earn excess profits while others become deficient in profitability.[25] Generally speaking, this freer interpretation of central place theory, with its emphasis much more on the structure of centres rather than pattern of trade areas, has been adopted as the main framework for most of the recent empirical work.[26]

Assessments of the Theory

The vast empirical literature which has grown up around central place theory may be broadly separated into two kinds:[27] first, those studies concerned primarily with testing and evaluating the various postulates of the theory; secondly, those studies which have been more concerned with utilising aspects of the theory for both descriptive and planning purposes. Several examples of the two sets of studies are examined in detail in later chapters;

the intention here is to introduce the general nature of the work and indicate the main limitations of the theory and the uses to which it has been put.

There has been considerable support both for and against the overall effectiveness of central place theory in explaining the locational relationships of centres and their trade areas. Unfortunately, much of the serious debate about its relevance has been coloured by a negative type of criticism which rejects outright the appropriateness of any high degree of abstraction for dealing with the real world. This criticism focuses particularly on the assumptions made about underlying isotropic conditions and the rational economic behaviour of consumers. Against this, there have been others who have tended to claim too much for the theory and who have taken it beyond its original limited intentions. Specifically, this has occurred when the theory has been used to provide a general explanation for the sizes and spacing of all settlements (or alternatively all shopping centres inside cities) regardless of the extent to which they actually function as central places or not.

The main weaknesses of the theory are that it is extremely rigid and deterministic and that it describes a mainly static set of locational relationships.[28] It refers exclusively to a range of business and related service activities that respond to the single process of centralisation and, within the context of real world situations, it is difficult to distinguish these from other activities which reflect much more on agglomerative and other forces. This inability to properly differentiate centralised versus non-centralised activities consequently means that it is virtually impossible to verify precise specifications about frequencies of centres and networks of trade areas without substantial statistical analyses and data transformations. Likewise, there are no summary mathematical formulae which can be easily manipulated and adapted to suit local conditions on the ground, for those models which have been formulated usually assume that a fixed K proportionality factor can be empirically derived.[29] Any forecasting or projection of the size relationships of centres in practical terms has therefore to be accomplished by other means (mainly regression analysis).[30]

In contrast to these limitations, the broader notions of the theory, particularly the hierarchy construct, have given extremely useful terms of reference and organisational concepts within which to examine systematic regularities in settlements and shopping centres. Indeed, many studies have utilised the hierarchy construct with little conscious reference to the theory that surrounds it.[31] The main purpose has been to provide a general classification of size orders within which individual settlements and/or shopping centres may be more consistently compared. Such studies have either been descriptive of the actual states of a system at any one time, or alternatively they have been prescriptive of optimum states to be realised in the future.

Many of the descriptive studies of hierarchies are similar both in their broad objectives and in their methodological perspective to those traditional and non theoretical studies which were reviewed earlier; in fact there has really been much blending of the two types of approach as we will elaborate in Chapter 4. For the moment, it is worth illustrating two examples of the more strict applications of the theoretical approach to describing hierarchies of centres. These are drawn from Christaller's own case study of settlements in Southern Germany[32] and Berry and Garrison's case study of settlements in Snohomish County, Washington State.[33] Figure 2.7 shows in map form the resulting hierarchy of central places obtained from ranking settlements according to the volume of their telephone calls; Figure 2.8 shows in graph profile the size differentiation of centres worked out from relationships between total numbers of business activities and population size.

The prescriptive studies of hierarchies undertaken in planning have been mainly used to provide guide-lines for the development control of centres. Occasionally, these have taken the form of master plan elements for the creation of new settlements (as in the Dutch polderlands) or new shopping centres (as in the case of New Towns in Britain); more commonly, they have been used as a broad format for notional standards about the future size capacities and spacing arrangements of existing settlements or shopping centres.[34] The hierarchy concept has been especially important in urban planning in Britain, where it represents the main organisational principle not only for retail provisions but also for educational, medical and other welfare services.

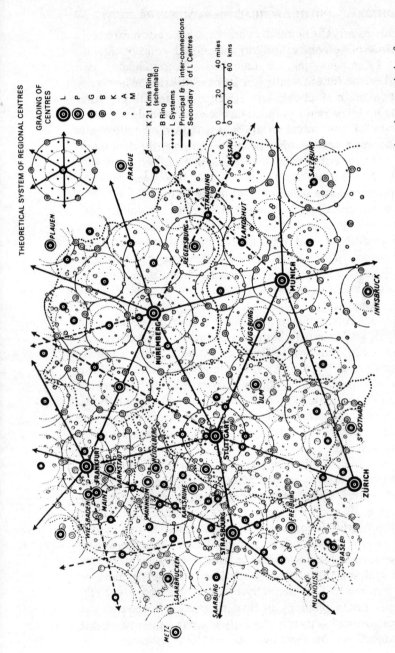

FIG. 2.7 *The hierarchy of central places in Southern Germany* (c. 1930). Some average-size characteristics for the places identified in the key are given in Table 1. The English name equivalents are: L. Regional capital city; P. Provincial head city; G. Small state capital; B. District city; K. County seat; A. Township centre; M. Market hamlet. (From Christaller, W., translated by Baskin, C., *Central Places in Southern Germany*, Prentice-Hall, 1966)

GENERAL INTERACTION THEORY

General interaction theory differs from central place theory in three fundamental respects. First, it provides less of an explanation for the growth processes behind centres and their trade areas than a simple account of the controls which affect the interaction between them. As the name implies, it is essentially a theory of movement rather than a theory of location.[35] Secondly, general interaction theory is a much less formally constituted theory with neither so strong and logical a sequence

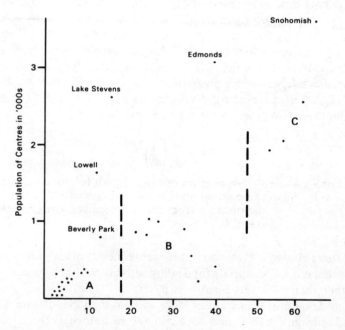

FIG. 2.8   *The hierarchy of central places in Snohomish County, Washington State.* Grouping tendencies amongst these settlements were first identified through 'nearest-neighbour' analysis techniques. Significant functional differences between the three size-orders shown were then confirmed by an analysis of variance. (After Berry, B. J. L. and Garrison, W. L., 'The Functional Bases of the Central Place Hierarchy', *Economic Geography*, **34**, 1958, 145–54)

of postulates nor so rigid a set of underlying assumptions as those contained in central place theory. It is mainly composed of a loose collection of mathematical equations, linked around a gravity concept analogous to Newton's law in physics. Thirdly, general interaction theory is a much broader body of theory to the extent that the so-called gravity models have been variously applied to many different kinds of interaction, including population migration, journeys to work, and assorted traffic flows, as well as shopping movements. Central place theory, on the other hand, is specifically formulated as a theory about marketing behaviour.

William Reilly was the first to demonstrate the applicability of gravity models to marketing geography in the early 1930s with his *Law of Retail Gravitation*.[36] Like other contemporary work this was specified in terms of the interaction between very large settlements. It states that 'two cities attract trade from an intermediate town in the vicinity of the breaking point approximately in direct proportion to the populations of the two cities and in inverse proportion to the squares of the distances from these two cities to the intermediate town'.

$$\frac{T_a}{T_b} = \frac{P_a}{P_b}\left(\frac{d_b}{d_a}\right)^2$$

where T_a, T_b = the proportion of trade drawn to cities a and b
P_a, P_b = the population sizes of cities a and b
d_a, d_b = the distance from the intermediate town to cities a and b

Three kinds of development have subsequently made the gravity concept more appropriate for dealing with urban shopping centres rather than with settlements as a whole.[37] The variables have been defined in terms much more specific than population size and mileage distance, and have come to be known as the attraction and deterrence factors. The relative decline in frequencies of trips away from centres, characterised as a 'distance-decay' function, has been shown to approximate a variety of negative exponential curves and hence can take on other values than the inverse square. The case of just two centres competing against each other has been expanded to accommodate a whole system of shopping centres. Most of the recent models particularly focus on the relationship between consumer expenditure and retail sales. The common root formula is:

$$S_{ij} = K_i E_i A_j F(d_{ij})$$

subject to the constraints

$$\sum_{i=1}^{n} S_{ij} = S_j; \ \sum_{i=1}^{n} S_{ij} = E_i$$

where S_{ij} = expenditure in a centre j by consumers in an area i
   E_i = expenditures available in area i
   A_j = a measure of shopping attractiveness at centre j
   S_j = retail sales generated at centre j
$F(d_{ij})$ = a measure of travel deterrence from i to j

   K_i = a constant of proportionality $\dfrac{1}{\sum_{j=1}^{n} A_j} F(d_{ij})$ which may

   also be interpreted as a competition term or balancing factor.

However, there have always been two particular types of problem to which both the older, general models and newer, specialised models have been applied. The first concerns the delimitation of trade area dimensions around centres. The second concerns an assessment of the growth potential for either urban places as a whole or specific shopping complexes.

Models of Trade Area Dimensions

Reilly's original gravity model has been reformulated to determine the exact position within an intermediate area where trade becomes split between two competing centres.[38] This has been described as a 'break-point' model and takes the form:

$$D_b = \frac{d_{ab}}{1 + \sqrt{\dfrac{P_a}{P_b}}}$$

where P_a, P_b = the sizes of centres a and b
   D_b = the break-point distance of trade to centre b
   d_{ab} = the distance between centres a and b

An example of the arithmetic involved in this is shown in Table 2.2. When such break-points are found for several pairs of places within a region they can be joined together by inter-polation and a set of trade area boundaries constructed. This is demonstrated in Figure 2.9. Such trade area delimitations, how-ever, are only meaningful for settlements of a broadly similar size, for single boundary lines cannot adequately represent the variability in shopping patterns for a wide range of goods. It has been found particularly useful to employ the break-point model in conjunction with a hierarchical classification of centres, for different levels of boundary lines can then be computed for different orders of goods.[39] In a perfect central place system of settlements, this would lead to the derivation of hexagonal-shaped trade areas as the diagram indicates.

The break-point model is further limited to the extent that it reveals little about the profile of the distance-decay curve in trip frequencies to centres. In addition, while it is often possible to identify precise breaks between trade areas, especially in rural situations and strongly planned urban environments, there also commonly exists an overlapping of trade areas which the model fails to depict. A more recent model by Huff,[40] initially tested against intra-urban shopping movements, gives greater scope to these considerations. It is formulated as a series of probabilities of consumers choosing to visit one centre from a set of competing centres:

$$P_{ij} = \frac{\dfrac{F_j}{d_{ij}^{\alpha}}}{\dfrac{F_1}{d_{i1}^{\alpha}} + \dfrac{F_2}{d_{i2}^{\alpha}} + \cdots \dfrac{F_m}{d_{im}^{\alpha}}} \quad \text{or} \quad P_{ij} = \frac{F_j/d_{ij}^{\alpha}}{\displaystyle\sum_{j=1}^{m} F_j/d_{ij}^{\alpha}}$$

subject to
$$\sum_{j=1}^{m} P_{ij} = 1 \cdot 0$$

where P_{ij} = the probability of a trip from area i to centre j
  F_j = the attractiveness of centre j (measured by floor-space)
  d_{ij} = the deterrence factor (measured by travelling times)
  α = an exponent calibrated for different trip purposes (e.g. convenience goods versus specialised goods)

TABLE 2.2

Computations of Gravity Models

Example I: The Break-Point Model

$$D_b = \frac{d_{ab}}{1 + \sqrt{\dfrac{P_a}{P_b}}} \qquad\qquad P_a = 160{,}000 \text{ population}; \; d_{ab} = 30 \text{ miles}$$
$$P_b = 40{,}000 \text{ population}$$

$$D_b = \frac{30}{1 + \sqrt{\dfrac{160{,}000}{40{,}000}}} = \frac{30}{1 + \sqrt{4}} = 10 \text{ miles}$$

Example II: The Retail Potential Model

$$S_j = \Sigma E_i \frac{F_j/d_{ij}^{\alpha}}{\Sigma(F_j/d_{ij}^{\alpha})} \qquad \begin{array}{l}\text{Suppose there are 3 centres, 3 areas and best} \\ \text{solutions are obtained when } \alpha = 2 \cdot 0\end{array}$$

For simplicity:

$F_{j1} = 16$ units	$E_{i1} = 80$ units	$d_{i1j1} = 2$ units
$F_{j2} = 45$ units	$E_{i2} = 60$ units	$d_{i1j2} = 3$ units
$F_{j3} = 20$ units	$E_{i3} = 40$ units	$d_{i1j3} = 2$ units

(*a*) Calculate the expenditure flows from one area to each centre

$$E_{i1j1} = 80 \frac{\dfrac{16}{2^2}}{\dfrac{16}{2^2} + \dfrac{45}{3^2} + \dfrac{20}{2^2}} = 19 \cdot 39$$

(*b*) Repeat for expenditure flows from E_{i1j2}; E_{i1j3}
(*c*) Calculate the expenditure flows from other areas to each centre
(*d*) Then sum the expenditures from all areas to any one centre to obtain $S_{j1} = E_{i1j1} + E_{i2j1} + E_{i3j1}$, etc.

Breakpoints Between Two Towns

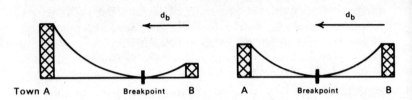

Trade Area Boundary Interpolations

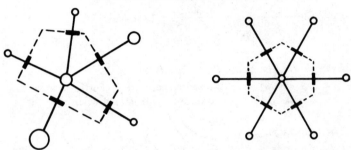

FIG. 2.9 *The derivation of trade area boundaries from a break-point model.* The top part of the diagram shows 'distance-decay' curves for the frequency of shopping trips to each of two towns. Where the curves intersect, a single position for a boundary line is given. In the lower part of the diagram, several such positions or break-points are shown and these can be joined up to approximate the overall sizes and shapes of the trade areas.

When the probability values for a series of areas are calculated they can be plotted on a map and interpolated by contour lines to indicate the relative use made of any centre by consumers (Figure 2.10). Where the same contour lines around two or more centres become tangential with each other (as for the probability values of 0·33 and 0·5 in the example) a point of equivalence in choice for visiting the centres is shown, which would be the boundary position obtained by a break-point model.

Models of Growth Potential

Some use has been made in the past of a general potential

model for indicating the growth prospects or alternatively accessibility conditions of large areas or cities. It has often been referred to as a market potential model and is similar to the population potential model extensively developed in demographic studies.[41] Most applications have referred to entire countries where the purpose has been to determine the relative proximity of provincial cities to the main national markets.[42] In this respect, it has also been usefully employed as a general guide to

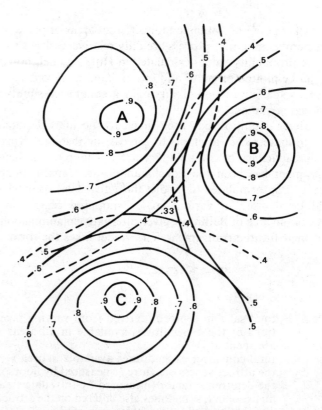

FIG. 2.10 *Probability contours for consumers choosing to shop in each of three centres.* (After Berry, B. J. L., *Geography of Market Centres and Retail Distribution*, Prentice-Hall, 1967; and Huff, D. L., 'A Probability Analysis of Shopping Centre Trade Areas', *Land Economics*, **53**, 1963, 81–9)

the location of manufacturing firms. A common expression is

$$M_i = \frac{Q_1}{t_{i1}^\alpha} + \frac{Q_2}{t_{i2}^\alpha} + \ldots \frac{Q_m}{t_{im}^\alpha} \quad \text{or} \quad M_i = \sum_{j=1}^{m} \frac{Q_j}{t_{ij}^\alpha}$$

where M_i = the relative market potential of an area i
   Q_j = the quantity of goods sold at centre j (e.g. retail sales)
   t_{ij} = the deterrence factor interpreted as transport costs from i to j
   α = an exponent, sometimes omitted from particular case studies.

The market potentials obtained for different areas or places from this general summation process are only relative abstract values. Like the probability values calculated in Huff's model, however, they can be plotted on maps and interpolated with contour lines to give a visual impression of varying degrees of accessibility and locational advantage.

A stricter definition has been given to the market potential model in more recent attempts to forecast in absolute terms the growth capacities of shopping centres. The most influential development has been the Lakshmanan and Hansen model.[43] This was first formulated to predict the actual sales volumes that would be realised in various major shopping centres in the metropolitan area of Baltimore given alternative planning policies about their future arrangement. The model takes the form:

$$S_j = \sum_{i=1}^{n} C_i \frac{F_j/d_{ij}^\alpha}{\sum_{j=1}^{m} F_j/d_{ij}^\alpha}$$

where S_j = total sales in centre j (derived from varying proportions of the expenditures available in all areas that are spent at j)
   C_i = total consumer expenditures available in area i
   F_j = the attractiveness of centre j (measured by floorspace)
   d_{ij} = the deterrence factor (measured by travelling times)
   α = an exponent, sometimes also entered on the attraction variable as well in particular case studies.

This has subsequently become a major vehicle for forecasting purposes in planning, particularly in Britain, and there are several similar types of model where the variables and their relationships have been changed to suit the circumstances of particular problems.[44] The procedure for computing the model is shown in Table 2.2 although it usually requires a computer to deal with the reiteration involved in real world applications. The general method of approach is to calibrate the model against the known sales performance of existing shopping centres or mean trip lengths in order to determine the nature of the parameters and the 'goodness-of-fit' before applying it to projected data about the state of retailing in the future. This is described in more detail in the chapter on forecasting and allocation techniques.

Assessments of the Theory

General interaction theory has become especially popular as a framework for practical work because it is seen to provide a kit-bag of tools for dealing directly with real world situations. It is the basis of an cperational approach to planning and marketing research when central place theory refers much more to an underlying strategy. In certain respects, however, the two theories establish complementary lines of approach, for gravity models are mainly used to test the consequences of alternative policy proposals, some of which may accord to a hierarchical organisation of centres. In addition, the structural mechanics involved in applying particular types of gravity models may incorporate features derived from central place theory, as has been indicated in the case of the break-point model and is further exemplified in the 'hierarchical-allocation' model (a variant on Lakshmanan and Hansen's model) recently developed at the Centre for Environmental Studies in Britain and extensively employed in their consultancy work.[45]

Nevertheless, the two theories diverge on certain conceptual matters. In particular, general interaction theory allows for a much greater variability in the directions of consumer movements, whereas central place theory dictates that consumers will always visit the nearest centre to them which offers their required goods. There is much conflicting evidence in support of each of these notions. Generally speaking, much greater variability in shopping patterns is found in the USA than occurs in Britain, not only because of higher levels of individual mobility and purchasing

power, but also because of less strict planning controls on the locations of centres.[46] Within urban areas, especially, British housewives are often severely constrained both in the number of centres made available to them and in their ability to use them. The net result is that shopping movements over small areas do not always approximate the negative exponential distance-decay curve assumed in general interaction theory, but rather that a 'plateau-like' effect is found around centres. In the British context, therefore, gravity models are seen to work best at a regional or subregional scale rather than at a intra-urban scale of enquiry.

Gravity models are further limited to simulating mainly aggregate consumer movements. This arises because it is extremely difficult to define in precise terms the nature of the attraction and deterrence factors when dealing with specific details about day-to-day shopping trips. Although there has been much research in this direction, the basic problem remains of an inability to properly quantify what are essentially qualitative controls.[47] The problem is especially acute when trying to forecast future patterns of behaviour rather than those of an existing or past time period.

FURTHER THEORETICAL AVENUES

Central place theory and general interaction theory are essentially macro-theories for describing and explaining the broad relationships between a system of centres and their trade areas. While they clearly provide the most thorough and comprehensive frameworks for study so far developed within marketing geography, the intense preoccupation with them in recent years has detracted from two major shortcomings. First, as has been indicated, the theories lack complete generality for they refer to only part (albeit the most ubiquitous and important part) of the total interplay of market forces. Secondly, they provide few guide-lines for more micro-scale studies of the internal structure of business centres or of the detailed composition of consumer trips.

There is a real need in current research to enlarge the perspectives taken in the study of marketing activity and at the same time to provide some unifying concepts by which to link empirical work at both the macro- and micro-scale levels of enquiry. One possible avenue is to establish some consistent classifications about major types of businesses and their locational requirements. This may be achieved by drawing analogies with those major taxonomic distinctions which have been made in the broader geographical literature on settlements and general urban land-use patterns.[48] These are described in Table 2.3.

TABLE 2.3

Analogous Classifications of Settlements, Urban Land-Use Forms and Business Complexes

	Locational Influences	
Arterial Accessibility	General Accessibility	Special Accessibility
	Settlement Types	
Transport-Based Places (e.g. Route Towns)	Central Places (e.g. Market Towns)	Resource-Based Places (e.g. Seaside Resorts)
	Land-Use Patterns	
Sector Pattern (Hoyt's Model)	Concentric Zone Pattern (Burgess' Model)	Multiple-Nuclei Pattern (Harris and Ullman's Model)
	Urban Business Complexes	
Linear Distributions ('String-Streets')	Compact Centres (Shopping Centres)	Special Districts (in Main Centres)
	Behavioural Influences	
Commercial and Travel Requirements	Household Shopping Requirements	Occasional or Specialised Requirements

In essence, there are three common kinds of economic activity which may be recognised at different scale levels of aggregation. These reflect in their locational requirements on three varying forms of accessibility conditions.

a. Certain activities exist to serve the everyday needs of a surrounding population and these require locations which command a 'general' level of accessibility. These are effectively centralised locations.

b. Other activities exist to fulfil a mainly service role by catering to the needs of a passing through-trade. These are activities which require proximity to major routeways or communications where there are enhanced levels of 'arterial' accessibility.

c. Further activities exist to provide a highly specialised set of either goods or services to a particular type of clientele. These require an assorted mixture of different locations but ones which reflect on a 'special' level of accessibility due to such things as physical site resources or prestige.

At the one end of this scale of analogies, combinations of these activities constitute the *raison d'être* for whole settlements, such as market towns, route towns and seaside resorts. These grow up in different locations for fundamentally different economic reasons. The differences between them, however, will be apparent not only in terms of their overall functions but also in terms of the detailed composition of their retail and related service trades. At the other end of the scale, the three types of activities might be represented inside any one settlement by the grocery shop, the petrol station and the high-class restaurant. Although these sometimes occur in isolation they more often group together with other like businesses to form distinct types of business complex. These may either be compact shopping centres in the middle of residential areas, linear distributions of businesses alongside major roads, or special districts found inside the main centre or central area.

The geographical literature alone, nevertheless, permits only a tenuous relationship to be drawn between these taxonomic distinctions and the differences in underlying accessibility conditions.[49] A more formal link is provided in the economics literature by rent theory. Rents are seen to be a direct reflection of varying locational advantages and different peakings in the urban rental surface have been directly equated with the three kinds of accessibility conditions.[50] Such peakings have also been related to the three types of business conformations we have recognised and the particular site requirements of certain activities found inside them. Rent theory therefore provides a much firmer basis for extending our analogies to the precise locational characteristics of individual firms. This is considered in more detail in Chapter 5.

The broad differences in business locations which we have

demonstrated at this stage also have clear implications for our later assessments of consumer behaviour. Table 2.3 indicates that the three main types of business conformations recognised bear a clear relationship to three main types of consumer movement. Thus we can distinguish between a set of trips for the main domestic needs of households, which will be primarily conducted by adult females; a set of more commercial or service-oriented trips, many of which will be inter-trade movements conducted by men; and a set of special-purpose trips for a variety of different requirements, many of which may be linked to particular age groups or socio-economic sections of the population. The detailed structure of consumer behaviour is extremely complicated, however, and at the micro-scale level of enquiry a greater understanding is necessary of the consumer decision-making processes involved rather than simply the overall influences of locational factors. Various different micro-theories about individual movements have been proposed and these are considered in more detail in Chapter 7.

REFERENCES

1. Dickinson, R. E., 'Markets and Market Areas of East Anglia', *Economic Geography*, **10** (1934), 172–82.

2. Smailes, A. E., 'The Urban Hierarchy in England and Wales', *Geography*, **29** (1944), 41–51.

3. Smailes, A. E., 'The Analysis and Delimitation of Urban Fields', *Geography*, **32** (1947), 151–61.

4. Green, H. L., 'Hinterland Boundaries of New York City and Boston in Southern New England', *Economic Geography*, **31** (1955), 282–300.

5. Green, F. H. W., 'Motor Bus Centres in S.W. England Considered in Relation to Population and Shopping Facilities', *Transactions of the Institute of British Geographers*, **14** (1948), 57–68; 'Urban Hinterlands in England and Wales: An Analysis of Bus Services', *The Geographical Journal*, **116** (1950), 64–88.

6. See, again, Green, F. H. W., 'A Commercial Application of Urban Hinterland Studies', *Lund Symposium in Urban Geography, University of Lund* (1962).

7. Geographia Ltd., *Marketing Areas Handbook* (London, 1960).

8. Rand McNally and Co. Ltd., *Commercial Atlas and Marketing Guide* (annual editions).

44   MARKETING GEOGRAPHY

9. Applebaum, W., *The Secondary Commercial Centres of Cincinnati* (University of Cincinnati, 1932).

10. Rolph, I. K., 'The Location Structure of Retail Trade', *U.S. Department of Commerce, Domestic Commerce Series, No. 80* (1933).

11. See, for example, Gruen, V., 'Planned Shopping Centres', *Dun's Review*, **61** (1953), 37–84.

12. See, for example, Jonassen, C. T., *The Shopping Centre Versus Downtown* (Ohio State University, 1955).

13. Several of the early survey techniques developed by Applebaum are reported in Kornblau, C. (ed.) *Guide to Store Location Research: With Emphasis on Supermarkets* (Addison-Wesley, 1968).

14. See Chapter 9 in Berry, B. J. L. and Garrison, W. L., *et al*, *Studies in Highway Development and Geographic Change* (University of Washington Press, 1959).

15. As, for example, in the above study, *ibid.*

16. Christaller, W., *Die zentralen Orte in Suddeutschland* (Verlag, 1933); translated by C. Baskin as *Central Places in Southern Germany* (Prentice-Hall, 1966).

17. Weber, A., *Über den Standort der Industrien* translated by C. J. Friedrich as *Alfred Weber's Theory of the Location of Industries* (University of Chicago Press, 1929).

18. Thunen, J. H. von, *Der Isolierte Staat in Beziehung auf Landwirtschaft und Nationalökonomie* (Schumacher-Zarchlin, 1926). Alternatively, see Hall, P. (ed.), *Von Thunen's Isolated State* (Pergamon, 1966).

19. A summary of the theory and references to other reviews are contained in Berry, B. J. L. and Pred, A., *Central Place Studies: A Bibliography of Theory and Applications* (Regional Science Research Institute, 1965).

20. These are further elaborated in Christaller, W., *Das Grundgerüst der räumlichen Ordnung in Europa: Die Systeme der europäischen zentralen Orte* (Frankfurter Geographische Hefte, 1950).

21. Lösch, A., *Die raumliche Ordnung der Wirtschaft* (Verlag, 1944) translated by W. H. Woglom and W. F. Stolper as *The Economics of Location* (Yale University Press, 1954).

22. Berry, B. J. L. and Garrison, W. L., 'Recent Developments of Central Place Theory', *Papers and Proceedings of the Regional Science Association*, **4** (1958), 107–20.

23. See, for example, Berry, B. J. L. and Garrison, W. L., 'Functional Bases of the Central Place Hierarchy', *Economic Geography*, **34** (1958), 145–54.

24. Berry, B. J. L. and Garrison, W. L., *et al, op. cit.*

25. Berry, B. J. L. and Garrison, W. L., 'A Note on Central Place Theory and the Range of a Good', *Economic Geography*, **34** (1958), 304–11.

26. The most complete assessment of recent work is found in Berry, B. J. L., *Geography of Market Centres and Retail Distribution* (Prentice-Hall, 1967). See also Marshall, J. U., 'The Location of Service

Centres', *University of Toronto, Department of Geography, Research Publication 3* (1969).

27. A more detailed classification of empirical studies is provided in Berry, B. J. L. and Pred, A., *op. cit.* This has recently been updated by Andrews, H. F., 'Working Notes and Bibliography on Central Place Studies', *University of Toronto, Department of Geography, Discussion Paper 8* (1970).

28. Several attempts have been made to reformulate the theory in probabilistic terms and provide for dynamic models. See, for example, Dacey, M. F., 'A Probability Model for Central Place Locations', *Annals of the Association of American Geographers*, **56** (1966), 550–68; Curry, L., 'Central Places in the Random Spatial Economy', *Journal of Regional Science*, **7** (1967), 217–38.

29. See, for example, Beckman, M. J., 'City Hierarchies and the Distribution of City Size', *Economic Development and Cultural Change*, **6** (1958), 243–8.

30. National Economic Development Office, Committee for the Distributive Trades, *Urban Models in Shopping Studies* (1970).

31. See, for example, the 'theory' of hierarchical shopping centres proposed by Wilfred Burns in *British Shopping Centres* (Leonard Hill, 1959).

32. Christaller, W., *Die zentralen Orte in Suddeutschland* (Verlag, 1933).

33. Berry, B. J. L. and Garrison, W. L., 'Functional Bases of the Central Place Hierarchy', *Economic Geography*, **34** (1958), 145–54.

34. Szumeluk, K., 'Central Place Theory: Its Role in Planning with Particular Reference to Retailing', *Centre for Environmental Studies, Working Paper No. 9* (1967).

35. Major reviews and bibliographies for the literature on general interaction theory are contained in: Carrothers, G. A. P., 'An Historical Review of the Gravity and Potential Concepts of Human Interaction', *Journal of the American Institute of Planners*, **22** (1956), 94–102; Olsson, G., *Distance and Human Interaction* (Regional Science Research Institute, 1965).

36. Reilly, W. J., *The Law of Retail Gravitation* (Knickerbocker Press, 1931).

37. Cordey-Hayes, M., 'Retail Location Models', *Centre for Environmental Studies, Working Paper 16* (1968); Lanchester Polytechnic, Department of Town Planning, *Gravity Models in Town Planning* (Coventry Corporation, 1969).

38. Converse, P. D., 'New Laws of Retail Gravitation', *Journal of Marketing*, **14** (1949), 379–84.

39. For a case-study example, see Manchester University, Department of Town Planning, *Regional Shopping Centres in North West England, Part I* (Manchester University, 1964).

40. Huff, D. L., 'A Probability Analysis of Shopping Centre Trade Areas', *Land Economics*, **53** (1963), 81–9.

41. See Stewart, J. Q., and Warntz, W., 'Physics of Population Distribution', *Journal of Regional Science*, **1** (1958), 99–123.

42. Two early case studies are: Harris, C. D., 'The Market as a Factor in the Localization of Industry in the United States', *Annals of the Association of American Geographers*, **44** (1954), 315–48; Dunn, E. S. 'The Market Potential Concept and the Analysis of Location', *Papers of the Regional Science Association*, **2** (1956), 183–94.

43. Lakshmanan, T. R. and Hansen, W. G., 'A Retail Market Potential Model', *Journal of the American Institute of Planners*, **31** (1965), 134–43.

44. A review of these is contained in National Economic Development Office, *op. cit.*

45. Broadbent, T. A., 'A Hierarchical Interaction-Allocation Model for a Two-Level Spatial System', *Centre for Environmental Studies, Working Paper 67* (1970).

46. Davies, R. L., 'Patterns and Profiles of Consumer Behaviour in Coventry', *University of Newcastle, Department of Geography, Research Series No. 10* (1973).

47. Davies, R. L., 'Variable Relationships in Central Place and Retail Potential Models', *Regional Studies*, **4** (1970), 49–61.

48. Davies, R. L., 'Structural Models of Retail Distribution: Analogies with Settlement and Urban Land-Use Theories', *Transactions of the Institute of British Geographers*, **57** (1972), 59–82.

49. *ibid.*

50. See, for example, Alonso, W., *Location and Land Use: Toward a General Theory of Land Rent* (Harvard University Press, 1964); Turvey, R., *The Economics of Real Property* (Allen and Unwin, 1957).

3 Growth and Developments in the Distributive Trades

The distributive trades are commonly defined as those intermediary activities involved in the transfer of goods from producers to consumers, namely wholesaling and retailing. Although these activities are generally small in their scale of operations, collectively they constitute one of the largest industries. In Britain, they account for approximately eleven per cent of the Gross Domestic Product and a similar proportion of the total national employment. Retailing alone generated sales of more than £15,000 million in 1971 and provided about two and a half million jobs, making it the third greatest contributor to national output behind manufacturing industry and a miscellaneous office services group.

The actual process of distribution within an economy, however, usually extends beyond the specific functions of wholesaling and retailing. It includes the transfer of many commodities which are normally identified as services, such as monetary transactions through a bank, car repairs through a garage, and even films shown in a cinema. The organisational structure involved in distribution also varies considerably, for the traditional roles and relationships of the wholesaler and retailer are rapidly changing. Many wholesalers are now owners of retail outlets and may also use their warehouse depots as discount shops; likewise, many retailers have increasingly developed their own system of wholesaling by dealing more directly with the producers. In addition, it is often found that the producers themselves distribute goods immediately to consumers without the aid of intermediaries, through the use of postal deliveries or direct shipments.

MAJOR COMPONENTS OF THE DISTRIBUTIVE TRADES

Wholesaling

It is difficult to give a precise definition for the function of
wholesaling for the term has been used in a variety of ways.[1]
There are also relatively few official statistics available to indicate
the amount as well as character of trade involved. In general,
wholesaling refers to the business of bulk commodity transactions,
ranging from the warehouse storage of industrial goods to the
traditional market exchanges of livestock and horticultural products. The minimum list headings of the Standard Industrial
Classification in Britain suggest three main staple groups: the
wholesale distribution of food and drink; the wholesale distribution of petroleum products; and other wholesale distribution,
including tobacco, clothing, paper, and general merchants.
Excluded from this classification, however, are dealers in coal,
builders' materials, industrial machinery and agricultural supplies, although these are incorporated into the basic categories
for wholesaling of the American Census of Business.

An alternative classification which cuts across these systematic
groupings and introduces some further dimensions has been
provided by Tietz.[2] He distinguishes between:

1. Wholesaling which is geared to the storage of goods
    a. with customers calling, e.g. general merchants serving
    mainly small shopkeepers.
    b. without customers calling, e.g. dealers delivering coal,
    builders' materials, and other heavy items.
2. Wholesaling which is geared to the disposition of goods
    a. with customers calling, e.g. wholesalers selling through
    samples, mainly in trade fairs and marts.
    b. without customers calling, e.g. agents and brokers (in-
    cluding importers and exporters) who oversee the transfer
    of goods.

The main geographical significance of these distinctions lies in
the different locational patterns that may be observed.[3] While
there are clearly many exceptions, storage wholesaling which

depends on customer visits remains much more strongly constrained to inner city locations whereas that which operates
through deliveries is much more widely dispersed. In Britain, a
marked contrast is emerging between those activities agglom-
erated on the fringe of the main centre or central area and those
linked with manufacturing firms on outlying trading estates and
new industrial sites. Dispositional wholesaling is altogether less
common in Britain compared to the USA and is mainly found
only in the largest cities. Trade fairs and marts, dealing with such
items as books, furniture and domestic appliances, often occupy
permanent exhibition halls; while agents and brokers commonly
associate with other general office activities in the central area or
are concentrated around the terminals of major transportation
lines.

The prevailing wind of change affecting wholesaling in recent
years concerns the growth of the multiple or chain organisations
at the expense of the small independent merchants. The most
spectacular, single development has been the emergence of the
cash and carry method of wholesaling predominantly in the food
trade. This is an American innovation which has created a
revolution in wholesaling as significant as that brought about in
retailing by the supermarket. The main impact in Britain has
been felt in just the last few years. Surveys conducted by
Crosse and Blackwell Ltd.,[4] for example, show that during the
eighteen months' period from January 1968 to July 1969 the
number of new cash and carry depots increased from 398 to 632.
Since then, there has been relatively little further numerical
increase, but the sizes of depots and their overall volumes of
sales have continued to expand rapidly. Nielsen surveys[5] have
revealed that depots of over 25,000 square feet increased their
share of trade from twenty-four per cent to forty-three per cent
between 1971 and 1972; the total turnover generated by all
depots more than doubled from £344 million in 1969 to
£707 million in 1972. The spread of these depots throughout the
country has been closely monitored by David Thorpe[6] and it is
clear that most of them are now concentrated in the largest urban
areas. They also typically locate alongside major roads on the
outskirts of cities rather than within close proximity to the central
area.

One of the major casualties of the growth in multiple organisations has been the horticultural wholesale market.[7] This has suffered particularly from the preference of supermarket chains for dealing directly with food producers. In addition, there has been a serious reduction in trade arising from changes in consumer demand towards processed rather than fresh foods. The future viability of many of the smaller markets will also depend on locational changes, for most of them were built in the last century and occupy congested sites in the main shopping areas of towns. New, more peripheral locations have recently been established for several of the largest markets in Britain, as in the movement of London's Covent Garden Market to Nine Elms and Newcastle's market to the Team Valley Trading Estate in Gateshead.[8]

Retailing

There is much more statistical information and concensus agreement about the structure of retailing than is the case for wholesaling. Three main categories are usually distinguished, based on their mode of organisation or ownership: the independents, the multiples, and the co-operatives. The department stores, mail order firms and retail markets may be further separated from these.

1. The Independents

These cover a wide range of shops from the itinerant stall-owner to the family business and the small chain group of half-a-dozen branches. They remain the most ubiquitous types of shops in Europe and North America, though they are increasingly becoming concentrated in the smaller shopping centres and the side streets of the central area. Like the independent wholesalers, they bore the brunt of the post-war supermarket revolution and the trend to mass-selling techniques in multiple stores, although those engaged in the convenience trades were more affected than those in specialist pursuits. In recent years the overall decline in the competitive position of independents has been improved by the formation of voluntary trading groups (or symbol groups), such as the Spar and VG grocery organisations, the Osmat hardware organisation and the Ardenn tailoring organisation.[9] These are effectively federations of retail stores operating through a common wholesaling firm and selling standardised, branded products while preserving the rights of individual ownership. Most progress has been made in the food trade and about one third of all independent grocers in Britain are now members of trading groups accounting for about one-quarter of the total retail grocery turnover.[10] Many of these groups are international organisations and most were initiated by wholesaling companies concerned over the declining proportions of trade commanded by their retail customers. Spar International (of Dutch origin), is the largest group operating in fourteen countries through 240 wholesalers and 34,691 retailers.[11] The leading groups in Britain are listed in Table 3.1.

TABLE 3.1

Leading Voluntary Chain Groups in Britain

Wholesaler-Sponsored Groups:			
	Wholesalers	Depots	Retailers
Mace	28	47	4800
Spar	23	26	3116
VG	10	23	2981
Alliance	1	8	1519
DBC	2	41	3807
APT	5	13	2000
Vivo	19	19	1286
Retailer-Sponsored Groups:			
	Buying Combines	Depots	Retailers
Londis	1	4	1171
SGF	1	1	1300
Bob	37	40	1430

Source: Fulop, C., *Retailing and the Consumer* (Longman, 1970).

2. The Multiples

These are defined in the Census of Distribution as retail firms with ten or more establishments. Although their prominence and importance has been linked with supermarkets, their existence in fact reaches far back into the last century. Such food chains as the Home and Colonial Tea Company, the Maypole Dairy Company and Lipton Ltd. had extensive networks of stores before the First World War.[12] The inter-war period in Britain saw the rise of the multiples in apparel and household goods, which tended to be more densely concentrated in the North rather than the South. By the mid-1950s Jeffreys and Knee[13] estimated that while eighty per cent of the multiples in continental Europe were engaged in the food trade only fifty-five per cent (of a proportionately greater overall number) of those in Britain were. A special feature of the British and also American multiples are the variety stores which grew out of the penny bazaars at the turn of the century. While these remain predominantly geared to mass selling of cheaper household goods in the USA a wider spectrum of customer orientation and specialisation in lines of trade has been developed in Britain. Marks and Spencer Ltd., for example, have gained such a high reputation for the quality of their textile goods that they are now the second largest organisation in the country after Associated British Foods (with sales of over £550 million in 1973 from 251 stores).[14] F. W. Woolworth, in contrast, generated about £378 million in 1973 from over 1,000 stores in Britain. For the most part these variety stores and other multiple organisations in specialist trades occupy the peak nodal positions in the main high streets of the largest shopping centres. The multiples engaged in the food trade tend to be found in more peripheral sites close to bus staging-points or car parks and also extensively in suburban centres.

3. The Co-operatives

The retail co-operatives were really the forerunners of the multiple organisations and were also the first to develop the technique of self-service trading.[15] From their inception in Rochdale in 1844, they spread rapidly through the country and became particularly concentrated in the North and Scotland. Jefferys[16] has estimated that in 1919, forty-five per cent of the 2,160,000 residents in Northumberland and Durham were registered with the local co-operative societies compared with only five per cent of 4,466,000 residents in London. The inter-war period saw a greater expansion in the Midlands and South, but they continued to remain pre-eminently geared towards the working classes of the traditional industrial areas. Curiously, while they are distinctly an urban trading group in Britain, in Scandinavia, which now has proportionately the strongest co-operative movement in Europe, they have mainly operated in rural areas. During the last two decades, the co-operatives in Britain have suffered from competition with the multiples in the same way as the independents. Despite the experience of self-service techniques and the advantages of having their own wholesaling system, the societies were slow to adapt to the modern methods of the supermarket and too much of their profits were dispersed as dividends rather than channelled as investments. Recent major improvements, however, have been the amalgamation of many individual town groups, the issue of trading stamps instead of dividends, and the adoption of a single brand name and advertising symbol. Some improvements have also been made in the locations of new branches, for many of the older stores now find themselves in isolated positions. There are currently about 14,000 shops operating from 243 separate societies.

4. The Department Stores

The department stores originated in the 1860s in Paris and London and were initially oriented to a middle-class clientele. Most of the growth in numbers and size took place in Britain in the inter-war period. There was less development in the larger cities of Europe primarily because of governmental restrictions designed to prevent any monopolies emerging in the retail field and also in some countries because of a fear of health hazards in serving several lines of trade together.[17] Interestingly, while indirect governmental measures in Britain in the form of the Selective Employment Tax and planning constraints have tended to curtail growth in the post-war period, department stores in Europe have expanded considerably. The most spectacular growth has been seen in the USA, however, where the number rose from 2,760 in 1954 to 4,250 in 1963.[18] This has mainly been associated with extensive decentralisation of department stores into the suburbs. In Britain, department stores remain tied to the central areas of the largest cities, where they usually form the main shopping magnet. There are four principal organisations which between them control about half of the total department stores in the country: Debenhams, the House of Fraser, the John Lewis Partnership, and Sears Holdings.

5. The Mail Order Firms

The early growth of mail order retailing was most conspicuous in the USA in the late nineteenth century, and is particularly linked with such firms as Montgomery Ward and Sears Roebuck of Chicago, who provided a wide range of household and agricultural supplies to the relatively isolated farming communities of the Mid-West and Great Plains. In Europe, mail order retailing tended to be much more small-scale and geared towards working-class families in industrial towns. There has been a recent and somewhat unexpected boom in this form of trading in the last decade, however, particularly in Germany and Britain and serving a wide cross-section of their populations.[19] Most sales are in textiles, especially women's and infant's wear, and in Britain there is a concentration of firms in Lancashire and the West Riding. Littlewoods and Great Universal Stores account for approximately half the total trade generated.

6. The Retail Markets

Although retail markets now account for less than one per cent of the total volume of retail trade, they remain a prominent feature in many British towns and a popular source for mainly fresh foods.[20] Historically, of course, they constituted the main forms of selling, and still have greater significance in many Mediterranean countries and especially in the under-developed world. In Britain, they remained the most important outlets for food until the middle of the nineteenth century. About one third of the existing markets are open only one day in the week, but most of the largest cities retain permanent, covered halls. Scott[21] has shown that there is a particular concentration of markets throughout east-central Britain, suggesting possible linkages with surrounding agricultural pursuits, although the nature of these are not entirely clear.

Services

Certain service activities are incorporated into the retail classification of the Census of Distribution because they obviously function in the same way as shops and exhibit similar locational characteristics. These are the domestic services of shoe repairers, hairdressers, dry cleaners and launderettes. In addition, statistics are reported for the utility services of the gas and electricity showrooms. There are numerous other service activities, however, which though associated with the functions and locations of conventional forms of retailing are treated separately and generally less well documented. These may be summarised as follows: the leisure services, including restaurants, cafés, public houses, bookmakers, cinemas, bingo halls and travel agencies; the business services, such as post offices, banks, insurance agencies and building societies; and the transport services, comprising a range of different types of garages and auto-accessory shops. Automotive dealers and petrol stations are listed in the retail classification of the American Census of Business.

THE MAIN CHANNELS OF DISTRIBUTION

Wholesaling and retailing and also service establishments act as agents in the transfer of commodities from producers to consumers. Their importance within this process obviously varies according to the nature of the commodities involved. In some cases they can be dispensed with altogether (as in the distribution of certain industrial products); in other cases, several different types of intermediaries may need to be utilised (as in the distribution of imported fresh food products). The extent of the interactions which take place particularly between wholesaling and retailing will also depend on the scale of operations and trading methods employed by various kinds of companies. A series of alternative channels of distribution, or distribution systems, can therefore be recognised, and the main sets of relationships involved in these are shown in Figure 3.1.

The Main Channels of Distribution Classified by Number of Ownership-Stages

		Notes:
One-stage channels	Manufacturer ——→ Consumer or industrial user	Direct delivery of industrial goods ; direct selling of consumer goods ; mail order ; Co-ops ; manufacturers sales branches.
Two-stage channels	Manufacturer ——→ Independant retailer ——┐ └——→ Consumer	High unit-value goods ; selectively distributed goods ; broad-line manufacturers.
	Manufacturer ——→ Voluntary group retailer ——┐ └——→ Consumer	Decreasing
	Manufacturer ——→ Multiple retail branch ——┐ ↘ Multiple wholesale warehouse ↗ ┘ └——→ Consumer	
	Manufacturer ——→ Mail order house ——→ Consumer	Mail order houses perform both wholesale and retail functions.
	Manufacturer ——→ Co-op retail outlets ——┐ └——→ Consumer	Independant negotiation by managers of Co-op retail branches decreasing.
	Manufacturer ——→ Franchise retailer ——┐ └——→ Consumer	Under exclusive distribution, direct to retailer is universal
	Manufacturer ——→ Industrial distributor ——┐ └——→ Industrial user	Growing in some industrial fields, e.g. electrical components
Three-stage channels	Manufacturer ——→ Wholesale merchant ——┐ └——→ Independent retailer ——→ Consumer	A declining channel, though still very important, especially for low unit-value, mass-distribution products.
	Manufacturer ——→ Wholesale merchant ——┐ └——→ Voluntary group retailer ——→ Consumer	Persists, but groups are trying to reduce it.
	Manufacturer ——→ Wholesale merchant ——┐ └——→ Co-op retail outlet ——→ Consumer	Persists, but Co-ops are trying to reduce it.
	Manufacturer ——→ Wholesale merchant ——┐ └——→ Multiple retail branch ——→ Consumer	Fill in orders
	Manufacturer ——→ Voluntary group wholesaler ——┐ └——→ Voluntary group retailer ——→ Consumer	Increasing ; mainly in groceries, also in pharmaceuticals.
	Manufacturer ——→ Voluntary group wholesaler ——┐ └——→ Independent retailer ——→ Consumer	Persists—(a) not enough group sales to keep wholesaler in business ; (b) cash-and-carry.
	Manufacturer ——→ Co-op wholesale Society ——┐ └——→ Co-op retail outlet ——→ Consumer	The Co-ops aim to increase this ; there are no sales by the C.W.S. to non-Co-op outlets.
Four-stage channels	Manufacturer ——→ Wholesaler ——→ Wholesaler ——┐ └——→ Retailer ——→ Consumer	There is considerable trade between wholesalers, to even out over-stock or under-stock positions.
	Producer ——→ Primary wholesaler ——┐ └——→ Secondary wholesaler ——→ Retailer ——┐ └——→ Consumer	e.g. white fish ; trawler ——→ coastal wholesaler and processor ——→ inland wholesaler ——→ fishmonger ——→ consumer
	Manufacturer ——→ Agent ——→ Wholesaler ——┐ ↘ ↓ Retailer ——→ Consumer	Physical distribution, ownership and selling are often separated when this channel is used.

FIG. 3.1 *The main channels of distribution.* (After Guirdham, M., *Marketing: The Management of Distribution Channels*, Pergamon, 1972)

Guirdham[22] has also examined the structural characteristics of different channels of distribution in terms of the degree of co-ordination and control exerted by participatory groups. She distinguishes between five types of organisational forms:

1. Consensus Channels

These are essentially the traditional forms of organisation which are based on the mutual co-operation of all the contributing agencies. There is no one group which exercises special authority over the distribution system. Consensus channels are epitomised in the relationships that extend between the independent merchant wholesalers (including cash and carry wholesalers) and the independent retailers.

2. Vertically Integrated Channels Commanded by Intermediaries

These are found most commonly when a multiple group, usually in retailing rather than wholesaling, imposes a management control over the entire distribution system and may even influence the nature of the goods that are produced. Most of the main supermarket chains have their own branded products and network of warehousing facilities; and some companies, like Marks and Spencer and Mothercare, can dictate exacting quality standards at the actual sources of production.

3. Vertically Co-ordinated Channels Led by Intermediaries

These occur when a large retailing or wholesaling firm is able to influence the distribution system, not through ownership of different agencies, but through the volume and strength of its commitments. The voluntary group associations in both wholesaling and retailing are the prime examples, although Guirdham suggests that the co-operative societies act in the same way. Theoretically, the distribution system within the co-operative movement should be the most fully integrated of any, but in practice there is considerable fragmentation and a separation of the levels of production, wholesaling and retailing.

4. Vertically Integrated and Vertically Co-ordinated Channels Commanded by Producers

These are found when the product companies organise their own distribution systems either through establishing warehouses and retail branch outlets for themselves or by conferring franchises on independent agencies. Examples of the former are the networks created by the Marley Tile company and Singer Sewing Machines; examples of the latter are the networks of 'Wimpy bars' established by Lyons and most of the petrol stations under licence from the oil companies.

5. Channels for Industrial Products

These involve more limited forms of distribution systems when producers deal directly with the public or through wholesaling intermediaries only. They incorporate such activities as builders' merchants, and manufacturers' own sales agencies.

TRENDS IN THE AGGREGATE STRUCTURE OF RETAILING

Most of the changes which have taken place in the organisational forms of distribution systems have been initiated from the retail sector or are a consequence of developments within it. There have been enormous upheavals in the methods of retail trading in the past two decades, which are epitomised by the revolution in self-service techniques and manifested in the growth of the giant supermarket chains.[23] The repercussions which have been felt in retailing itself, however, have varied considerably amongst different lines of trade and in different parts of the country. In addition, the developments that have been experienced in Britain have often proceeded at a different pace and scale of change compared to those in other European countries and the USA.

The Impact of the Supermarket

Until the 1950s, there had always been a steady growth in the number of retail establishments throughout Britain. During the decade of the 1950s, the first signs of a dramatic reversal in these trends were observed. These occurred in the convenience lines of trade where an increasing proportion of small independent grocers and other food vendors began to close in the face of opposition from supermarkets. During the 1960s, what had been a trickle of closures became almost a flood-tide as more and more small independent retailers in every line of trade found it impossible to cope with the competition of self-servicing.

The root causes for the overall decline in numbers of establishments since the 1960s are primarily explained by the expansion of chain stores which offered a greater range of products at generally lower prices because of the economies of scale that could be achieved in operating through large outlets. At the same time, there were a series of credit squeezes imposed by successive governments which, together with the introduction of the Selective Employment Tax, tended to mitigate against the marginal businessman. The 1960s also saw the beginnings of some massive central area redevelopment schemes and other programmes aimed at the removal or renovation of commercial slums, and small businesses displaced in these ways found it difficult to re-establish in new shopping areas because of the high rents incurred.

Specific details about the nature of these trends in different lines of trade are summarised in Figure 3.2. The major exception to the overall decline occurs in certain specialist and household goods shops (such as electrical and television shops) which have obviously continued to increase in response to the demand for new types of products. The number of independently-owned shops declined by 9·7 per cent between 1961 and 1971 with a loss of more than 43,000 establishments engaged in some form of food trade. It has been calculated that on average any new supermarket now replaces 10–15 of the traditional independent food shops.[24] In 1973, there were estimated to be 5,000 supermarkets proper (defined as those self-service outlets with more than 2,000 square feet) and these are expected to increase in number to 7,200 by 1980.[25]

While there has been an overall increase in the volume of turnover generated by each of the main types of stores, the propor-

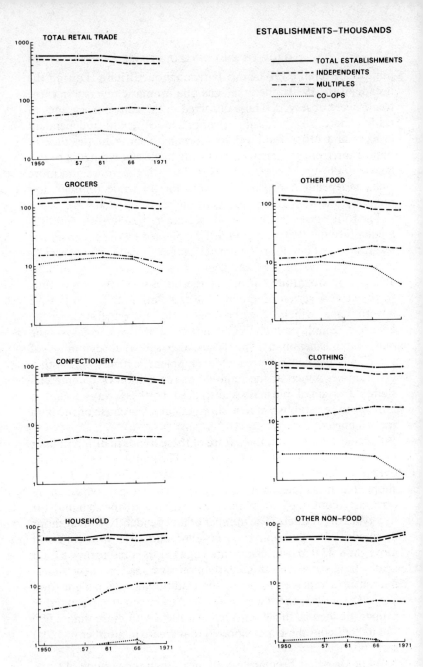

FIG. 3.2 *Trends in the numbers of retail establishments in Great Britain, 1950–1971.*

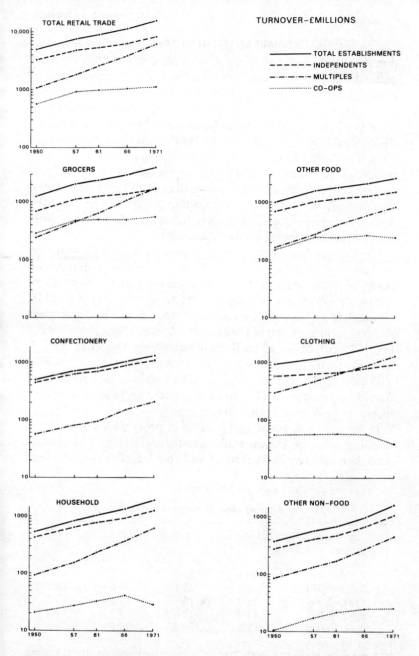

FIG. 3.3 *Trends in the volume of retail turnover in Great Britain, 1950–1971.*

tionate shares captured of the total trade available has changed quite dramatically. These are described in absolute terms in Figure 3.3. The multiples, which commanded only twenty-nine per cent of total retail sales in 1961, increased their share to forty per cent in 1971. The independents, by contrast, reduced their share from sixty per cent in 1961 to fifty-three per cent in 1971. The bulk of this change has again taken place in the food trades where the chain groups already command a higher percentage of the grocery sales available than all of the independents. The formation of the voluntary trading groups has arrested the decline in some respects, but mainly only within the ranks of those stores operating under symbol names.[26]

The independent stores are not alone in experiencing a depletion of their relative economic strength, of course. The proportionate share of total retail sales commanded by the co-operatives declined from eleven per cent in 1961 to seven per cent in 1971, although there has been a levelling off since then. The department stores (included as part of the multiples quoted above) held a static five per cent share of total retail sales over the same period. Only the mail order stores have shown a growth rate comparable with that of the chain food groups, having increased their share from two per cent in 1957 to four per cent in 1966 and an estimated five per cent at the current time.[27]

In general, the trend to larger-scale economies continues in retailing, and the largest trading outlets will show the greatest growth in turnover in the future (see Table 3.2). The precise role of

TABLE 3.2

Typical Sizes of New Supermarkets in Britain

Sq. Ft. of Selling Area	1969 %	1970 %	1971 %	1972 %
2,000–3,999	30·1	25·1	11·5	19·7
4,000–5,999	22·2	25·1	26·1	18·8
6,000–7,999	15·9	13·8	20·4	17·1
8,000–9,999	15·9	12·0	14·6	17·9
over 10,000	15·9	24·0	27·4	26·5

Source: A survey of forty-five retail organisations by the Institute of Grocery Distribution, 1973.

hypermarkets, superstores and discount houses in this is difficult to ascertain as yet because of the limited developments that have taken place and the uncertainties involved over planning constraints. So far only three hypermarkets in a proper sense have been built in Britain (the most notable being at Caerphilly in South Wales), although there are estimated to be fifty-six superstores with an average selling area of 34,685 square feet.[28] If the experience of continental countries and the USA are invoked, then clearly this type of store will become the main forerunner in overall growth. Such prospects and the planning problems involved are pursued in Chapter 6.

Regional Variations in Britain

Retailing characteristics and growth trends within the regions of Britain tend to reflect on the overall economic and cultural differences which are found. This is not adequately portrayed by comparisons of aggregate statistics alone, for these conceal important variations in the quality levels of shops and the local physical environments in which they occur. The Census of Distribution, however, provides the only standardised body of information available and hence considerable attention must be given to it. In considering the tables and graphs which accompany this section, it should be remembered that the 1957 and 1966 censuses were based on sample surveys rather than total inventories, and there have been changes between them in the categorisation of regions for which statistics are collated.

There is a conspicuous difference between the regions in terms of the densities of shops and the strength of various types of trading methods. These characteristics are summarised in Table 3.3. The North-West and Wales have the highest incidence of shops in relation to the population served, and the South-East, Scotland and the Northern region the lowest. These differences are not easily accounted for, but tend to reflect on variations in population growth rates and the distribution of the population. In general, lower numbers of shops are found whenever there has been a substantial population increase over the last two decades of stricter planning control, or alternatively where a large section of the population is widely dispersed throughout a region.

TABLE 3.3

Average Population Served per Establishment in 1971

	Total Retail Trade	Co-op Societies	Multiple Groups	Independent Stores
East Anglia	118	3516	1071	137
East Midlands	113	1922	1086	135
South West	106	4328	829	125
South East	124	5629	731	154
Greater London	109	6904	580	136
West Midlands	116	3781	833	140
Scotland	121	2029	847	151
North West	93	3572	858	108
Wales	97	3289	903	113
Yorks and Humber	108	3397	956	126
Northern	122	2994	817	150

Source: Provisional Figures of the Census of Distribution, 1971.

In cities, a high incidence of shops in relation to the population served will often reflect on retailing inefficiencies and be due to an historical legacy of uncontrolled growth in the first part of this century. The lower numbers of shops in Scotland and the Northern region are also partly explained by the entrenchment of the co-operative societies which operate through relatively large store premises. In contrast, there is a much greater tradition of small, family business concerns in the North-West and Wales. The multiple stores, whilst often originating from the provinces, have now become most densely concentrated in the South-East and particularly London. Generally speaking, there is always a much greater incidence of multiple stores in the larger cities compared to the smaller ones.

Relative differences in business performance between the regions, as indicated by the amount of turnover generated per head of population, are summarised in Table 3.4. These tend to equate with the overall levels of prosperity experienced in the regions. The particular strengths and weaknesses of the co-operative societies and multiple groups are again conspicuous in these statistics. The general inequalities to be observed may be

TABLE 3.4

Average Turnover per Head of Population in 1971

	Total Retail Trade	Co-op Societies	Multiple Groups	Independent Stores
East Anglia	268	23	93	151
East Midlands	252	35	81	135
South West	264	17	102	145
South East	294	16	139	138
Greater London	368	16	170	181
West Midlands	256	20	100	135
Scotland	273	26	95	150
North West	276	21	92	162
Wales	249	20	82	146
Yorks and Humber	257	18	91	147
Northern	250	19	100	130

Source: Provisional Figures of the Census of Distribution, 1971.

further considered by reference to the Family Expenditure Surveys which are now undertaken by the government each year. These are based on the diary records kept over a two week period of approximately 7,000 sample households scattered throughout the country. For the period 1965–67, for example, they showed that the average total weekly household expenditure in the South-East was £24·56 compared to £20·11 for the Northern Region. In 1971, the figures for the same regions were £34·82 and £27·81, indicating that in recent years the gap in purchasing power or disposable income has actually widened.

Some examples of the changes which have taken place in numbers of shops, turnover and also retail employment within the regions are shown in Figures 3.4 and 3.5. The graphs refer to the years 1957 to 1961 and 1961 to 1966 when the impact of the revolution in business methods was most pronounced. It is clear from the trends in numbers of shops that the effects of the general movement to larger-scale and mass-merchandising techniques were first felt in the southern parts of the country. These were the only areas which experienced a substantial decline in establishments in the late 1950s. Between 1961 and 1966, how-

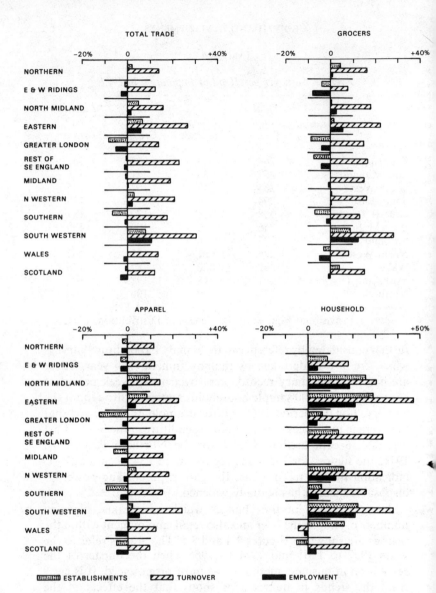

FIG. 3.4 *Regional variations in retail establishments, turnover and employment for Great Britain, 1957–1961.* (From the *Censuses of Distribution*)

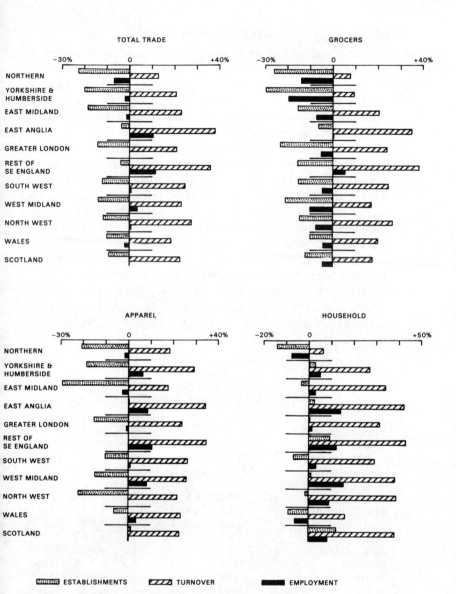

FIG. 3.5 *Regional variations in retail establishments, turnover and employment for Great Britain, 1961–1966.* (From the *Censuses of Distribution*)

ever, every region and particularly those in the North experienced a massive reduction, especially in the food and apparel trades. The trends in employment are significant for indicating the specific effects of the growth in supermarkets. It is only in the food category that there has been a sustained decline in numbers of employees throughout all the regions over the last fifteen years. The trends in turnover show a marked increase in all the regions, of course, but with most growth in the eastern and south-western parts of the country and the suburban areas of London. This mainly reflects a response to rapid population increases and higher levels of income. Table 3.5 updates the trends in total numbers of shops, turnover and employment to the latest period for which statistics are available.

Further regional variations may be seen in terms of the distribution and territorial market penetration of particular major chain organisations. These tend to reflect the general spread of firms originating from different source areas. In grocery business, for example, Sainsbury's are essentially a southern-based company

TABLE 3.5

Recent Growth Trends in the Regions

Per cent Increases or Decreases (Except for Income in £s)	*No. of Shops 1966–71*	*Total Sales 1966–71*	*Total Employ-ment 1966–71*	*Popula-tion Size 1966–71*	*Average Income 1968*
East Anglia	−8·1	+35·0	−2·0	+8·44	1211·1
East Midlands	−1·3	+35·7	+10·2	+3·91	1212·3
South West	+6·4	+40·0	+7·1	+5·90	1197·2
South East	+0·1	+47·2	+3·5	+2·87	1325·5
West Midlands	−3·9	+35·6	−1·2	+3·88	1251·2
Scotland	−12·0	+33·7	−3·3	+1·18	1136·5
North West	−11·9	+35·4	−1·1	+1·73	1166·9
Wales	−1·9	+43·3	+4·1	+2·12	1136·6
Yorks and Humber	−3·2	+36·1	−1·9	+2·59	1186·4
Northern	+2·3	+38·3	+2·5	+0·78	1136·6

Source: Provisional Figures of the Census of Distribution, 1971 and the Family Expenditures Survey, 1968–69.

whereas Moores' Stores are almost exclusive to the North-East; in the clothing trade, Jackson-the-Tailors are more heavily concentrated in the North-East and Scotland while Alexandre's are mainly concentrated in Yorkshire and the North-West. Scott[29] has described some further interesting spatial patterns for other lines of trade, including the distinct territorial claims of the two largest jewellers of H. Samuel Ltd., emanating from the Midlands and spreading to the North, and James Walker Ltd., predominantly concentrated in the South-East. While these regional distinctions exist, however, there are proportionately more retailing companies in Britain which are fully national in their network of operations than occurs in most other European countries and the USA. These are usually the single largest firms in particular lines of trade, of course, such as Tesco in groceries and Montague Burton in tailoring.

Contrasts with Europe and the USA

There have always been considerable differences in retailing characteristics between Europe and the USA, especially in the numbers of shops found and the sizes of individual outlets.[30] In many respects, Britain has occupied a position somewhat intermediate between the two extremes. The differences which occur are mainly an expression of broader differences in population densities, purchasing power, levels of mobility and shopping habits, and also degrees of planning control. Prior to the major period of revolutionary changes in retailing methods, the following comparisons were drawn by Jefferys and Knee.[31] In 1954–55, the average number of people served per establishment in continental Europe was 72, in Britain 86, and the USA 152. The average number of employees per establishment, as an index of size, was respectively 2·7, 4·3 and 5·7. There were and remain further, substantial variations inside Europe, of course, and generally speaking shops are larger and less numerous in the northern and western countries compared to those in the east and south. Even within the major countries of the Common Market there remain considerable differences in the organisational structure of trade as Table 3.6 indicates.

Table 3.6

Percentage Share of Total Turnover by Different Retail Organisations in Western Europe

	Belgium (1970)	France (1969)	Italy (1969)	Nether-lands (1970)	W. Germany (1970)	Britain (1971)
Co-op Societies	2·1	2·7	1·1	1·5	2·9	7·2
Multiple Groups	6·5	6·3	1·0	↑	13·3	25·8
Variety and Dept. Stores	6·4	6·2	2·7	25·6 ↓	10·3	10·2
Independent Stores	84·3	75·0	95·2	70·5	63·3	52·9
Mail Order	0·7	1·1	—	0·7	4·7	3·8
Miscellaneous	—	8·7	—	1·7	5·5	—

Source: A collation of various statistics in the Economist Intelligence Unit, 'Retail Distribution in the Common Market', *Special Supplement on Marketing* (London, 1971).

Since the mid-1950s, however, there has been a common experience amongst nearly all countries in the emergence of new mass-merchandising techniques and the consequent trends to fewer but larger new types of outlets. The changes which have taken place, nevertheless, have proceeded at different rates and different levels and have become manifest in different kinds of retail forms. These new differences are best indicated by some reference to case examples.

1. In France, there have been dramatic developments in the form of hypermarkets (hypermarchés), which constitute free-standing superstores on the outskirts of towns and measure anything up to 250,000 square feet in size. They tend to combine the functions of variety stores and supermarkets, but are physically more akin to large discount stores and even cash and carry warehouses. Essentially, they offer convenience in access and low prices for a wide range of goods, but in surroundings which are often stark and lacking visual appeal. Their growth in number has been spectacular from just four in 1967 to 212 in

1973[32] and the average selling area is now 63,000 square feet. A summary of their characteristics in comparison with other European countries is given in Table 3.7.

Until the advent of the hypermarket, however, retailing in France remained much less affected by new methods of selling than might have been anticipated. The independent retailers still accounted for about ninety per cent of the shops and eighty per cent of total turnover in the mid-1960s. Multiple chain groups have remained small in corporate size and localised to particular areas, and in 1970 there were only 1,500 supermarkets proper, less than a half of the total number in Britain.[33] Traditional conservative attitudes have also hampered the development of voluntary group-trading methods amongst the independents who continue to specialise to a greater degree than those in Britain and often engage in extensive processing of goods (as in the case of the boulangeries with bread and the pâtisseries with cakes). This overall fragmentation of the retail system extends into wholesaling where several intermediaries are commonly employed in distributing goods.

2. Germany's experience of retail change has been more similar to that in Britain although there remain certain basic differences. Most important amongst these are the recent developments in large discount and variety stores in 'out-of-town' locations. Some of these resemble the French hypermarkets and have been referred to in these terms. About 406 such hypermarkets were estimated to be in existence at the beginning of 1973, averaging nearly 70,000 square feet in selling area and capturing 6·8 per cent of total retail turnover.[34] Other types of new superstores resemble more closely conventional department stores but with substantial self-service food halls. Collectively, there are over 1,000 superstores at the present time with forecasts for 3,000 by 1980.[35]

It is partly because of an earlier growth of discount stores in Germany that supermarkets tend to be fairly small in size. There is also generally less multiple chain ownership in both food and specialist goods trade. The stronger hold of independent owner-ship has not led to fragmentation as in France, however, and voluntary group-trading practices are probably stronger here than in any other country except the Netherlands. They command

TABLE 3.7

Characteristics of Hypermarkets in Western Europe

	Belgium	Denmark	France	Italy	Netherlands	Switzerland	West Germany	Britain
No. of Hypermarkets	46	2	212	3	7	10	406	1
Total Selling Area (sq. ft.)	3,303,214	232,370	13,334,800	303,540	364,000	632,000	27,942,138	56,000
Average Selling Area (sq. ft.)	71,809	116,185	62,900	101,180	52,000	63,200	68,823	56,000
Average Car Parking (sq. ft.)	214,200	373,500	364,700	446,792	160,000	291,600	200,000	288,000
Average No. of Employees	140	195	205	165	78	108	142	240
% Total Retail Trade	4·6	<1	4·8	unknown	<1	1·5	6·8	unknown

Source: MPC and Associates, *The Changing Pattern of Retailing in Western Europe 1973* (Worcester, 1973) and Smith, B. V., 'Retail Planning in France: The Changing Pattern of French Retailing', *Town Planning Review*, **44** (1973), 279–306.

about sixty per cent of total grocery sales and are also much more important in the non-food trades than is the case in Britain. Retailer co-operatives, organised to effect bulk purchasing through their own wholesaling channels on a non-profit making basis, are again much more strongly developed than in Britain. According to Guirdham,[36] the largest retailer co-operative, Edeka, comprised 115 local associations and 37,000 independent retailers in 1970 accounting for some twenty per cent of total food sales in Germany. In contrast, the consumer co-operatives have had a similar history to those in Britain and command about the same relative percentage share of total retail sales at the present time.

3. The innovations in modern methods of retailing that have taken place in the USA are different from those in Europe in three basic respects. First, they occurred at a much earlier time and often preceded those in Europe by as much as a decade. Secondly, they have resulted in many more and altogether larger-scale developments than those in Europe. Thirdly, they have had a much greater spatial impact in changing the pattern of retail distribution. (See, for example, Figure 3.6.)

The supermarket revolution that took hold in Britain in the early 1960s had its most conspicuous effects in the USA in the early 1950s.[37] Comparisons of the Census of Business for 1948 and 1963 reveal a tremendous decline in the total numbers of food stores from 537,000 to 319,000. Over the same period, however, the numbers of the largest food stores (with annual sales of more than a million dollars) increased from 2,315 to 14,518. Unlike the origins in Britain, nevertheless, much of the impetus for supermarket development came from independent vendors rather than the chain organisations. This was facilitated by the growth of retailer co-operatives, as in Germany, although most expansion in the last decade has been made by the multiples. Currently, there are estimated to be just over 40,000 supermarkets proper, and the majority of these are in excess of 15,000 square feet in floor space size[38] (virtually the maximum size of the single largest supermarkets in Britain). In addition, there are a further 36,000 superettes, an American term for smaller self-service grocery stores. Supermarkets and superettes together accounted for only

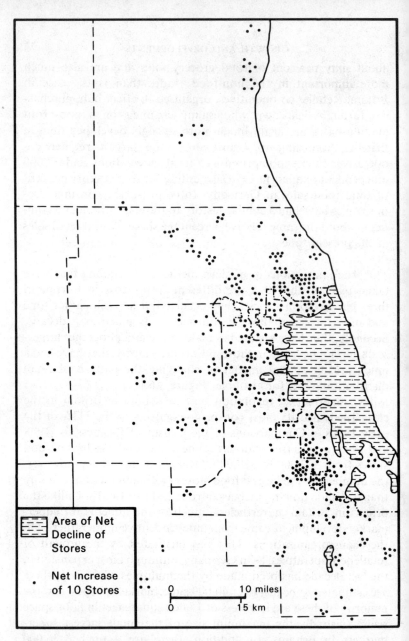

FIG. 3.6 *Spatial changes in the number of retail establishments in Chicago, 1948–58.* (After Berry, B. J. L., 'Commercial Structure and Commercial Blight', *University of Chicago, Department of Geography, Research Paper No. 85*, 1963)

thirty-eight per cent of the total number of all grocery stores in 1973 but commanded eighty-nine per cent of total grocery sales.

During the 1950s there was also considerable growth in the numbers of variety and department stores, particularly in suburban areas. These formed the nuclei for new, planned 'out-of-town' shopping centres and reflected a response to the massive shifts in population distribution that had taken place since the war. The suburban population doubled in size from 1945 to 1965 and, because it comprised mainly the higher and middle-class social groups, generated an enormous reservoir of purchasing power. Consequently, between 1955 and 1965, the market share of retail sales commanded by the suburbs increased from twenty-five per cent to fifty per cent of total metropolitan sales. The 1963 Census of Business recorded 3,153 new shopping centres with more than 100,000 square feet, and twenty-five of these had more than a million square feet.[39] These and subsequent developments and their impact on the central area are discussed in more detail at a later stage.

The most recent trend in new retailing methods has been the growth of discount stores. These initially penetrated the market for hardware and appliance goods but have increasingly moved into the food trade. In the early 1960s they were often excluded from new shopping centres on the grounds that they might have reduced the overall quality image, but such restrictions did not last long. By 1966, there were estimated to be 2,685 discount stores with an average total floorspace of 64,000 square feet.[40] They constitute the nearest American equivalent to the European hypermarket, and in Britain their counterpart would be the Woolco, Gem and Co-op superstores.

THE PROCESS OF ORGANISATIONAL CHANGE

Although there are considerable international differences in the rate and form of retail change the general trend to a larger-scale economy is a common feature of all the westernised countries. The immediate causes for this trend are to be found in the changing technology within distribution itself. Consumers require an increasing degree of convenience in shopping and an increasing choice in the selection of goods and services; firms can provide this and at relatively cheaper costs by building larger stores in new types of locations. The recent phenomenon of mass-selling techniques, however, is part of a more general process of organisational change, the explanation of which has followed a number of different interpretations.[41]

The simplest interpretation likens the evolution of the retail system to the process of natural selection or Darwin's theory concerning the 'survival of the fittest'. Those companies which are most likely to survive or prosper over a long period of time are those which best perceive and subsequently adapt to the changing demands of consumers and the changing technology of distribution. Department stores are often cited as an example of stores which have been slow to respond to new circumstances, while certain of the grocery chains responsible for the development of supermarkets are examples of more progressive elements. Survival may sometimes require the re-location of a store when there are major changes in the physical environment, such as a re-distribution of population or the diversion of traffic through a road-improvement scheme.

A second interpretation refers to the 'wheel of retailing' or the wave-like cycle of change which follows from the development of a new business innovation.[42] The innovation is usually slowly adopted at first, then gains increasing popularity, and finally settles to a position of general acceptance before retreating into relative obscurity. The department store, supermarket and more recent discount store are each an expression of an innovation at a different stage in the cycle. Not all innovations are successful of course, and the main determinant of success has tended to be whether the new form of selling is more competitive over prices or not.

A third interpretation suggests that the entire retail system, and particularly that in North America, has undergone a complete cycle in terms of the type and range of merchandise which is offered by stores.[43] This is described as a 'general-specific-general' cycle, referring to the way in which consumers in the nineteenth century were served predominantly by general stores, then in the first half of the twentieth century by speciality stores, and now increasingly by general stores again. Discount stores, hypermarkets and superstores are seen to be comparable in size and function to entire shopping centres but to play essentially the same role for the community as the old rural trading-posts used to.

Finally, there is a Marxian or dialectic interpretation which views the process of change as a series of stages, within each of which there is some degree of rejection or negation of elements of the retail system in the previous stage.[44] In the Marxian context, these stages are represented by an existing thesis, a future anti-thesis, and an eventual synthesis. If the trading philosophy of small independent grocery stores constituted an original thesis, the trading philosophy of supermarkets would represent the anti-thesis and the resulting melting of these in terms of the trading philosophy of self-service stores and supercttes would be an equivalent to their synthesis. An alternative example is the difference in trading philosophies between the high profit margin/low sales turnover concept of the department stores and the low profit margin/high sales turnover concept of the discount stores, the resulting synthesis of which is the discount department store.

With the exception of the wheel theory, however, there has been relatively little geographical interest shown in these theories of organisational change and primarily because they are difficult to examine from a spatial perspective. Most geographical studies have centred on the environmental consequences involved rather than the causes or origins of change. Certain recent geographical enquiries, nevertheless, indicate the emergence of two new areas of interest into growth aspects of the distributive trades. The first concerns the patterns and processes which are involved in the spread or diffusion of new business innovations. This has obviously been derived from the general popularity of 'diffusion models' in geography as a whole. The second area of interest is more difficult to define in such a succinct way but has to do with assessments of the relative costs and benefits involved in new forms of business organisations. This includes the costs and benefits accruing to consumers or the public at large as well as to the companies which are directly concerned.

So far, most of the research into the diffusion of new business innovations has been descriptive of various patterns to be observed rather than explanatory about the underlying forces at work. Not unexpectedly, there have been several case-studies dealing with the spatial evolution of the supermarket and the spread of branch stores of chain groups.[45] Perhaps the most authoritative case-study to date, however, is Yehoshua Cohen's investigation of the spatial evolution of planned regional shopping centres in the United States.[46] This traced the development and subsequent concentration of 422 'out-of-town' shopping centres throughout the country between 1949 and 1968. Figure 3.6 indicates that, although the first development took place in Raleigh, North Carolina, most of the initial concentration or 'adoption' of the innovation occurred in the Mid-West and Far-West. It was only after 1955 that the major cities of the North-East became adopters (with the exception of Boston) and not until after 1959 that the majority of the southern cities followed suit. Cohen hypothesised that these differences in the times, and also magnitude and intensity of the adoptions could be explained by a variability in the market conditions of the cities involved. In testing the hypothesis through correlation and regression analyses, however, he found that the relative influence of such factors as population sizes, income levels and the economic strength of the central areas of cities changed considerably through each of the four main periods of growth, although generally speaking they had more effect in the earliest stages than in the later ones. His conclusion was that a fuller understanding of the complexity of the diffusion process requires a much more detailed examination of the entrepreneur's perception of development prospects than was possible in his own study.

The studies concerned with the costs and benefits accruing from business innovations have been much more disparate and piece-meal than those linked around the methodology of diffusion research. They have an obvious connection, however, with traditional considerations in the economics and business science fields. Indicative of the work which has focused on the supply side is a study by David Thorpe and associates[47] into the relative costs and benefits to be found in different forms of grocery distribution. A comparison is essentially made between the relative levels of efficiency involved in the relationships between independent grocers and wholesalers on the one hand and multiple food chains and manufacturers on the other. Specific examples are given about

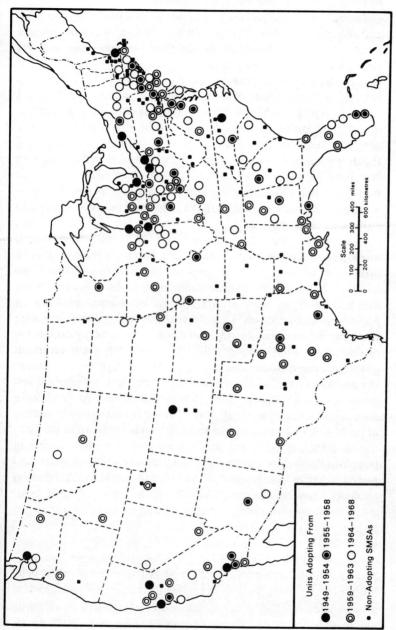

Fig. 3.7 *The spread of planned regional shopping centres in the United States, 1949–1968. (After Cohen, Y. S., 'Diffusion of an Innovation in an Urban System', University of Chicago, Dept. of Geography, Research Paper No. 140, 1972)*

Units Adopting From

● 1949–1954   ◉ 1955–1958
◎ 1959–1963   ○ 1964–1968
■ Non-Adopting SMSAs

Scale

100 200 300 400 miles
200 400 600 kilometres

differences in organisational systems and methods of deliveries and the physical as well as economic consequences that tend to result. Most of the work on the demand side has dealt with the problems of price variations for particular kinds of goods. Certain studies have concentrated on a comparison of prices between different types of new stores, such as between discount shops and supermarkets;[48] others have looked at the areal pattern of prices in different parts of the city or drawn even broader contrasts between urban and rural situations.[49] In combining these approaches to a study of selected food items throughout Northern Ireland, O'Farrell and Poole[50] somewhat surprisingly found a much closer relationship between the prices of goods and the locations of stores than was obtained between prices and store sizes or ownership.

Apart from these new and special areas of interest, however, most of the geographical work which has been bound up with growth trends and developments in the distributive trades has focused simply on the overall differences to be observed in the business composition of centres. These have been most widely considered in the context of different sizes and types of towns or in terms of a national or regional system of centres. The Census of Distribution has again provided the most important statistical source for these studies, furnishing summary figures on retailing for all towns over 2,500 in population size, and a more detailed breakdown for different lines of trade for those over 20,000. In addition, further separate statistics for the main centres or central areas of towns, as against the total figures for the urban authorities as a whole, are given in the case of towns over 50,000 in population size. The way in which such data have been utilised and linked to the major theoretical concerns of marketing geography forms the basis of the next chapter.

REFERENCES

1. A detailed discussion on the major characteristics of wholesaling is contained in Beckman, T. N. and Engle, N. H., *Wholesaling, Principles and Practice* (Ronald Press, 1939).

2. Tietz, B., 'Future Development of Retail and Wholesale Distribution in Western Europe', *British Journal of Marketing*, **5** (1971), 42–55.

3. There has been relatively little geographical study of the locational patterns of wholesaling. The most important summary work to-date is Vance, J. E., *The Merchant's World: The Geography of Wholesaling* (Prentice-Hall, 1970).

4. Crosse and Blackwell Ltd., Survey of Cash and Carry Depots.

5. Nielsen Co. Ltd., 'Cash and Carry Survey', *Nielsen Researcher*, **13** (1972).

6. Thorpe, D. and Kirby, D. A., 'The Density of Cash and Carry Wholesaling', *Manchester University Business School, Retail Outlets Research Unit, Report No. 4* (1972).

7. Chambers, J. H., 'Wholesale Markets for Horticultural Produce in Cities and Towns', *Horticultural Marketing Council, Report 14* (London, 1963).

8. Hardman, Sir H., 'The New Covent Garden Market Scheme', *Journal of the Royal Society of Arts* (October, 1971), 762–77.

9. McFadyen, E., *Voluntary Group Trading: Six Case Studies* (HMSO, 1971).

10. National Economic Development Office, Committee for the Distributive Trades, *The Future Pattern of Shopping* (HMSO, 1971).

11. McFadyen, E., *op. cit.*

12. Jefferys, J. B., *Retail Trading in Britain 1850–1950: A Study of Trends in Retailing with Special Reference to the Development of Cooperative, Multiple and Department Store Methods of Trading* (Cambridge University Press, 1954).

13. Jefferys, J. B. and Knee, D., *Retailing in Europe: Present Structure and Future Trends* (Macmillan, 1962).

14. Gower Economic Publications, *Retail Trade Developments in Great Britain 1973–4* (Gower Press, 1973).

15. There have been numerous books on the history of the co-operative movement. See, for example, Cole, G. D. M., *A Century of Cooperation* (Co-op Union Ltd., 1944); Flanigan, D., *A Centenary Story of the Cooperative Union of Great Britain and Ireland* (Co-op Union Ltd., 1969).

16. Jefferys, J. B., *op. cit.*

17. Jefferys, J. B. and Knee, D., *op. cit.*

18. Hoyt, H., 'US Metropolitan Area Retail Shopping Patterns', Part I, *Urban Land*, **25**, No. 3 (1966), 3–15.

19. Johnson, P., 'The Development of British and American Mail Order Trading', *British Journal of Marketing,* **4** (1971), 220–6.

20. Kirk, J. H., Ellis, P. G. and Medland, J. R., 'Retail Stall Markets in Great Britain', *Wye College Marketing Series No. 8* (1973).

21. Scott, P., *Geography and Retailing* (Hutchinson, 1970).

22. Guirdham, M., *Marketing: The Management of Distribution Channels* (Pergamon, 1972).

23. For a general summary of recent developments, see Wilkens, W. H. (ed.), *Modern Retailing: Evolution and Revolution in the West European Distributive Trades* (Business Publications, 1967).

24. National Economic Development Office, *op. cit.*

25. Gower Economic Publications, *op. cit.* Further estimates (with slightly higher figures) are to be found in the Institute of Grocery Distribution, *Report on the Physical Characteristics of New Supermarkets* (1972).

26. Nielsen surveys indicate that the share of grocery trade held by the symbol shops rose from thirteen per cent in 1961 to twenty-one per cent in 1966, but there has been little further growth since then. See Nielsen Co. Ltd., 'Annual Grocery Review', *Nielsen Researcher*, **14** (1973).

27. Gower Economic Publications, *op. cit.*

28. MPC and Associates Ltd., *The Changing Pattern of Retailing in Western Europe 1973* (Worcester, 1973).

29. Scott, P., *op. cit.*

30. A major, though slightly outdated, comparative study is Hall, M., Knapp, J. and Winsten, C., *Distribution in Great Britain and North America: A Study in Structure and Productivity* (Oxford University Press, 1961).

31. Jefferys, J. B. and Knee, D., *op. cit.*

32. Smith, B. V., 'Retail Planning in France: The Changing Pattern of French Retailing', *Town Planning Review*, **44** (1973), 279–306.

33. Guirdham, M., *op. cit.*

34. MPC and Associates Ltd., *op. cit.*

35. Tanburn, J., *Superstores in the 70s: A Comparison of Shopping Developments in Britain and the Common Market* (Lintas Ltd., 1972).

36. Guirdham, M., *op. cit.*

37. Zimmerman, M. M., *The Supermarket: A Revolution in Retailing* (McGraw-Hill, 1955).

38. Supermarket Institute, *Facts About New Supermarkets Opened in 1971* (Chicago, 1972); 'Annual Report on Grocery Store Sales', *The Progressive Grocer*, April (1973).

39. Hoyt, H., 'U.S. Metropolitan Area Retail Shopping Patterns', Part II, *Urban Land*, **25**, No. 4 (1966), 3–16.

40. Applebaum, W., 'Consumption and the Geography of Retail Distribution in the United States', *Proceedings of an International Congress on Distribution and Town Planning*, 1966, Brussels, Belgium.

41. For a general discussion of these, see Gist, R. E., *Retailing: Concepts and Decisions* (Wiley, 1968).

42. Hollender, S. C., 'The Wheel of Retailing', *Journal of Marketing*, **24** (1960), 37–42.

43. Brand, E. A., *Modern Supermarket Management* (Fairchild, 1965).

44. For a detailed discussion of dialectics, see Blake, W. J., *Elements of Marxian Economic Theory and its Criticisms* (Garden, 1939).

45. For example, Dawson, J. A., 'The Development of Self-Service and Supermarket Retailing in Ireland', *Irish Geography*, **6** (1970), 194–9; 'The Development of Self-Service Retailing in Nottingham', *East Midland Geographer* (1973).

46. Cohen, Y. S., 'Diffusion of an innovation in an Urban System: The Spread of Planned Regional Shopping Centres in the United States 1949–68', *University of Chicago, Dept. of Geography, Research Paper No. 140* (1972). See also Berry, B. J. L., 'Hierarchical Diffusion: the Basis of Development Filtering and Spread in a System of Growth Centres' in Hensen, N. (ed.), *Growth Centres in Regional Economic Development* (Free Press: Collier-Macmillan, 1972).

47. Thorpe, D., Kirby, D. A. and Thompson, C. H., 'Channels and Costs of Grocery Distribution', *Manchester University Business School, Retail Outlets Research Unit, Report No. 6* (1973).

48. For example, Thorpe, D., 'Food Prices: A Study of Some Northern Discount and Super Stores', *Manchester University Business School, Retail Outlets Research Unit, Report No. 4* (1972).

49. For example, Campbell, W. and Chisholm, M., 'Local Variation in Retail Grocery Prices', *Urban Studies*, **7** (1970), 76–81; Parker, A. J., 'An Analysis of Retail Grocery Price Variations', *Area*, **6** (1974), 117–20.

50. O'Farrell, P. N. and Poole, M. A., 'Retail Grocery Price Variations in Northern Ireland', *Regional Studies*, **6** (1971), 83–92.

4 National and Regional Systems of Centres

There have been literally scores of geographical studies during the last two decades concerned with describing broad differences in business provisions between towns. This remarkable flood of work seems to be due to the coincident growth of interest in both theoretical and practical research over the same period in which detailed published statistics about the distributive trades had at last become available and numerous techniques of analysis had been developed to deal with them. The majority of the studies, however, have continued to reflect the traditional predilection in marketing geography for distinguishing between the rank levels in business status of places. The main new feature lies in a common adherence to the notion of the hierarchy as the preferred framework for summarising these distinctions.

Nevertheless, two separate kinds of hierarchy studies have emerged in the modern literature. On the one hand, there remains a group of studies which is primarily concerned with differentiating between overall levels of centrality of places to surrounding areas, and hence with the derivation of a hierarchy of service centres or central places. On the other hand, there is a newer group of studies concerned much more specifically with differentiating only the retail importance of towns and the designation of a hierarchy of major shopping centres (viz., the central areas of towns). Both sorts of studies have been involved with testing aspects of central place theory and both have also been used for practical purposes in applications to marketing and planning. In both cases, too, a number of methodological issues have been raised about the nature of the hierarchy as a general concept and considerable discussion has been generated about the proper meaning of centrality and also shopping centre attractiveness.

Some of the more valuable work in recent times, however, has concentrated less on defining a precise structure to the hierarchy than using it simply as a loose guide-line within which to compare variations and changes in business characteristics.

HIERARCHIES OF SETTLEMENTS CLASSIFIED BY CENTRALITY

Hierarchies of settlements as general service centres have been described in many different parts of the world, in under-developed economies as well as in the more advanced countries, and in a historical context as well as the modern-day setting.[1] The range of these studies can only be indicated in the next few pages by selected examples which are limited to Britain and the USA. The selection is intended to reflect on the general growth and development of this kind of work as well as the more specific interests which different researchers have held.

Case Studies in Britain

Brief mention has already been made of the pioneering work of Arthur Smailes in describing a hierarchy of the main service centres throughout England and Wales before the last war.[2] This had considerable influence on subsequent research in Britain in two main respects. First, it established a concise methodology for measuring the relative centrality of urban places and one which could be easily duplicated elsewhere. Essentially, this involved the selection of representative functions or 'urban traits' which increased in frequency of occurrence with the general increase in sizes of centres. Secondly, the resultant classification provided the first national yardstick against which more in-depth regional assessments could be made. Five major size-orders of centres were defined and the nomenclature of major cities, cities, minor cities or major towns, towns, and sub-towns used to describe them.

The detailed specifications involved in Smailes' study are now clearly out-of-date, however, and it is preferable to dwell on a more recent study that has adopted the same mode of approach. R. D. P. Smith has provided the most comparable modern counterpart in two separate studies of England and Wales.[3] The differences that arise in Smith's studies are due to the much greater assortment of data on which he has been able to draw and also to a considerable body of experience gained from other researchers following in Smailes' wake.[4] Thus Smith expanded Smailes' original five indices of centrality to a total of thirty-five, involving such specialised criteria as the incidence of Boots, Woolworth's and Marks and Spencer's stores, the 'star' class of the best hotel and the league division of the local football team, but generally aiming for the same balance in social and economic factors as before. Similarly, he was able to increase the sample of places studied from 750 to 2,500 and to subdivide the major categories of size orders in the resultant classifications. The classi- fication of service centres for England is shown in Figure 4.1.

Smith's studies also provide a unique opportunity for examin- ing the nature of changes which have taken place in the hier- archies for England and Wales over more than a quarter of a century. The general conclusion which he has drawn, however, is that 'centres of all types are remarkably stable in their distri- bution and relative status'. It is only in a relative few cases that substantial increases or decreases in rank level of importance can be seen. The specific changes which have occurred in England since Smailes' study are summarised in Figure 4.2. Of the major cities classified by Smailes, only Bradford has declined in overall status and this has been replaced by Coventry. All the centres of Smailes' third order size (equivalent to 3A centres in Smith's scheme) retain their rank importance, with the exception of Coventry, although several new centres have been upgraded to this level in 1965 and mainly from a northern belt (such as Bolton, Huddersfield, Doncaster, Chester and Lincoln). Most change has clearly taken place amongst the smaller centres. The greatest concentration of growth has occurred in the outer metro- politan area of London, and the greatest concentration of decline is to be found within the towns bordering the Pennines. Altogether, 138 places increased their status as against 78 which declined, with the difference in figures here reflecting on the general growth of the urban population in the country as a whole.

A comprehensive study of the relative status of service centres throughout Wales was also undertaken by Harold Carter in the

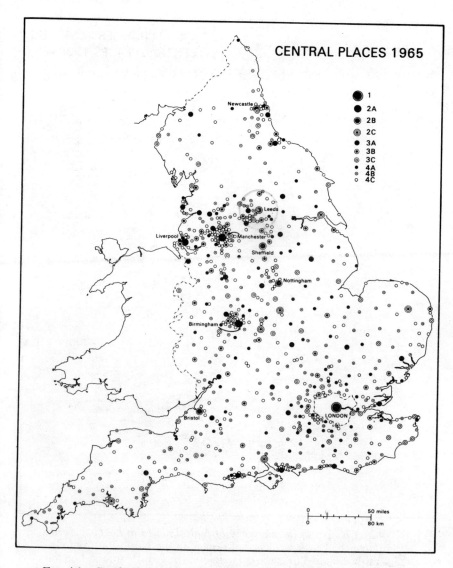

FIG. 4.1 *Smith's hierarchical classification of central places in England, 1965.* Four main size-orders of centres are shown, with the largest ones concentrated in the main conurbations and industrial areas and the smallest ones more widely distributed throughout the country. (After Smith, R. D. P., 'The Changing Urban Hierarchy', *Regional Studies*, **2**, 1968, 1–19)

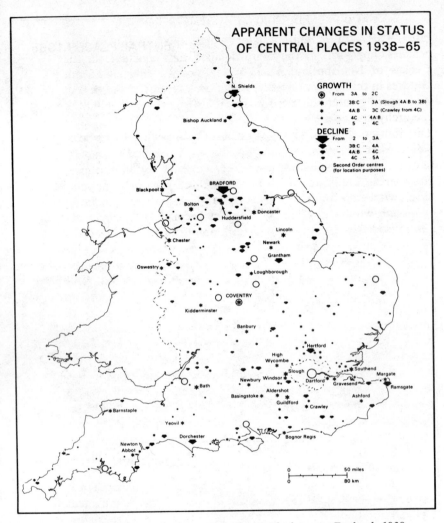

FIG. 4.2 *Changes in the hierarchy of central places in England, 1938–1965.* Note the heavy incidence of decline in the North-East and also the West Riding of Yorkshire compared to the growth around London and the Home Counties. It is primarily the small centres based on a single and depleted economic resource (such as mining towns) which have experienced most decline; the growth points tend to be new or planned expansion towns or those with an increasing commuter population. (Adapted from Smith, R. D. P., 'The Changing Urban Hierarchy', *Regional Studies*, **2**, 1968, 1–19)

late 1950s.[5] Like Smith's later work, this sought to link Smailes' approach to the more detailed data available in the Census of Distribution. There were two new and significant features in this study, however, which considered together reflect on a much greater concern for the underlying theory behind the hierarchy concept. First, the statistics from the 1950 Census of Distribution that Carter relied on most fully referred to whole-saling establishments rather than shops. He argued 'it can be shown that wholesale trade is a good index of urban importance, for whereas retail trade varies locally in direct relation to population, wholesale trade is an essentially centralised function'. Although wholesaling has now in fact become increasingly de-centralised the relevance of Carter's point remains that indices of service importance or the centrality of places should reflect on the territorial extent of the trade area influence rather than the particular characteristics of the local urban population. The second feature relates to this in that he stressed the difficulty of using any single kind of centrality index for producing a universal hierarchical scheme when the types of towns under consideration in the study clearly varied in their major underlying economic bases. Specifically, he argued that such variability in the root functions of towns 'is the main factor breaking down the idealised concept of a clearly defined hierarchical system'. While this has often been noted in other studies[6] it has never been so fully made explicit. Carter attempted to show these effects by cross-referencing his rank orders for the service component of towns with a classification of their major functions. This is summarised in Table 4.1.

The towns of Wales have also been examined in more depth in a series of regional and sub-regional studies principally conducted by former students of Carter.[7] The most important of these is by W. K. D. Davies who focused on the smaller valley settlements in the Rhondda.[8] This is distinctive because it represents the first major study in Britain specifically concerned with central place theory and with testing the notion of the hierarchy through more rigorous statistical analysis. The study follows Carter's lead in searching for a more accurate and objective measurement of centrality but returns to the use of retail trade figures from the census rather than wholesaling. Since the study was conducted in a

TABLE 4.1

Carter's Hierarchy and Functional Classification of Welsh Towns

Grade		Example	No. of Wholesale Establishments
A	Major city and national capital	Cardiff	over 500
B	Major towns dominating both immediate industrial and outlying rural areas	Swansea	over 150
C	Regional centres dominating large rural areas	Aberystwyth	20–60
Cxi	Industrial centres dominating marked tributary areas which are intensively developed	Merthyr Tydfil	
Cxii	Resorts of major importance	Rhyl	
D	Major local centres dominating well defined but limited areas	Brecon	10–19
Dx	Industrial centres with limited tributary areas	Aberdare	
E	Local centres dominating strictly limited and immediate rural areas	Denbigh	
Exi	Industrial centres strictly limited in areas tributary to them	Ebbw Vale	
Exii	Resorts of minor importance	Tenby	
Exiii	Ports	Fishguard	
F	Subtowns (these were further sub-divided)	Pontardawe	

Source: Carter, H., *The Towns of Wales* (University of Wales Press, 1965).

predominantly mining and industrial area there is less regard for variations in economic base amongst the settlements. However, the attempt to identify a hierarchy of central places within an area that has developed through special resource factors has drawn considerable criticism.

Davies' index of centrality was derived from the family of localisation coefficients used in industrial geography.[9] These essentially provide a ratio of the number of particular activities found in any one place to the average calculated for a whole system of places. He constructed the formula:

$$C = \frac{t}{T} \cdot 100 \quad \text{where } C = \text{the location coefficient of function } t$$

$$t = \text{one outlet of function } t$$

$$T = \text{the total number of outlets of function } t$$
$$\text{in the whole system}$$

When each coefficient is multiplied by the number of outlets of each functional type a centrality value is obtained. The addition of all the centrality values obtained within a settlement provides a summary measure of the degree of centrality or its functional index.

In the actual case-study application, Davies used the number of employees within establishments to represent the number of outlets since this allows for size differences to be included. The functional indices for fifty-one settlements were then plotted on graphs and five groupings were derived. The validity of these groupings was confirmed by correlation analyses of the extreme members of each group. A further graph plot of the average centrality values for the forty-nine functions within each group provided a more vivid indication of the latent structure of the hierarchy (Figure 4.3).

There have been many other descriptions of regional hierarchies of central places in other parts of Britain.[10] While there is insufficient space here to mention all of these some reference should be given to the work of Howard Bracey.[11] Bracey conducted several studies in southern and south-western England in the 1950s which are noteworthy in three respects. First, he concentrated primarily on the identification of a hierarchy of service centres in predominantly rural areas where an ideal central place system is usually best developed. Secondly, besides using the incidence of specific service activities within settlements as an index of centrality he conducted questionnaire surveys of people's movements and hence differentiated between the relative importance of centres according to their functional use. Thirdly, he made an interesting international comparison with John Brush of the spacing of rural service centres in southern England and those in south-western Wisconsin.[12] A remarkable similarity in spacing standards of three size-orders of centres in the two areas was found (occurring at 21 mile, 8–10 mile, and 4–6 mile intervals) despite the differences in cultural and economic conditions between the two countries.

Case Studies in the USA

One of the few and most comprehensive studies which have been made of the urban hierarchy at the national scale in the USA is that by the Rand McNally Company in its publication *City*

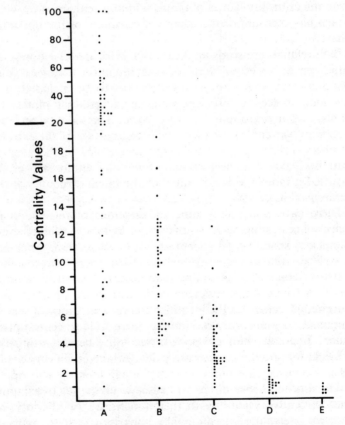

FIG. 4.3   *Average centrality values for retail activities in the Rhondda settlement hierarchy.* The letters refer to the five size-orders of centres identified. The method used for defining the centrality values is explained in the text. (After Davies, W. K. D., 'Centrality and the Central Place Hierarchy', *Urban Studies*, **4**, 1967, 61–79)

Rating Guide: The Nation's Markets at a Glance.[13] This is a study which illustrates the usefulness of the hierarchy concept in practical work since it is specifically oriented to businessmen and marketing personnel engaged in such pursuits as planning advertising campaigns, sales promotions and the like. It is also interesting from an academic viewpoint, however, to the extent that it combines a ranking of the business importance of the largest towns with a functional classification of their major economic functions. It is probably the most exhaustive exercise which has ever been undertaken to link these two sets of urban characteristics together.[14]

The relative business importance in 1964 of 1,090 towns and cities (generally those over 20,000 population size) was determined through a composite index based on seven variables of retailing, wholesaling and banking activities. Four main size-orders of towns were derived, according to whether they commanded a national, regional, significant local, or limited local business importance. These are exemplified in the map of Illinois (Figure 4.4) by the numbers 1 to 4. Each town was also further categorised according to the particular trade area characteristics of its major shopping centres, whether these acted as the primary centres for a large surrounding area, as secondary centres for a large surrounding area (as in the case of Rock Island and Moline in the urban complex focused on Davenport), as localised centres within a larger city's trade area but outside its metropolitan limits, or as suburban centres found inside a larger city's metropolitan boundaries. The letters A, B, C and S represented these categories and were used in different sets of frequency to give some additional indication of levels of importance. Thus, in reference to Figure 4.4, Chicago was rated 1-AAA, Rockford 2-A, Evanston 2-S, Moline 3-BB and Dixon 4-C.

The functional classification of types of towns was based on an economic activity code of the number of people employed in different occupations. Altogether, eighteen separate types of towns were distinguished, a selection of which are shown in Figure 4.4. By far the most common types of towns are those which function primarily as manufacturing, retailing, residential or diversified towns.

While the Rand McNally study serves to illustrate both a national assessment of towns and a special practical application of geographical concepts, most of the research conducted in the USA over the last two decades has been based on a theoretical interpretation of regional systems of centres. The Mid-West, and especially the State of Iowa, has drawn most attention since the physical conditions within this part of the country and the rich agricultural economy which they support most nearly reflect on the isotropic conditions of a plane surface and uniform purchasing power assumed in central place theory.[15] Many studies have therefore been made in this region with the specific objective of evaluating the real existence of a hierarchy of centres and examining its structural form.

Considerable reference has already been made in this connection in Chapter Two to the work of Brian Berry. Those studies of his which have so far been mentioned, however, have principally been concerned with extending or modifying the relevance of Christaller's theory. An alternative investigation may be considered here which provides much more empirical description about the actual business composition of the hierarchy and various other characteristics to be found in the real world. This is a study which was undertaken in south-western Iowa, where a five-tier hierarchy of central places was identified and described in terms of hamlets, villages, towns, small cities and regional capitals.[16]

It should be noted that the nomenclature used to describe settlements in the American literature differs from that conventionally used in Britain, to the extent that the terms 'town' and 'city' and also 'metropolis' often refer to much smaller settlements than would be the case in our own connotation. In Berry's study, the average population sizes equated with the five-tier hierarchy are 100, 500, 1,500, 6,000 and 60,000. A regional metropolis would contain an average of 250,000 people.

The hamlet in Iowa, however, is clearly comparable in its limited service role with the hamlet that exists in East Anglia. Only one or two stores are usually found and seldom more than four or five. These tend to be grocery or general stores which command a catchment area of up to three miles in one direction and a total population of 500. The village in Berry's study typically

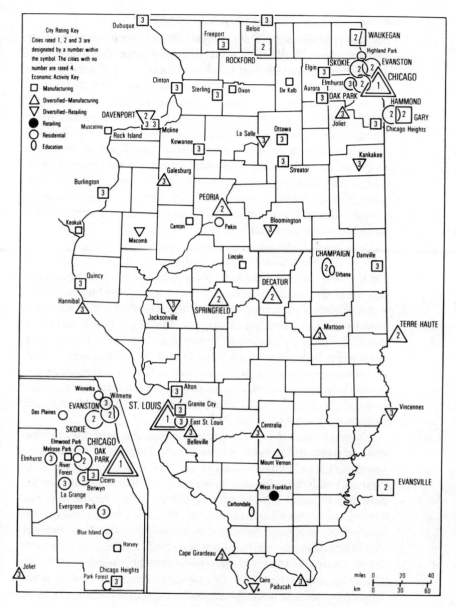

FIG. 4.4 *Rand McNally's city rating indices and economic activity codes for towns in Illinois.* (Adapted from Forstall, R. (ed.), *City Rating Guide: the Nation's Markets at a Glance*, Rand McNally, 1965)

contains 30–40 separate establishments which between them provide about 25 different kinds of service activities. The sorts of activities representative of this level of centres are: a post office, church, petrol station, farm elevator and more than one food shop. The catchment area extends on average five miles and up to 1,200 people are served. The town typically contains 90–100 separate establishments which perform about 40–50 different activities. Besides the activities found in the village, the town also provides: a doctor and dentist, dry cleaner, hardware store, bank and funeral parlour. The catchment area extends to eight miles and up to 4,000 people are served. The term 'small city' in Berry's study really refers to the county seats which are often similar in their overall functional role to the larger, traditional type of market town in Britain. These may have 300–400 establishments engaged in 90–100 different activities. The diagnostic activities for this level of centre include: local (county) government offices, a jewellers, small department store, cinema, auto showroom, and a wide range of clothing shops. The catchment area extends to twenty miles and encompasses up to 30,000 people. The regional capital, which in this case is Council Bluffs, a twin city of Omaha in Nebraska, contains over 1,000 establishments which are engaged in more than 200 different activities. These include a wide range of specialised retail shops, professional services and cultural facilities. The catchment area extends to about forty miles and encompasses over 100,000 people.

In summary, the relative importance of the hierarchy in Iowa may be described in these general terms: hamlets and villages are essentially local convenience centres; towns are full convenience centres; small cities (or county seats) are shopping-goods centres; and the regional capital is a specialty-goods centre and also secondary wholesale centre. We will show later, in connection with studies of shopping movements, that the distinction between convenience-goods trade, shopping-goods trade, and specialty-goods trade has provided the most common though not always the most useful basis for describing differences in the actual functional use made of the hierarchy of centres by consumers.

HIERARCHIES OF THE MAIN SHOPPING CENTRES OF TOWNS

There have been many more studies in Britain than in other countries specifically concerned with ranking just the retail importance of towns and cities. This particular penchant on the part of British academics is not altogether easily explained but has to do with the fact that the major shopping centres in this country are more conspicuously linked together as a system of activities than is the case elsewhere. This can be seen in two ways. First, as has been stated in Chapter Three, there is a much stronger entrenchment of national and regional chain groups of companies than is found in other countries so that all the larger shopping centres contain a high proportion of virtually the same kinds of stores. Secondly, there has been a much more conscious attempt by the planning profession to establish a rigid and stable hierarchical organisation of shopping centres both nationally and regionally, through the universal application of some strict development controls.

There have been two separate assessments of the hierarchy of major shopping centres at the national scale in recent years: one by David Thorpe[17] and the other by William Carruthers.[18] Despite the fact that these were conducted about the same time in the mid-1960s and both were specifically based on the new data contained in the 1961 Census of Distribution, different conclusions were reached about the structure of the hierarchy. This was partly due to a difference in the kinds of techniques used to measure retail importance; it was also partly due to a basic difference in objectives concerning the potential usefulness of a size classification of shopping centres.

Thorpe's approach was altogether much simpler than Carruthers. He took as his index of retail importance the total turnover or sales generated by all types of trade in the main shopping centres of towns. The sample essentially comprised all those towns in England, Wales and Scotland for which published statistics were available. Graph plots were then made of the rank-size distribution of turnover figures and arbitrary breaks determined in a subjective way, mainly by inspection of the marginal cases. Seven grades of centres were obtained and described as: regional centres, sub-regional centres, area centres, major centres, district centres, local or suburban centres, and village or small suburban centres. The arrangements of the four largest groups of centres are shown in Figure 4.5 in relation to the concentration of population in surrounding areas.

Thorpe's study was really less concerned with describing the hierarchy in precise terms, however, than with establishing a classificatory framework (consistent with many other regional hierarchy assessments) within which a wide range of retailing characteristics could be compared. In particular, Thorpe was interested in identifying spatial variations in the organisational mix of centres and the differences which could be seen in the locational policies of firms. This tends to reflect on a general theme throughout all his work, namely the practical extension of spatial enquiries to problems of a business kind. Carruthers' study, by contrast, has as its end product a detailed definition of the hierarchy. There is consequently much more in-depth analysis of those factors which contribute to a shopping centre's importance and much more critical evaluation of the relative effectiveness of the scheme as a whole. This perspective may be explained by Carruthers' involvement with regional planning and hence a professional concern for assessing the degree of balance in shopping provisions throughout the country.

Carruthers devised a composite index to measure the retail importance of each of 240 towns. This was based on the number of points awarded for three separate criteria: the amount and type of trade conducted within the central area; the net attraction of the town as a whole to surrounding areas; and the provision that was made in certain specialised facilities. In the first of these criteria, type of trade was represented by the proportion of total turnover which was captured by the non-food trades. Points were then allocated according to how far above or below the national average this proportion was found to be. The second criterion was represented as the difference between the total turnover actually generated throughout the urban area and the theoretical turnover that might be expected (from multiplying the resident population by an average regional expenditure figure per head). This difference provides an estimate of the net trade gained, and hence points were allocated according to the size of the gain. The third

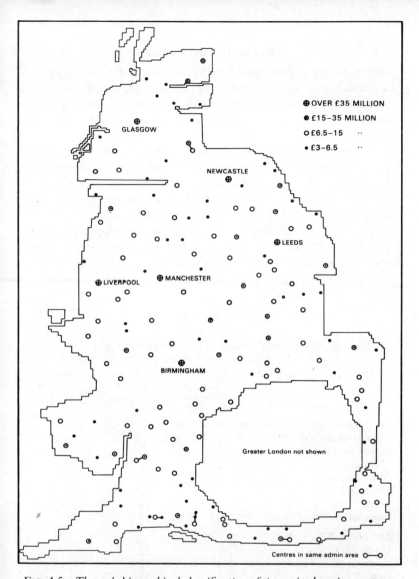

FIG. 4.5 *Thorpe's hierarchical classification of the main shopping centres in Great Britain, 1961.* The four size-orders of centres have been plotted on a population cartogram, which dramatically alters the shape of the country according to the concentration of population. Thus Wales and the Highlands of Scotland are virtually eradicated, and London accounts for an enormous proportion of the territory which is occupied. The effect on the distribution of centres is that these are seen to be much more evenly spaced than would otherwise be the case. (Adapted from Thorpe, D., 'The Main Shopping Centres of Great Britain in 1961', *Urban Studies*, **5**, 1968, 165–206)

criterion was represented by the degree of concentration of durable-goods shops within the central area. This was expressed as a percentage of the national total of these types of shops and points were assigned on the basis of the percentage figures obtained.

A hierarchical classification of shopping centres was finally derived from inspection of the total number of points awarded each town.Three main size-orders were recognised, each of which could be subdivided. These were simply given an alpha-numeric label rather than being described in qualitative terms. A detailed listing of the categorisations of the largest shopping centres is given in Table 4.2. It should be noted that Carruthers felt that the size gap between London and the major regional centres is so large that this should be indicated by omitting a class of 2A centres.

TABLE 4.2

Major Shopping Centres in England and Wales, 1961
Classified by Carruthers

Centre	Points for Selected Facilities	Points for Amount of Trade	Points for External Attraction
SECOND-ORDER CENTRES			
Sub-order 2B			
Manchester	24	25	25
Birmingham	23	25	24
Liverpool	24	25	22
Leeds	24	24	21
Newcastle	22	23	25
Sub-order 2C			
Nottingham	23	22	22
Leicester	20	21	22
Cardiff	20	21	21
Sheffield	20	21	20
THIRD-ORDER CENTRES			
Sub-order 3A			
Bristol (City)	18	20	20
Hull	20	20	18
Bradford	20	20	17
Wolverhampton	19	20	21

TABLE 4.2—*Continued*

Centre	Points for Selected Facilities		Points for Amount of Trade		Points for External Attraction	
Coventry	19		20		18	
Plymouth	19		20		17	
Southampton	18		20		19	
Croydon		19		20	—	
Kingston		19		20	—	
Blackpool	19R		19R		20R	
Derby	19		19		20	
Doncaster	19		19		19	
Bournemouth (The Square)	18R		19		21R	
Norwich	18		19		20	
Reading	17		19		20	
Swansea	18		19		18	
Sunderland		18		19		16
Middlesbrough		18		19		16
York	20		18		18	
Preston	19		18		18	
Huddersfield		19		18		16
Bolton		19		18		16
Brighton (Town Centre)	18R		19R		19R	
Chester	18		18		19	
Cheltenham	18		18		18	
Gloucester	18		18		18	
Newport	18		18		18	
Northampton	18		18		18	
Romford	18		18		18	
Brixton		18		18	—	
Bath	18		18		17	
Watford	17		18		19	
Exeter	17		18		18	
Southend	17R		18		18	
Stoke (Hanley)		17		18		14
Luton		17		18		14
Ilford		17		18	—	
Wood Green		17		18	—	
Cambridge	16		18		19	
Oxford	16		18		19	
Carlisle	18		17		17	
Worcester	18		17		17	

Source: Carruthers, W. I., 'Major Shopping Centres in England and Wales', *Regional Studies*, **1** (1967), 65–81.

A comparison of Table 4.2 with Thorpe's map (Figure 4.5) shows that the two classifications are the same only with respect to the five major regional shopping centres. Thorpe's class of sub-regional centres includes all of Carruthers' 2C centres and nearly a half of his 3A centres. There is less general correspondence between the two schemes in fact than occurs between Carruthers' classification of shopping centres and Smith's classification of the overall service role of towns (Figure 4.1). Somewhat significantly, there is considerable agreement between this classification of Carruthers and an earlier one he himself had undertaken of the overall service role of towns in the mid-1950s.[19] This enabled him to make some assessment of the kinds of changes taking place in the shopping hierarchy, though generally speaking, his conclusions were much the same as those of Smith. Carruthers' study, however, gave more tacit recognition to varying rates of change amongst towns which differ substantially in their underlying economic base. The towns which are indented in the listings of Table 4.2 indicate those particular cases where retail performance was considered to be seriously affected by special economic conditions.

Besides these major national enquiries, there have, of course, been several more detailed studies of the hierarchical arrangements of shopping centres within the regions.[20] While each of these is interesting in its own right, two particular case-studies will be mentioned here which give a further indication of the practical uses to which a size classification can be put. The first of these comprises an application to planning problems in the North-West;[21] the second involves a relationship with store location research in the North-East.[22]

The study of the North-West was conducted by a research team at the University of Manchester in relation to a county planning enquiry. The specific objective was to assess the likely effects on existing shopping centres of a proposal for a new, large 'out-of-town' shopping centre to be built at Haydock Park, between Liverpool and Manchester. The approach taken by the research team was to describe the existing hierarchy of shopping centres and then project this into the future given a variety of assumptions about the precise size of the new development. The existing hierarchy was established along fairly conventional lines.

A functional index of relative retail importance was used, based principally on the incidence of twenty-one different kinds of stores. A set of alternative future hierarchies was then determined by a variety of means. Essentially, a detailed examination was made of trends in consumer behaviour and purchasing power and consideration was given to the individual effects of urban redevelopment schemes and major road improvements. This allowed for changes in the sizes of trade areas to be computed which could then be translated back into terms of the relative rank status of shopping centres. Given that a very large development was allowed to take place at Haydock Park, the study predicted that the shopping centres to suffer most in decline would be St. Helens, Wigan and Warrington. In the event, however, the proposal for the 'out-of-town' centre was refused by Lancashire County Council.

In contrast, Thorpe and Rhodes' study in the North-East was undertaken in association with a local chain group of food stores. The specific objective in this case was to identify the trading practices of different competing firms in and around Tyneside with a view to establishing the best sorts of locations for their own sponsoring company. The first step in the exercise was again a description of the hierarchy of shopping centres. This involved a much more rigorous analysis, however, and included a large number of very small centres. A complex index of shopping attractiveness was used, based on the number of non-food shops which were found in a centre weighted by the number of multiple traders (viz., the non-food multiples, banks, food multiples, and co-operatives). Once the hierarchy was established, a series of comparisons were then made of the degree of concentration in different size-orders of centres of the principal grocery firms. This was extended to consider the apparent preferences of firms for locating in planned versus unplanned centres and the density of their operations in different parts of the region.

METHODOLOGICAL ISSUES INVOLVED

The assortment of studies that have been reviewed in the last two sections indicate that the hierarchy concept has been used for a

variety of purposes. It is mainly because of this variability in underlying objectives, together with the unique circumstances of business activities within any area, that there has been relatively little consistency in methods of approach. This has meant that it is difficult to compare the findings of one study with another except in the broadest of terms. Certain common problems have been encountered, however, which have to do with the technical procedures involved in ranking centres and the taxonomy employed in grouping these together. Specifically, there have been two methodological issues at the heart of these studies: what is the proper meaning of the centrality of places and the attractiveness of shopping centres and how can these be best interpreted; is there a natural order to the size levels of centres in reality or is the hierarchy concept just a convenient but arbitrary means of classification?

Measurements of Centrality and Shopping Centre Attractiveness

The centrality of a settlement (and the attractiveness of a shopping centre) refers in a strict theoretical sense to the location of a centre as well as its size. It reflects on a territorial drawing capacity rather than simply the volume of consumers served. This becomes manifest in the range as well as numbers of activities which are performed and hence the degree of centrality of any place is indicated by the degree of complexity and overall character of its business provisions.

The problem which confronts the case-study investigator is that this complexity can never ever be fully measured or represented. Time and cost constraints in field research and the limitations of published statistics are such that only selected indices of centrality can be used. The problem is compounded in the case of defining more specifically the attractiveness of shopping centres, since attractiveness depends on additional considerations to do with the amenities found and the imagery involved and these are not easily translated into quantitative terms. The result is that numerous different criteria have been used to index both centrality and shopping attractiveness and there has been much critical discussion in the literature about the relative merits of these.[23]

Some recent comparative evaluations of the effectiveness of alternative indices, however, have shown that there is often little to choose between them. One such study, by the present author, examined the degree of correspondence found in the rankings of several centres in different regions using those indices advocated by several of the people whose work has been reviewed earlier.[24] These rankings were also compared against those produced by an assortment of raw census statistics. An example, for the North-West region, is shown in Table 4.3. No consistent agreement was found in the rank placements of centres using the different indices and no greater degree of similarity existed between them than could be seen amongst the rankings obtained from the raw census statistics. It was concluded that, for broader scale levels of enquiry, no single best index can really be identified, and that indices based on aggregate data are just as suitable for differentiating the relative business importance of places as those indices of a more specific kind.

A further finding of this study, and one that has been widely confirmed elsewhere, was that a ranking of towns by their urban population size usually closely resembled the rankings produced by different sets of business criteria.[25] This is significant because, given the variable economic functions of towns, we are usually led to believe that there will be an imbalance between these: 'Population alone is not a true measure of the central importance of a city: a large mining, industrial, or other specialised-function town might have a small tributary area and exercise few central functions.[26] The theoretical expectation is that there will be a much closer relationship between rankings by business criteria and those by the trade-area population sizes of towns. In practice, however, this is rarely attained. Table 4.3 shows that there are higher degrees of correlation between the rankings of towns in the North-West according to urban population sizes and the indices of Carruthers, Davies and the Manchester University research team than occurs between these same indices and estimated trade-area population sizes.

The main weakness common to all indices of centrality and also shopping centre attractiveness, therefore, lies in their inability to properly distinguish between that proportion of trade which accrues from the local population as against that which is

TABLE 4.3

Rank Correlation Coefficients of Indices of Centrality in the North West

Example (a) for 21 most important places

	Hay-dock	Car-ruthers	7-fold	City pop.	Hint. pop.	Total ests.	Total sales	Employ.	CA sales	CAD sales
Haydock method	1·00	0·93	0·84	0·78	0·71	0·81	0·92	0·92	0·84	0·88
Carruthers' method		1·00	0·84	0·80	0·79	0·78	0·96	0·97	0·96	0·95
7-fold method			1·00	0·93	0·73	0·99	0·90	0·89	0·73	0·75
Population size				1·00	0·67	0·93	0·89	0·88	0·73	0·69
Hinterland population					1·00	0·67	0·80	0·79	0·71	0·65
Total establishments						1·00	0·85	0·84	0·67	0·70
Total sales							1·00	0·99	0·90	0·88
Full employment								1·00	0·92	0·90
Central area sales									1·00	0·94
CA durable sales										1·00

Example (b) for 44 most important places

	Hay-dock	City pop.	Hint. pop.	Total ests.	Total sales	Employ.
Haydock method	1·00	0·81	0·87	0·89	0·91	0·91
Population size		1·00	0·83	0·90	0·92	0·90
Hinterland population			1·00	0·85	0·90	0·90
Total establishments				1·00	0·93	0·93
Total sales					1·00	0·99
Full employment						1·00

Source: Davies, R. L., 'Variable Relationships in Central Place and Retail Potential Models', Regional Studies, 4 (1970), 49–61.

drawn from people in surrounding areas. Linked with this is their failure to allow for the influence of particular tastes and preferences amongst different groups of consumers. It is often claimed, for example, that an excess of trade can be recognised for certain centres which can then be taken to reflect on a wider catchment area. In fact, this excess trade could also be explained by a greater propensity to spend on the part of the local population.

The root cause of the deficiencies in these indices, of course, is to be found in the data which are utilised. Neither selected types of activities nor aggregate statistics can ever be expected to reveal the nature of the clientele which is served. The only effective way of making some assessment of the types of consumers to be found is to conduct extensive surveys; and this is usually impractical in a regional context.[27] An alternative is to include other data about the socio-economic structure of towns. A framework for this kind of approach has been described in Chapter Two and we have seen some rudimentary steps in this direction in the case-studies reviewed earlier. This is essentially the combination of a hierarchical size classification of the business importance of places with a functional classification of their underlying economic bases.

The Form of the Hierarchy

The issue concerning the form of the hierarchy can be traced back to the different theoretical propositions of Christaller and Lösch. Christaller, as we have seen, asserted that the general process of centralisation would always lead to a stepped-like arrangement of different size groups of centres within a region. Lösch, on the other hand, contended that the influence of other location factors in the real world would be such that these distinct size groups would become blurred and a distribution would result that is more akin to a continuum. While these propositions are not in themselves conflicting, they tend to crystallise the two sides of a debate which has often been confused in its meaning. Essentially, there are on the one side a set of empirical studies which have been specifically concerned with testing this aspect of central place theory (for example, those by Davies and Berry) and these have mainly produced evidence to support the existence of a stepped-like hierarchy. On the other side are a set of case-studies which have been less concerned with the theory as such (for example, those by Smailes and Carruthers) but which have nevertheless made detailed assessments of the size relationships of centres and frequently concluded that they form a continuum. The debate has been conducted both in the context of whole settlements and in terms of the major shopping centres of towns; and there have been some investigators who have claimed that both forms of the hierarchy exist. Thus Thorpe and Rhodes found in their study of the North-East that 'the values of the index of centrality for all shopping centres show a dispersion (on a graph) which is more akin to a stepped continuum than to a hierarchy of grades', while at the same time suggesting that 'there is evidence, however, that discrete grades of such a hierarchy do exist in reality'.

The confusion that has entered the debate arises from the assortment of indices which have been used to measure centrality. What many studies have really shown is not the true form of the hierarchy in any area but the type of hierarchy that accrues from the particular ranking method employed. This is the point of Vining's criticism concerning the apparent evidence in support of discrete size-orders of centres.[28] Rather than rejecting Christaller's theoretical proposition he has rejected the acceptability of various criteria used in empirical studies for properly distinguishing the central functions of towns. Given our previous discussion about the general deficiencies of all ranking methods, the amount of hard evidence on both sides of the debate would seem to be quite small.

Looked at in these terms, there appears to be much justification for the claim that both forms of the hierarchy can be recognised. However, there are also some strong logical arguments as to why this should be so. Whether the hierarchy is seen as a distinct stepped-like structure or tending to a continuum depends essentially on the underlying economic character of an area. This in turn may vary according to the scale level of the enquiry. Thus it is much more likely that the system of centralised activity we are concerned with will be more conspicuous in a rural than in an industrial area where the influences of other location factors will be particularly marked.[29] Similarly, a much more clear-cut arrangement of central functions will be apparent in small and homogeneous areas rather than in large ones with a mixed economy.[30] Berry and Barnum have neatly summarised these distinctions by contrasting those studies which deal with the basic *elements* of the central place hierarchy and those that deal with its *aggregate* relations.[31] Such views are clearly much more in keeping with the real differences in proposition of Christaller and Lösch.

CORRELATES OF CENTRE SIZE AND DIFFERENT TYPES OF TOWNS

Irrespective of the methodological issues which may be involved, several of the case-studies reviewed point to the practical value of the hierarchy concept as a size classification. While the size of a centre is obviously not the only factor of interest to a regional planner or store location researcher, it usually becomes the first consideration in any assessment of the state or relative 'health' of business activities within an area. There are clearly many different manifestations of size itself, but equally important perhaps are the concomitant effects. These include the volume of traffic that may be generated, public services and amenities that will be required, the extent to which nuisance conditions may arise and so on.

Generally speaking, the larger centres are growing at the expense of the smaller. In terms of business performance, where this may be measured by turnover per establishment, the central areas for the biggest towns in Britain are clearly the most efficient of all shopping centres to be found.[32] They continue to attract the greatest proportion of new types of store and remain the leaders in fashion changes and selling ideas. The single main cause for their increasing prosperity, however, is to be found in the growth in mobility of the population at large. The explosion in car ownership over the last ten years has radically improved the accessibility of the largest shopping centres to all but those in the most isolated communities.

These trends have raised some difficult planning problems. On the one hand, there is a clear need to protect the smaller, weaker components of the overall hierarchy, many of which have suffered an acute decline. On the other hand, there is the additional responsibility of easing traffic congestion and preventing building decay in the largest shopping centres. A dilemma exists in that the implementation of massive redevelopment schemes leads to a further increase in the attractiveness of the largest shopping centres when ideally such extra growth should probably be curtailed.

Some reference has already been made to the locational preferences of different types of firms. In general, the multiple organisations are more heavily concentrated in the largest shopping centres, whereas the co-ops and independent stores remain tied to the smaller ones. This pattern is distorted to some extent, however, by the obvious relationship between the sizes of individual business establishments and the sizes of the centres in which they are found. Thus Table 4.4 shows that while there is overall a greater number of co-ops in the smaller shopping centres of Tyneside the single biggest co-operative stores are to be found in the largest shopping centres. To a considerable extent, the sizes of individual business establishments reflect basic differences in methods of trading operations. It is essentially the chain stores engaged in mass-selling practices which are the largest, while those still geared to counter-top services remain small and hence more locally-bound.

The importance of the size variable needs to be qualified by many other considerations, such as the ages and locations of particular shopping centres. There are some enormous differences

TABLE 4.4

Size and Location of Large-Scale Grocery Shops in Tyneside

Centre	Multiples			Co-operatives		
	1,000 sq. ft.	1–2,000 sq. ft.	2,000 sq. ft.	1,000 sq. ft.	1–2,000 sq. ft.	2,000 sq. ft.
A	105	28	23	7	2	20
B	97	11	10	18	11	1
C	114	10	8	46	11	8
D	94	4	1	79	13	3

Source: Thorpe, D. and Rhodes, T. C., 'The Shopping Centres of the Tyneside Region and Large Scale Grocery Retailing', *Economic Geography*, **42** (1966), 53–73.

in relative business performance between say the new towns around London and the old towns in the Tyneside conurbation.[33] Common to all towns in close proximity to a major regional shopping centre, however, is a relative depletion of those specialist provisions that might otherwise be found.[34] Thus Bradford does not have such a full complement of the highest quality shops that might be expected, given its population size, because of the neighbouring dominance of Leeds. Likewise, Coventry lacks status in these respects because of its nearness to Birmingham.

The range in quality levels of shops within any centre is further significant in reflecting the socio-economic conditions of the consumers who are served. R. Schiller has furnished some interesting examples of this in case-studies of the suburban centres around London.[35] He examined the distribution of luxury clothes shops, high-class restaurants, dealers in foreign cars and other similar criteria in relation to the structure of the outer metropolitan population. While a town such as Slough, with a population of 93,000 and a thriving main shopping centre, contained only four of his highest status businesses, places like Beaconsfield, with a population of 12,000 and a much smaller main shopping centre, contained twenty-seven of these kinds of businesses. The difference is explained by the fact that, whereas the population in Slough is predominantly working-class, thirty-six per cent of Beaconsfield's population are employed in management or the professions.

Variations in the structure of business composition in relation to the socio-economic structure of the population can be seen in a more general way by reference to a functional classification of towns. Table 4.5 compares some aggregate retail statistics for those different types of towns classified by Moser and Scott from a factor analysis of fifty-seven socio-economic variables.[36] The main differences to be found in these figures bear a close resemblance to those regional variations which were discussed in Chapter Three. Thus co-ops are particularly strong in the mining towns of the North-East and the older industrial towns in the Midlands and the North-West. Generally speaking, there is a much healthier business economy amongst middle-class towns than those which are predominantly working-class, insofar as this

TABLE 4.5

Retailing Characteristics for Different Types of Towns

	Average Sales Per Shops	% No. of Food Shops	% Total Sales for Multiples	% Total Sales for Co-ops	% Total Sales for Independents
Major Service Centres	20,336	59·1	46·1	9·5	44·4
Seaside and Other Resorts	18,340	53·7	44·6	5·8	49·6
Spas and Admin. Centres	22,443	54·3	41·4	1·1	57·5
INDUSTRIAL TOWNS					
Mainly Railway Centres	16,560	58·7	37·7	14·4	47·9
Mainly Ports	19,305	60·1	42·4	12·7	44·9
Mainly Textile Centres	14,410	58·9	38·2	10·2	51·6
Mainly Mining Centres	15,065	62·5	37·5	16·1	46·4
Mainly Metal Centres	15,851	60·5	38·9	13·9	47·2
SUBURBAN TOWNS					
Exclusive Residential	21,458	53·9	—	—	42·3
Older, Mixed Residential	20,721	55·6	—	—	42·4
Newer, Mixed Residential	21,367	55·2	—	—	42·9
Light Industry Towns	22,027	56·0	—	—	40·3
Older, Working Class	17,048	56·2	—	—	52·4

is indicated by average levels of turnover and the proportionate numbers and types of shops to be found. It should be noted that in this classification the category of service centres comes closest to what might be properly called a system of central places.

SUMMARY

The literature dealing with the hierarchy concept at the regional scale contains a bewildering variety of studies, the objectives of which are predominantly oriented to problems of a unique or localised kind. Given the enormous number of individual case-studies which have been made, however, it is surprising that there has been relatively little synthesis of or generalisation about their collective findings, particularly with respect to the factual validity of the concept and its relevance to practical work. We have sought to stress in this chapter that there are several important considerations that need to be kept in mind in seeking to distinguish the wood from the trees. Primarily, it is necessary to discriminate between those studies which are essentially concerned with describing the overall levels of business importance or the centrality of settlements from those which are exclusively concerned with just shopping centres or the retail component of towns. The precise form that a hierarchy will take in each of these two contexts will then depend on several additional factors, mainly the ranking methods that are employed, the type of areas in which the centres occur, and the character as well as the sizes of the populations that are served. Whether the hierarchy emerges as a real or imaginary one will also depend on the extent to which the actual body of centralised activity is disaggregated from the total mix of businesses to be found. The main value in properly identifying a hierarchy, nevertheless, lies not so much in being able to give a literal interpretation to the system of centralised activity itself as in using the hierarchy as the basis of a more comprehensive classification of the entire spectrum of business activities contained within towns. Planners and marketing specialists alike require a reliable and consistent framework for the comparison of all aspects of the tertiary economy and the ordering of towns in terms of the size or status of their centralised activities should be simply the first step in a whole series of comparative assessments.

REFERENCES

1. Berry, B. J. L. and Pred, A., *Central Place Studies: A Bibliography of Theory and Applications* (Regional Science Research Institute, 1965); Andrews, M. F., 'Working Notes and Bibliography on Central Place Studies', University of Toronto, Department of Geography, Discussion Paper 8 (1970).
2. Smailes, A. E., 'The Urban Hierarchy in England and Wales', *Geography*, **29** (1944), 41–51.
3. Smith, R. D. P., 'The Changing Urban Hierarchy', *Regional Studies*, **2** (1968), 1–19; 'The Changing Urban Hierarchy in Wales', *Regional Studies*, **4** (1970), 85–96.

4. For example, Green, F. H. W., 'Urban Hinterlands in England and Wales: An Analysis of Bus Services', *The Geographical Journal*, **116** (1950), 64–88; Carruthers, W. I., 'A Classification of Service Centres in England and Wales', *The Geographical Journal*, **123** (1957), 371–85.

5. Carter, H., *The Towns of Wales* (University of Wales Press, 1965).

6. Smailes referred to the distorting influences of different urban economic functions but without incorporating them into his hierarchical classification; Smailes, A. E. *op. cit.*

7. Some of these are contained in Carter, H. and Davies, W. K. D., *Urban Essays: Studies in the Geography of Wales* (Longman, 1970).

8. Davies, W. K. D., 'Centrality and the Central Place Hierarchy', *Urban Studies*, **4** (1967), 61–79.

9. For a summary of these kinds of techniques see Smith, D. M., *Industrial Location* (Wiley, 1971).

10. See, for example, Tarrant, J. R., 'Retail Distribution in Eastern Yorkshire in Relation to Central Place Theory', *University of Hull, Occasional Papers in Geography 8* (1967); Fullerton, B., 'The Pattern of Service Industries in North East England', *University of Newcastle, Department of Geography, Research Series 3* (1960).

11. Bracey, H. E., *Social Provision in Wiltshire* (Methuen, 1952); 'Towns as Rural Service Centres', *Transactions of the Institute of British Geographers*, **19** (1953), 95–105.

12. Brush, J. E. and Bracey, H. E., 'Rural Service Centres in South-western Wisconsin and Southern England', *The Geographical Review*, **45** (1955), 559–69.

13. Forstall, R. (ed.), *City Rating Guide: the Nation's Markets at a Glance* (Rand McNally, 1965). An interesting alternative study of the national hierarchy in the USA is: Taaffe, E. J., 'The Urban Hierarchy: An Air Passenger Definition', *Economic Geography*, **38** (1962), 1–14.

14. There have been several detailed functional classifications of American towns. See, for example, Berry, B. J. L. (ed.) *City Classification Handbook* (Wiley, 1972).

15. For example, Berry, B. J. L. and Mayer, H. M., *Comparative Studies of Central Place Systems* (U.S. Office of Naval Research, Washington, 1962); Borchert, J. R. and Adams, R. B., 'Trade Centres and Trade Areas of the Upper Midwest', *University of Minnesota, Upper Midwest Economic Study Urban Report 3* (1963).

16. Berry, B. J. L., 'Central Place Theory' in Kornblau, C. (ed.) *Guide to Store Location Research: With Emphasis on Supermarkets* (Addison-Wesley, 1968). This study is also summarised in Berry, B. J. L., *Geography of Market Centres and Retail Distribution* (Prentice-Hall, 1967).

17. Thorpe, D., 'The Main Shopping Centres of Great Britain in 1961: their Locational and Structural Characteristics', *Urban Studies*, **5** (1968), 165–206.

18. Carruthers, W. I., 'Major Shopping Centres in England and Wales, 1961', *Regional Studies*, **1** (1967), 65–81.

19. Carruthers, W. I., 'A Classification of Service Centres in England and Wales', *The Geographical Journal*, **123** (1957), 371–85.

20. For example, Lomas, G. M., 'Retail Trading Centres in the Midlands', *Journal of the Royal Town Planning Institute*, **50** (1964), 104–19; Richardson, C. and Burkitt, R., 'Main Shopping Catchments of the West Yorkshire Conurbation', *European Journal of Marketing*, **6** (1972), 51–9.

21. Manchester University, Department of Town Planning, *Regional Shopping Centres in Northwest England, Part I* (Manchester University, 1964).

22. Thorpe, D. and Rhodes, T. C., 'The Shopping Centres of the Tyneside Region and Large Scale Grocery Retailing', *Economic Geography*, **42** (1966), 53–73.

23. See, for example, Davies, W. K. D., 'The Ranking of Service Centres: A Critical Review', *Transactions of the Institute of British Geographers*, **40** (1966), 51–6.

24. Davies, R. L., 'Variable Relationships in Central Place and Retail Potential Models', *Regional Studies*, **4** (1970), 49–61. See also, McEvoy, D., 'Alternative Methods of Ranking Shopping Centres', *Tijdschrift voor Economische en Sociale Geografie*, **59** (1968), 211–17.

25. Davies, R. L., 'A Note on Centrality and Population Size', *Professional Geographer*, **21** (1969), 108–12; Haggett, P. and Gunarwadena, K., 'Determination of Population Thresholds for Settlement Functions by the Reed-Muench Method', *Professional Geographer*, **16** (1964), 6–9.

26. Ullman, E. L., 'A Theory of Location for Cities', *American Journal of Sociology*, **46** (1941), 853–64.

27. Where researchers like Bracey have undertaken consumer surveys to indicate the functional use of the hierarchy, this has usually been in terms of the movements of people from one settlement to another. There has been little differentiation of local versus external movements.

28. Vining, R., 'A Description of Certain Spatial Aspects of an Economic System', *Economic Development and Cultural Change*, **3** (1955), 147–95.

29. Davies, R. L., 'Structural Models of Retail Distribution: Analogies with Settlement and Urban Land Use Theories,' *Transactions of the Institute of British Geographers*, **57** (1972), 59–82.

30. Carter, H., 'Structure and Scale in the City System', Chapter 5 in Chisholm, M. and Rodgers, B. (eds.), *Studies in Human Geography* (Heinemann, 1973), 172–202.

31. Berry, B. J. L. and Barnum H. G., 'Aggregate Relations and Elemental Components of Central Place Systems', *Journal of Regional Science*, **4** (1962), 35–48. See also, O'Farrell, P., 'Continuous Regularities and Discontinuities in the Central Place System', *Geografiska Annaler*, **52** (1969), 104–14.

32. Price, D. G., 'An Analysis of Retail Turnover in England and Wales', *Regional Studies*, **4** (1970), 459–72.

33. Price, D. G., *op. cit.* See also Carruthers, W. I., 'Major Shopping

Centres in England and Wales, 1961', *Regional Studies*, **1** (1967), 65–81.

34. Thorpe, D., *op. cit.* See also, Berry, B. J. L., 'The Impact of Expanding Metropolitan Communities Upon the Central Place Hierarchy', *Annals of the Association of American Geographers*, **50** (1960), 112–16.

35. Schiller, R., 'Location Trends of Specialist Services', *Regional Studies*, **5** (1971), 1–10.

36. Moser, G. A. and Scott, W., *British Towns: A Statistical Study of Their Social and Economic Differences* (Oliver and Boyd, 1961). Factor analyses have also been made of retail characteristics themselves as in Dawson, J. A., 'Retail Structure in Groups of Towns', *Regional and Urban Economics*, **2** (1972), 25–65.

5 Business Land Uses Inside the City

The spatial pattern of commercial activity inside the city continues to be dominated by a concentration of the largest and most important business establishments in the main centre, or central area, or central business district (CBD). Throughout the rest of the urban area there seems to be a rather haphazard arrangement of mainly retail activities grouped together in different kinds of business configurations. These configurations appear to be particularly numerous and irregular in form in the inner city, when they are much more isolated and physically compact in the suburban fringe (Figure 5.1). The differences that might be perceived in terms of their size, age, shape and functional character are mainly an expression of underlying differences in locational processes at work. They have also been affected by special historical circumstances, including the degree of planning control involved, and variations in the influences of individual companies and the clientele which they serve.

CLASSIFICATIONS OF BUSINESS CONFIGURATIONS

There have been two alternative theoretical approaches to classifying different types of business complexes throughout the city. First, because a majority of shops are seen to require central locations with respect to their potential trade areas, the hierarchy concept in central place theory has been used as the basis to a size differentiation of shopping centres in the same way that it has at the regional scale.[1] There has been a similar kind of discussion about the best ranking methods to employ and a similar kind of

117

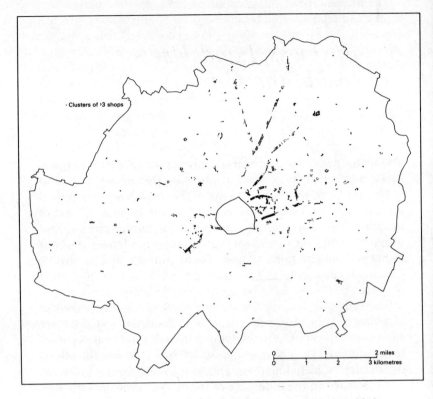

FIG. 5.1 *The distribution of shops and related service establishments in Coventry, 1969.* The high density of shops in the inner parts of the city reflects on a legacy of uncontrolled growth in retailing in the first half of the century. The relative sparseness of shops in the outer areas reflects on the more recent period of tighter planning regulations. The alignment of certain main roads towards the north and east of the city is conspicuous from the linear distributions of shops.

debate about the real form of the hierarchy. To a greater extent in the urban context, however, there have been many studies which have used the hierarchy concept with little regard for the underlying theory. It has often been applied, especially in planning, to a wide range of business configurations irrespective of whether these occupy central positions and function equivalently as central places or not.[2]

The second type of classification has its roots in economic rent theory and relates to the broader notion of accessibility.[3] In this approach, there is much more attempt to discriminate between the different ages, shapes, and functional roles of business complexes as well as their overall importance or size. Three sets of locational processes are assumed to exist which lead to the formation of three kinds of business conformations. There is a set of compact shopping centres found mainly in the middle of residential areas which act as distinct central places in providing a general range of household goods and services to a surrounding population. Next is a set of linear distributions which straggle alongside major roads and contain a high proportion of commercial establishments geared to passing motorised trade rather than local consumers. Lastly, there is a set of special 'districts' found mainly inside or adjacent to the central area which comprise groups of like-kinds of activities catering for the particular demands of certain sections of the population. This approach has a clear parallel with those functional classifications of towns which have been made at the regional scale as we have tried to show in Chapter Two.

The relevance and application of these two types of classifications may again be illustrated by some case-studies drawn from Britain and the USA. A comparison between these two countries is particularly interesting at the urban scale because the effects of societal differences on the nature of business activities are much more clear. In general, a much greater use has been made of the comprehensive functional approach in the USA whereas the simpler, hierarchical approach has been favoured in Britain. Partly, this is because the different kinds of business conformations we have described are more conspicuous in the USA due to the greater influences of the motor car. Partly, it is also explained by the stricter enforcement of planning controls in Britain which have tended to promote considerable uniformity especially within the system of shopping centres.

The Business Pattern in the USA

Just as the State of Iowa has become the 'classical' case area for studies of the regional pattern of business activities, Chicago has emerged as the 'classical' case city for studies of the urban

pattern. This link was first forged in some important work by
Proudfoot[4] and Mayer[5] more than thirty years ago. Both sought
to discriminate between different typologies of business configurations, though Proudfoot gave more attention to their locational
characteristics while Mayer looked more closely at their functions
and forms. Proudfoot's classification contained five main
elements: the CBD, outlying business districts, principal business
thoroughfares, neighbourhood business streets, and isolated store
clusters. Mayer's classification, by contrast, sought to cross-
tabulate four size-orders of business complexes with six different
kinds of shape: an intersection, cruciform, attentuated cruciform,
bimodal, cruciform modified by diagonal, and quadrilateral.

These studies (along with certain others) had a considerable
influence on the recent work of Brian Berry who has provided
the most definitive classification of the modern business pattern in
Chicago.[6] Berry used sophisticated multi-variate statistical techniques (viz., factor analysis) to analyse the functional compositions of more than 125 business complexes in the metropolitan
area. Three main typologies were recognised of the kind we have
already described and these he called nucleated centres, ribbon
developments and specialised functional areas. Further sub-
divisions of these are shown in Figure 5.2.

1. The nucleated centres constitute the main body of shopping
centres proper in the city. It is these which lend themselves most
appropriately to a size differentiation in terms of the hierarchy
concept. We have previously noted that these effectively represent
the urban equivalent to the rural hierarchy that Berry recognised
in Iowa. The urban hierarchy is subject to even greater internal
variations than its rural counterpart, however, and a clear distinction needs to be made between the older, unplanned centres of
the inner city and the newer, planned centres of the suburbs.
Berry therefore described two kinds of hierarchies of nucleated
shopping centres in Chicago and certain differences between these
are summarised in Table 5.1. While the hierarchy of planned
centres displays a similar overall structure to that for the unplanned centres, within any one individual size-order there is
usually found only half the number of shops, a proportionately
much greater average floorspace size to shops, fewer individual
lines of trade, and little use of second and third storeys for business

purposes. Further differences pertain to the free-standing sites of the new planned centres, their greater uniformity in architectural styles and the surrounding expanses of car-parking lots.

2. Ribbon developments are a particularly conspicuous feature in most American cities but they tend to assume a variety of forms.[7] Berry's sub-divisions refer mainly to differences arising from location and age. Traditional shopping streets are essentially former nucleated shopping centres which have expanded alongside major roads in the inner parts of the city and changed in functional role from serving predominantly a local residential clientele to catering much more for passing through-traffic. They have often degenerated to become slum areas and 'skid rows'. Urban arterial developments are ribbons likewise found in the older parts of the city but which have grown up separately from shopping centres and reflect a need for independent locations on the busiest roads where large space-users and affiliated service activities can group together and still command considerable

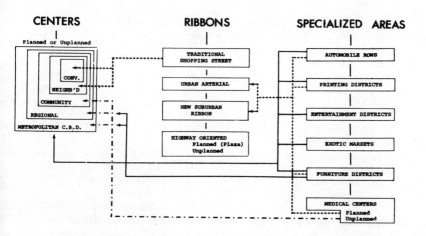

Fig. 5.2 *Berry's classification of urban business conformations.* The lines and arrows indicate that there are often strong functional linkages between shopping centres, ribbon developments and specialised areas. For example, many of the same activities occur in 'traditional shopping streets' as are found in convenience and neighbourhood centres; certain specialised areas can be recognised inside community and regional centres as well as inside the central area.

accessibility to a large segment of the urban market. Typical activities include garage and auto-repair shops, appliance stores, office equipment outlets, funeral houses, lumber yards, electrical supply shops etc., which involve consumers who are often engaged in commercial enterprises themselves or making more occasional specific-purpose trips. New suburban ribbons represent the emergence on the outskirts of the city of linear groupings of garage and auto-repair establishments, mixed with leisure facilities such as ice-cream parlours, drive-in snack-bars, cocktail lounges (in particular), and also with discount houses. Highway-oriented ribbons are 'strip' developments which have emerged alongside the most important trunk roads, comprising activities such as motels, restaurants and service plazas, which are often geared towards inter-city traffic. While some regularities in the size differences of these types of ribbons have been found, Berry made no attempt to describe them in terms of a hierarchy

TABLE 5.1

Characteristics of Nucleated Centres in Chicago

	No. of Ests.	Ground Floor Area Sq. Ft.	Frontage in Feet	Trade Area Population
A. Unplanned Centres				
Major Regional Centres	200	600,000	6,000	300,000
Smaller Shopping Goods Centres				
High-Income Areas	150	330,000	3,600	77,000
Low-Income Areas	100	300,000	3,100	135,000
Community Centres	77	170,000	2,000	60,000
Neighbourhood Centres				
High-Income Areas	40	75,000	1,000	—
Low-Income Areas	55	125,000	1,500	—
B. Planned Centres				
Major Regional Centres	60	400,000	—	—
Shopping Goods Centres	35	150,000	—	—
Community Centres	25	100,000	—	—

Source: Berry, B. J. L., 'Commercial Structure and Commercial Blight', *University of Chicago, Department of Geography, Research Paper 85*, (1963).

or to relate them to equivalent business forms in the rural settlement system.

3. The specialised functional areas which Berry has described are fairly self-evident. Entertainment districts are probably the most obvious and universal examples to be found in any city and reflect the interdependencies between theatres, restaurants, bars and the like. Retail markets constitute a traditional specialised functional area but they have almost entirely disappeared from the American city. A more unique feature in the USA is the 'automobile row' which exists only in embryonic form in European countries. This represents a dense concentration of garages and auto-dealers usually on the edge of the central area where considerable benefits from comparative shopping and other economies of scale can be achieved. The medical district is a further feature found only in the very largest of European cities. This comprises not simply hospitals and associated medical schools, but blocks of offices given over to the surgeries of doctors, dentists and more specialised practitioners whom we would expect to find widely scattered throughout the urban area in Britain.* Other specialised functional areas may be perceived in terms of particular concentrations of like kinds of shops, such as streets distinct for their high-class fashion stores or those made up of tourist facilities and *avant-garde* pursuits. In Chicago, Michigan Avenue represents one such high-class fashion street, and Old Town is renowned as a centre of tourist and 'underground' activities.

Although Berry has provided the most comprehensive classification yet made for the American city, it is to be remembered that the urban business pattern in that country continues to experience dramatic change. The suburbs and its stock of new regional shopping centres continue to expand; the inner city with its legacies of ribbon development is increasingly blighted and becoming decayed; the central area is no longer the magnet of major shopping activities and many specialised functional areas are beginning to break down. The result is that many researchers have felt that an even stronger distinction needs to be made

*There is a growing trend towards health centres and group practices in Britain but these remain relatively small in size compared with the medical complexes in the USA.

between old and new elements of the business system.[8] At the same time, paradoxically, the differences which have hitherto been drawn in new types of business complexes are rapidly becoming blurred. Thus Cohen and Lewis[9] have concluded from their study of retailing in Boston '. . . cross shopping has brought higher-order goods into association with lower-order goods in the same shopping centres, and even the same stores. We find centres of the same functions beginning to take on different sizes and orders, and centres of essentially different functions beginning to take on the same sizes and orders. The result is not the clear nesting pattern comprised of rank-size schemes that had formerly been so characteristic of the landscape, but rather patterns which reveal a diffusion of clusters of various sized but similarly functioning centres.'

The Business Pattern in Britain

There has been relatively little attempt to apply Berry's type of classification to the business pattern of British cities. This is curious because any map of the actual distribution of establishments (such as Figure 5.1) will suggest that the main components of the classification are appropriate, if not the scheme in its entirety. There is a clear difference between the linear concentrations of activities alongside major roads in the inner city and the compact forms of shopping centres in the middle of new housing estates.[10] We also know from experience that the central areas of our largest towns contain specialised functional areas similar to those described for Chicago. The best-known examples are to be found in London, of course, such as the markets of Smithfield, Billingsgate and Covent Garden, the entertainment districts of Piccadilly and Soho, the fashion streets of Bond Street and the King's Road, the specialist medical areas of Harley Street and Wimpole Street, the printing district of Fleet Street, and so on.

The major issue, however, rests on whether ribbons and nucleations in British cities differ fundamentally in their functional roles in the same way as their larger American counterparts. A multivariate statistical analysis of the business configurations in Coventry suggests that they do.[11] The difference in types of activities found in this study were not nearly so clear-cut, nevertheless, and many of the older business configurations appeared to be rather mixtures of the two. These frequently appeared to be original nucleated centres which grew up around a major tram- or bus-stop in the past and which subsequently expanded in a linear fashion in response to the growth in demands of private vehicular traffic. In addition, many of the smaller ribbons were no more than closely spaced corner-stores interspersed with a few repair establishments or garages and were not really cohesive or unitary business complexes in any functional sense. No direct equivalents to the different sub-categories of ribbon developments described by Berry could therefore be recognised in Coventry. Two separate size groupings for the nucleations and ribbons were discriminated, however, and these are shown in Figure 5.3. A significant by-product of the study was that the size groupings for the nucleations displayed much more of a stepped-like hierarchical form than was the case when the total mixture of all types of business configurations were ranked together and plotted on graphs.

There have been numerous studies of British towns, nevertheless, which have treated the diversity of business configurations collectively together and then purported to show a common hierarchical size differentiation of shopping centres.[12] These include a large number of studies conducted by planning departments as well as by academic geographers.[13] As in the case of the regional hierarchies there has been little consistency in methods of approach and it is difficult to compare them and synthesise their findings. This is particularly well-illustrated in two well-known studies for London, by Carruthers[14] on the one hand and Smailes and Hartley[15] on the other, which were conducted at about the same time at the beginning of the 1960s. Carruthers used a sophisticated, composite index of shopping status based on the incidence of certain store types, the rateable values of all stores found, and the frequency of bus services each hour, but his study was restricted to ninety-eight centres representing the upper strata of the hierarchy and was based on information largely extracted from directories. Smailes' and Hartley's study was more firmly rooted in field observation and treated the larger sample of 269 centres, but distinguished between the functional importance of these centres only in terms of the numerical occurrence of a few selected business activities. Needless to say, the two resulting hierarchies were widely diverging. Of incidental interest in these studies is the terminology that the authors employed. Thus Carruthers referred to the set of business complexes he dealt with as service centres, though his index of centrality was based essentially on retail activities (with the exception of banks and cinemas). Smailes and Hartley, in contrast, talked specifically

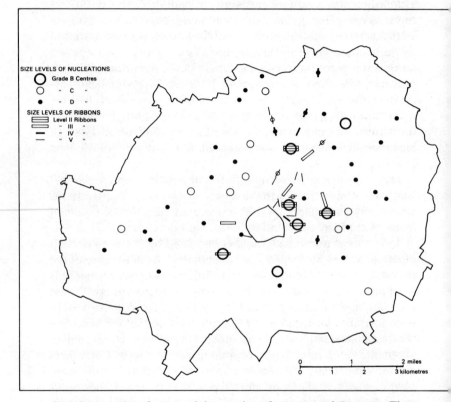

FIG. 5.3 *A classification of the retail configurations of Coventry.* Three types of retail conformations have been recognised from the distributions of shops shown in Figure 5.1: nucleated centres, ribbon developments and a set of mixed centres. In the hierarchy of nucleations, grade B centres are essentially district centres; grade C centres are large neighbourhood centres; and grade D centres are small neighbourhood centres. (From Davies, R. L., 'Nucleated and Ribbon Components of the Urban Retail System in Britain', *Town Planning Review*, 1974, 91–111)

about shopping centres, although their index of centrality comprised few separate types of stores and embraced such things as dance halls, theatres, local government offices, as well as banks and cinemas.

Most of the urban-planning studies for the smaller cities in Britain, however, have shown some conformity for demarcating five main structural levels to the hierarchy of shopping centres.[16] This relates to the five-tier structure typical of smaller American cities, although the grade of regional-type centres is usually weaker in this country (especially outside the conurbations) and the nomenclature of district centres is preferred to community centres. It is more commonly the planning profession, in fact, who have used the terms local centres (or sub-centres), neighbourhood centres, district centres, regional centres and the central area (or main centre), whereas British geographers have tended to distinguish between size categories in the nondescript form of alphabetical letters or roman numerals. This similarity in hierarchical designations lies at the heart of an atlas of shopping centres for most of the major towns and cities of Britain compiled by David Thorpe and associates.[17] Most of the source material for the individual maps produced was obtained from local planning departments.

The basis to the five-tier hierarchy utilised in planning is a set of notional standards regarding the sizes of residential areas that each type of shopping centre should serve (Table 5.2). Burns[18] suggested several years ago that these need revision given the growth in car ownership and consumer mobility taking place. In particular, he advocated that the three lower grades of shopping centres in the hierarchy should be reduced to two so that a more clear-cut distinction between convenience and more specialist shopping can be achieved. Within his scheme, local centres would be made up of only a very few corner-type shops serving catchment areas of about 5,000 people; neighbourhood centres would be decreased in number and upgraded to the size of conventional district centres, comprising (in 1960) over 100 shops and catering to a population of between 20,000 and 40,000. Curiously, however, despite the attractiveness of the scheme it has rarely been used in practice. This is primarily because of the entrenched position of the neighbourhood concept in planning as a whole. It should also be mentioned that Homer Hoyt, one of the foremost developers of shopping centres in the USA, has recently suggested that within America there is likely to be a much greater trend towards rather than away from the provision of neighbourhood shopping centres in the future.[19]

THE INTERNAL CHARACTERISTICS OF SHOPPING CENTRES

The varying accessibility requirements of individual business activities that lead to the emergence of the three different kinds of business complexes also determine at the micro-scale level the precise sites that are occupied inside them: such internal arrangements are mainly explained in terms of the rents which they can afford. Rents are essentially a function of the competition between different groups of activities for particular types of sites. In general, such competition is greatest inside the nucleated centres, for nearly all those activities concerned with domestic shopping

TABLE 5.2

Traditional Planning Norms for Shopping Centres in British Towns

Central Area	This obviously varies in size, but normally a population of 150,000 is required to support district centres in surrounding areas.
Regional Centres	These are normally found only in conurbations and represent former town centres that have been absorbed into a wider urban area (e.g. Gateshead in the Tyneside Conurbation).
District Centres	These relate to a catchment area of 30,000 and contain about 100 shops in the inter-war and early post-war centres.
Neighbourhood Centres	These relate to a catchment area of 10,000 and contain about 35 shops in the older centres.
Local or Sub-Centres	These vary from isolated corner stores to small local parades and cater to a population of 500–5,000.

There is much more flexibility in the current approach to planned provision of shopping centres and such norms have really now become outdated. The consequence, however, is that many new developments are planned on an *ad hoc* basis.

provision would like to be as close as possible to the peak nodal position of greatest crowd convergence. In the case of ribbon developments and specialised functional areas, competition is weaker and rent levels are usually lower because proximity to a single point location is less critical for those activities concerned with only certain sections of the population. The consequence is that a much greater degree of order and stratification occurs in the rental surface of nucleated centres whereas those for ribbon developments and specialised functional areas are fragmented and uneven.[20] The corollary effects of a greater degree of regularity in the pattern of shops inside nucleated centres are discussed in the next two sections.

The Rental Surface of Nucleated Centres

The structure of the rental surface inside nucleated centres may be explained by reference to the graph profiles of bid-rent curves.[21] Bid-rent curves reflect on the rent-paying abilities of different types of activities. The highest bid-rent curves are commanded by those activities which can exploit most fully the advantages that accrue from crowd convergence, such as comparison shopping. Thus clothes shops will normally out-bid furniture shops for the single most accessible sites; furniture shops will normally out-bid hardware shops for the next most accessible sites; these in turn will then out-bid certain food shops and so on. From the cumulative interactions of such bid-rent curves for each activity, an overall rent gradient can be constructed from the peak nodal position of the centre outwards. While this may vary in its degree of steepness from one side of a centre to another it will always tend to contribute to a pyramid shape in the total rental surface.

Barry Garner[22] has used the methodology of bid-rent curves to relate the internal arrangement of retail activities to the structural characteristics of the hierarchy of nucleated centres. The elements of his model are shown in Figure 5.4. Those retail activities which occupy the highest rental sites are those which, at any one size level within the hierarchy, exhibit the highest threshold values in terms of the volume of consumers that are served. In small centres, such as neighbourhood centres, convenience functions will actually occupy the most central positions because it is only

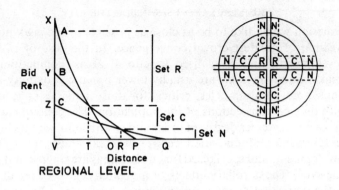

REGIONAL LEVEL

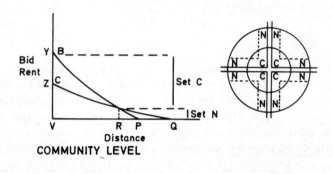

COMMUNITY LEVEL

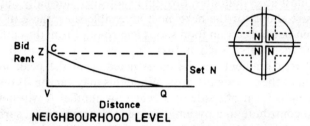

NEIGHBOURHOOD LEVEL

FIG. 5.4 *Garner's model of the internal locational characteristics of nucleated shopping centres.* R indicates those functions which have high threshold values and are diagnostic of the regional level of centres in the hierarchy. The bid-rent curve X to O shows their relative competitive ability for central sites. C refers to community level functions with medium threshold values and their competitive ability is shown by the curve Y to P. N refers to neighbourhood level functions with low threshold values and their competitive ability is shown by the curve Z to Q. (After Garner, B. J., 'The Internal Structure of Retail Nucleations', *Northwestern University, Dept. of Geography, Research Series 12*, 1966)

these that are found at this size level in the hierarchy. In large centres, however, such as regional centres, more specialised activities will take control of the most central positions and force the convenience functions into peripheral sites. This leads to a distinct spatial order in the pattern of retail activities inside the largest centres, where a series of belts indicative of different threshold values provide a horizontal reflection of the vertical differentiation inherent in the hierarchy.

Garner's model is obviously a generalisation, nevertheless, and needs to be modified in application to particular situations. The concentric belts do not really represent discrete areas where certain kinds of activities alone will be found; rather, they are gradational zones in which the frequency or incidence of particular types is more prominent than elsewhere. The unique characteristics of the street layout in different centres will distort these zones, as will minor peaks in the rental surface created by exceptionally large stores and those occupying corner sites. In many new planned shopping centres there is a much greater uniformity in the rental surface than is found in the older, unplanned ones, because of a standardisation in the sizes of the establishments. In addition, the interpretation that is given to the notion of threshold values (in equating them with different lines of trade) is rather crude to the extent that it ignores the important qualitative aspects of shops and the locational variations that derive from these.[23] Thus the high-class restaurant is treated in the same way as the café, and the multiple tailor like the specialist outfitter, but we know that in practice these prefer completely different kinds of sites.

Functional Variations Inside Nucleated Centres

The types of shops which are found inside nucleated centres vary considerably according to the tastes, needs and preferences of the surrounding population. This is most apparent when there are strong differences in the ethnic and socio-economic composition of a city. For example, Allen Pred[24] has shown that the shopping centres in Negro areas of Chicago contain a much higher proportion of bars, 'pool-parlours', cafés and general stores than is found in predominantly white areas. Brian Berry[25] and Barry Garner[26] have both shown that the shopping centres in the high

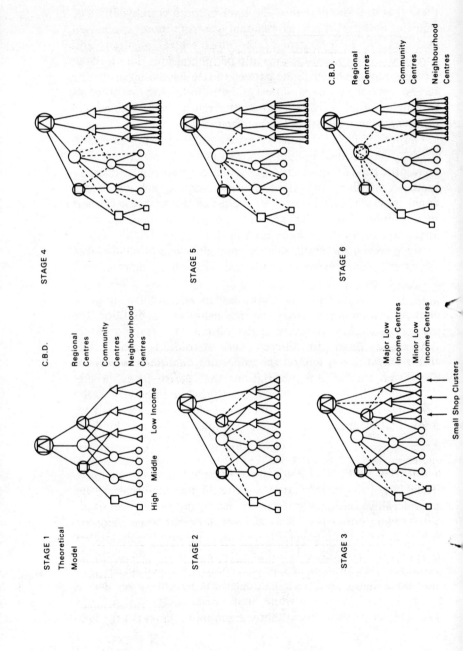

STAGE 1
Theoretical
Model

C.B.D.

Regional
Centres

Community
Centres

Neighbourhood
Centres

High   Middle   Low Income

STAGE 2

STAGE 3

Major Low
Income Centres

Minor Low
Income Centres

Small Shop Clusters

STAGE 4

C.B.D.

Regional
Centres

Community
Centres

Neighbourhood
Centres

STAGE 5

STAGE 6

C.B.D.

Regional
Centres

Community
Centres

Neighbourhood
Centres

FIG. 5.5   *The development of hierarchical sub-systems of shopping centres.*
Stage 1: the general theoretical model.
   This represents the aggregate system of shopping epitomised in central place theory. No importance is attached to the frequencies of centres at each hierarchical level, although there will usually be more centres serving lower-income consumer groups than middle- or higher-income groups. The different consumer groups share the facilities of higher order centres as indicated by the superimposed symbols.

Stage 2: effects of varying locational relationships.
   Allowance is made for the fact that shopping centres are more densely concentrated in the inner parts of the city compared to the outskirts. However, the regional centres catering mainly to low-income consumers are overshadowed by the central area, such that they are often by-passed on shopping excursions. Regional centres serving mainly the middle-income consumers are more central to the urban market and hence attract extra trade.

Stage 3: emergence of variant hierarchies.
   As the viability of low-income regional centres diminishes, the smaller centres in low-income areas are able to increase their standing in the hierarchical sub-system by taking on more specialised roles. The enhanced importance of the lower levels of this sub-system then allows for numerous isolated store clusters, which are very dense in the inner, older parts of the city, to be supported.

Stage 4: distinction of the low-income hierarchy.
   An almost separate hierarchy of centres emerges for the low-income areas since consumers here are less mobile than those in other parts of the city and visit either locally-based centres or the C.B.D. Considerable cross movements for shopping in other parts of the city, however, tends to increase the strength of middle-income regional centres.

Stage 5: competition with the central area.
   In the absence of planning intervention, it is possible for a middle-income regional centre to create severe competition with the central area and undermine its functional role (as in the USA). Some consumers in middle-income areas may also begin to by-pass their smaller shopping centres and erode the lower levels of their own hierarchical sub-system.

Stage 6: the empirical model.
   The emergence of three distinct but related sub-systems of shopping centres is complete. The high-income areas have shown the greatest stability in form although, because there are fewer centres, the full structural levels of the hierarchy are not always found. The middle-income areas exhibit the largest types of regional centres; and the low-income areas exhibit the greatest strength in smaller orders of centres.

(From Davies, R. L., 'Structural Models of Retail Distribution', *Transactions of the Institute of British Geographers*, **57**, 1972, 59–82)

income areas of Chicago usually contain a greater number of stores and are larger in floorspace terms than equivalent shopping centres in low income areas (see Table 5.1). A more specific case-study of the effects of income differences on the retail structure of two housing estates in Leeds[27] has indicated that although there may be more numbers of establishments in the centres of high income areas they tend also to be more specialised such that the centres of low income areas provide a greater range of functions and may fulfill a more important overall functional role for the communities that they serve. Lower-income people have both a more limited purchasing power and lower levels of mobility than higher-income people and are consequently more dependent on the local facilities available to them for a greater proportion of their shopping goods.

The wider implications of these socio-economic effects for the whole system of shopping centres throughout the city need to be considered against the background of varying locational condi-tions. Relative proximity to the central area is especially im-portant in this respect as are the imbalances in population densities to be found.[28] A model is described in Figure 5.5 which attempts to draw these considerations together and show how they lead to a distortion of the normal hierarchy. Three variant hier-archical structures are seen to emerge in fact as a result of the concentration of three different income groups in separate parts of the city.

The model also indicates that the functional variations amongst shopping centres are more clear-cut in the case of the smallest ones, because the larger ones become shared by different income groups. Nevertheless, within the larger shopping centres the dif-ferent types of consumers will still continue to patronise a different range of shops. A strong indication of these variations in store patronisation is to be found in the quality levels or images associated with shops.[29] Thus high-quality shops will usually reflect on a high-income clientele, low-quality shops on a low-income clientele. Medium-quality shops will tend to reflect not only on a bulk middle-income clientele but also the greater sharing of these kinds of establishments by all sections of the population.

It is in the context of quality levels of shops that a second interpretation to the meaning of threshold values may be given. In the usage so far màde, medium-quality shops would normally be assigned the highest threshold values because they serve the greatest volume of consumers and become concentrated at the peak nodal positions inside shopping centres. The highest quality shops, however, exhibit the greatest territorial trade areas, for though they serve limited numbers of people, these are mainly scattered in outer parts of the city. It is in terms of extent of territorial trade areas that classical central place theory strictly distinguishes between the relative levels in importance of activities, and hence, in keeping with this, the highest quality shops should really be assigned the highest threshold values. Inside of shopping centres, nevertheless, the highest quality shops do not necessarily require the single most accessible sites to the heaviest pedestrian flows since they can usually remain sufficiently central to their own select clientele in a variety of prestige positions. The lowest quality shops retain the lowest threshold values through serving limited numbers of people with low purchasing power; and their locations inside shopping centres are usually constrained to peripheral sites adjacent or close to the poorer housing areas. These distinctions are summarised in Figure 5.6

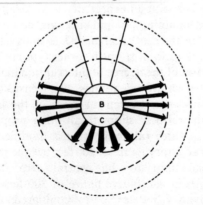

FIG. 5.6   *The relationship between the relative locations of shops and their trade area characteristics.* A. indicates high-quality shops; B. medium-quality shops; C. low-quality shops. (From Davies, R. L., 'Structural Models of Retail Distribution', *Transactions of the Institute of British Geographers*, **57**, 1972, 59–82)

PROBLEMS OF CENTRAL AREA DELIMITATION

Most business configurations within the city are difficult to define in terms of their precise areal extent and degree of separateness from other land use agglomerations. The problem is particularly acute in the case of the central area because of its overall size. The necessity for some kind of definition arises because of the various planning and administrative policies that have to be applied. The sheer quantity of traffic, density of buildings and concentration of services that are found require much more intensive zoning controls, police and fire protection, public health inspection and so on than any other part of the city. While there has been considerable research into various methods for demarcating boundary lines, however, there have been few common or standardised procedures which have actually been used in practice. The result, especially in the largest cities, is that a plethora of special-purpose boundary lines exist, suitable perhaps for the unique circumstances of particular problems but bearing little relationship with each other and ineffective for those problems which are essentially inter-related.

Most researchers not unexpectedly have dealt with retailing criteria when attempting to find a single best or compromise boundary line for the central area.[30] The simplest methods used have comprised a ratio of shops to other types of establishments found or measures of the degree of interruption in the distribution of shops by other land-use activities. The Census of Distribution defines boundaries for the central areas of the largest cities in Britain when the ratio of shops to all other properties becomes less than one in three (although this is modified in individual situations). An arbitrary figure of 200 feet between shops was used as the physical limit to the central area in a study of Cedar Rapids,[31] an alternative figure of 300 feet has been used in the case of Sydney.[32] Peter Scott[33] compared all three of these particular indices and found them surprisingly consistent for delimiting the central area of Melbourne. His general conclusion, however, was that 'a shopping area cannot be satisfactorily demarcated without data additional to that on the spatial patterning of retail establishments'.

Such additional data may relate to the behaviour of consumers in and around the central area, property or land values, the physical dimensions of buildings and the nature of other kinds of land uses found. Many American planning departments have made use of pedestrian counts from pavement surveys in conjunction with broader transportation studies.[34] Many British planning departments have considered the street listings of rateable values that are publicly available.[35] Murphy and Vance pioneered attempts to construct a consistent boundary index linking the floorspace size of establishments with the types of activities they perform.[36] In particular, they proposed two indices applicable to comparing the central areas of medium-sized American cities: the Central Business Height Index (CBHI) and the Central Business Intensity Index (CBII). The CBHI is calculated as the total floorspace of central business activities found within a street block divided by the ground level floorspace of the same block. If a value greater than one is achieved the street block can normally be said to be part of the central area, or central business district. The CBII is calculated as the percentage amount of total floorspace available that is given over to central business activities. In this case, a value greater than fifty per cent is usually taken as the limit of inclusion of a street block in the central area. The use of the two indices for determining the boundary of the central area in Worcester, Massachusetts is shown in Figure 5.7.

The Murphy-Vance indices have been extensively employed and evaluated in the context of other countries.[37] The main topics of contention have been the use of street blocks and the definition given to central business activities. Street blocks are clearly an appropriate unit of measurement to work with in the grid-iron pattern of American and also in colonial-type cities, but they tend to have less relevance to British and European cities and do not allow for much precision in the demarcation of boundary lines. Murphy and Vance predominantly referred to retailing and office activities in their interpretation of central business activities and excluded such functions as wholesaling, industry and residential accommodation which are often conspicuous features of the central areas of older cities. There has also been some considerable criticism about the real value of these numerous boun-

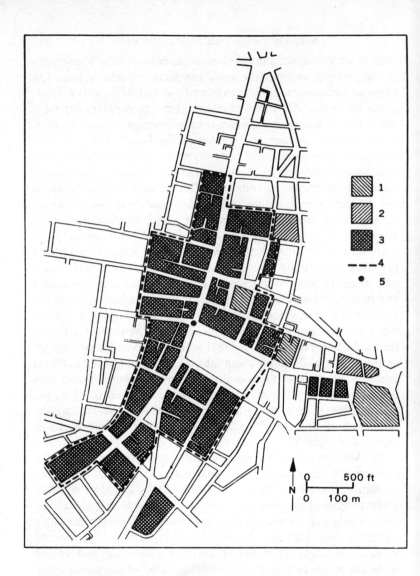

Fig. 5.7 *The boundary of the central area in Worcester, Massachusetts.*
Key: 1. Central Business Height Index of 1 or more; 2. Central
Business Intensity Index of 50 or more; 3. Central Business Height
Index of 1 or more and Central Business Intensity Index of 50 or
more; 4. CBD boundary; 5. Peak land value intersection. (After Murphy,
R. E. and Vance, J. E., 'Delimiting the CBD', *Economic Geography*, **30**,
1954, 301–36)

dary studies. Harold Carter[38] has commented: 'To a large extent the fixing of a boundary has become an end in itself, devoid of purpose and academically barren.' Not only has there been little relationship to those problems confronting planners and service administrators but there have been few attempts to compare the growth characteristics or relative economic health of central areas delimited in a consistent way. Several historical studies of changing boundary lines through time have been made but these remain primarily descriptive in their objectives.[39] Two exceptions are the work of Hartenstein and Stack[40] in Germany and R. W. Thomas[41] in Britain. The former showed that in floorspace terms it is office functions which are growing much more rapidly than those in retailing. The latter showed that as retailing becomes proportionately less important as an overall central business land use, its distribution within the central area becomes much more compact, more isolated and generally more centralised.

The physical limits of central areas are becoming increasingly more distinct, however. This is mainly because of the extensive redevelopment which is now taking place. While the inner parts of the central area are usually renovated through new building construction the outer parts are removed of their former land uses and usually left clear for transportation improvements. In many cities in Britain, in fact, the central area has already become conspicuously 'contained' within an inner ring-road expressway system.

Redevelopment plans have also often clearly distinguished between two separate parts to the central area, a core and frame, by virtue of their designating a precinct or pedestrianised zone which is then surrounded by a distributory road network linking the major traffic arteries to multi-storey car parks. Such a core and frame are implicit in the conceptual design models of Keeble[42] and Buchanan[43] and also fully realised in the built form of such cities as Coventry, which is the forerunner to most of the central area schemes in Britain. Figure 5.8 shows the original design model that was conceived for Coventry and the way it has actually been implemented in practice. Other cities still in the major stages of redevelopment, such as Birmingham, Glasgow and Newcastle, reveal a similar arrangement of land uses emerging. In general, the core is given over to mainly shopping

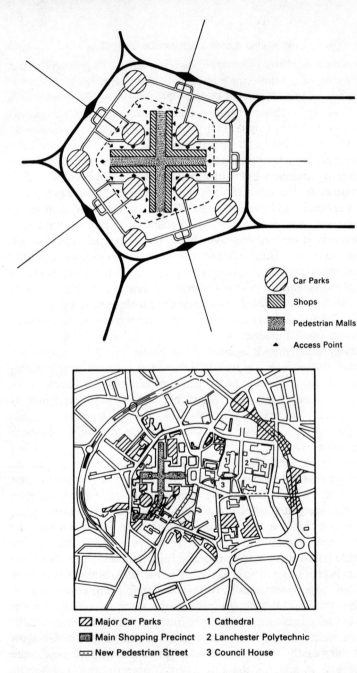

Car Parks

Shops

Pedestrian Malls

▲ Access Point

Major Car Parks   1 Cathedral

Main Shopping Precinct   2 Lanchester Polytechnic

New Pedestrian Street   3 Council House

Fig. 5.8 *The form of the central area in Coventry.* The top diagram indicates the city planning department's original design model for re-developing the central area after it was blitzed during the last war. The bottom diagram indicates the built-form that has now been realised.

and office functions, whereas the frame is characterised by a variety of segregated activities such as wholesaling, educational facilities, local government institutions and transport provisions.

THE SPATIAL STRUCTURE OF THE CENTRAL AREA

Curiously, there has been little relationship between geographical studies of central area land-use patterns and the various plan proposals put forward for major redevelopment schemes. Most geographical studies have had an historical perspective, examining the current spatial structure of business activities as an expression of 'natural' processes which have operated in the past.[44] Likewise, there have been few attempts to construct theories or concepts about the particular locational attributes of business activities inside the central area, despite the importance of the area to the city as a whole and the dramatic changes which have been taking place. Significantly, where there have been some developments in geographical concepts, these tend to link well with those planning design models which we have referred to. They also tie up with those classificatory distinctions we have made in connection with studies of the urban business pattern as a whole.

The General Pattern of Land Uses

The notion of a core and frame to the central area has been widely discussed for a long time in geography. It is only comparatively recently, however, that a core-frame model in a geographical rather than planning sense has been formulated. Only within the last decade have geographers systematically endeavoured to identify the common and recurrent functional components of the central area and to assess the degree of spatial orderliness in the pattern of land-use arrangements. The core-frame model, proposed by Horwood and Boyce[45] in 1959, is shown schematically in Figure 5.9. Interestingly, Horwood and Boyce themselves have been more closely identified in the past with planning rather than geographical studies. However, the intention of the model was to provide a descriptive framework of existing situations rather than a design format for the optimum arrangement of land uses in the future.

The general properties which are considered to be diagnostic of the core and frame are listed in Tables 5.3 and 5.4. Most of these are appropriate to the British central area although certain qualifications need to be given because of the differences in cultural and historical effects. The scale of activities and physical size dimensions of establishments are altogether much smaller than in the American case, but within any one street there is likely to be a much greater variety of functions and building morphology. The medieval nucleus of many British towns has often been a

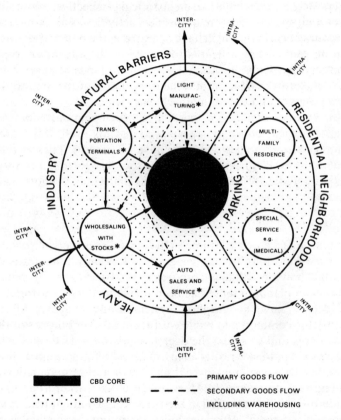

FIG. 5.9 *The central area core-frame model of Horwood and Boyce.* (After Horwood, E. M. and Boyce, R. R., *Studies of the Central Business District and Urban Freeway Development*, University of Washington Press, 1959)

particularly strong influence on the character of the central area, becoming the core of modern shopping and office activities and at the same time retaining scattered legacies of other, formerly prominent pursuits. There is generally less distinct segregation of different types of land uses in the frame area than in the American counterpart, mainly because of a smaller overall spatial extent and because the effects of the motor car have not been so great.

Many of the largest cities display more than one core. This is particularly conspicuous in the older capital cities where the office and shopping quarters have become physically separated. In some cases there may also be two or more office cores and two or more shopping cores. These often reflect on basic differences between clusters of financial and governmental office activities on the one hand and clusters of high quality and low quality shopping activities on the other.

The example of London has recently been examined by John Goddard using multi-variate statistical procedures (viz., factor analysis and cluster analysis). In a general study[46] of the overall land-use pattern three major core areas were defined: the City, as the obvious financial centre; Westminster, as the main governmental centre; and the West End, as the main retailing centre. Surrounding these, a set of frame areas were described in terms of the following: areas with mixed commercial activities; areas in a state of decay; areas predominantly given over to residential accommodation; and areas experiencing a change in the composition of land uses. While the frame by no means contained the clear-cut groupings of different functions depicted in Horwood and Boyce's model, a broad resemblance to the underlying principles involved was acknowledged. A more specific study[47] of the City core office area also revealed that this comprises a series of distinct sub-areas of functional specialisations. The definition and spatial demarcation that may be given to these sub-areas, however, was shown to vary according to the nature of the classificatory methods employed. When non-contiguous types of office activities were considered, five main sub-areas could be described: a central node of financial activities; a surrounding ring of other financial activities; a district dominated by publishing and professional services; a

TABLE 5.3

General Properties of the CBD Core

Property	Definition	General Characteristics
Intensive land-use	Area of most intensive land-use and highest concentration of social and economic activities within metropolitan complex	Multi-storied buildings Highest retail productivity per unit ground area Land-use characterised by offices, retail sales, consumer services, hotels, theatres, and banks
Extended vertical scale	Area of highest buildings within metropolitan complex	Easily distinguishable by aerial observation Elevator personnel linkages Grows vertically, rather than horizontally
Limited horizontal scale	Horizontal dimensions limited by walking distance scale	Greatest horizontal dimension rarely more than 1 mile Geared to walking scale
Limited horizontal change	Horizontal movement minor and not significantly affected by metropolitan population distribution	Very gradual horizontal change Zones of assimilation and discard limited to a few blocks over long periods of time
Concentrated daytime population	Area of greatest concentration of daytime population within metropolitan complex	Location of highest concentration of foot traffic Absence of permanent residential population
Focus of intracity mass transit	Single area of convergence of city mass transit system	Major mass transit interchange location for entire city
Centre of specialised functions	Focus of headquarters offices for business, government, and industrial activities	Extensive use of office space for executive and policy making functions Centre of specialised professional and business services
Internally conditioned boundaries	Excluding natural barriers, CBD boundaries confined only by pedestrian scale of distance	Pedestrian and personnel linkages between establishments govern horizontal expansion Dependency on mass transit inhibits lateral expansion

TABLE 5.4

General Properties of the CBD Frame

Property	Definition	General Characteristics
Semi-intensive land-use	Area of most intensive non-retail land use outside CBD core	Building height geared to walk-up scale Site only partially built on
Prominent functional sub-regions	Area of observable nodes of land utilisation surrounding CBD core	Sub-foci characterised mainly by wholesaling with stocks, warehousing, off-street parking, automobile sales and services, multi-family dwelling, inter-city transportation terminals and facilities, light manufacturing, and some institutional uses
Extended horizontal scale	Horizontal scale geared to accommodation of motor vehicles and to handling of goods	Most establishments have off-street parking and docking facilities Movements between establishments vehicular
Unlinked functional sub-regions	Activity nodes essentially linked to areas outside CBD frame, except transportation terminals	Important establishment linkages to CBD core (e.g. inter-city transportation terminals, warehousing) and to outlying urban regions (e.g. wholesale distribution to suburban shopping areas and to service industries)
Externally conditioned boundaries	Boundaries affected by natural barriers and presence of large homogeneous areas with distinguishable internal linkages (e.g. residential areas with schools, shopping, and community facilities)	Commercial uses generally limited to flat land Growth tends to extend into areas of dilapidated housing CBD frame uses fill in interstices of central focus of highway and rail transportation routes

Source: Horwood, E. M. and Boyce, R. R., *Studies of the Central Business District and Urban Freeway Development* (University of Washington Press, 1959).

district of concentrated general trading activities; and a district of mainly manufacturing and textile trading activities. When contiguous types of office activities were considered, thirteen separate sub-areas could be described representing various assorted mixtures of activities with less clear emphasis on any single type.

Spatial Regularities in the Retail Sector

While most shops are concentrated in the core part of the central area there are considerable ribbon extensions through the frame especially in those cities which have not been extensively re-developed. A transect through the central area as a whole will normally reveal that the largest and most specialised shops are concentrated together at the most central positions of the core and outwards there is a gradual decline towards smaller, more general trade and often physically blighted shops in the frame. This change in the general character of shops relates to a rental surface of the kind discussed in the context of smaller shopping centres. The rental surface will sometimes be seriously interrupted, how-ever, by districts of specialised retailing activities at prestige locations and there will be a tendency to much greater uniformity where ribbons occur. There will therefore be much less continuity and smoothness in the slopes of the surface than is found in the outlying nucleations. The central area, by virtue of its greater complexity and size, manifests in itself a mixture of all those different types of business conformations that we have recognised in the rest of the city.[48]

The locational arrangements of shops inside the central area may thus be interpreted by first distinguishing the three separate components or sub-systems of retailing activity that exist. This is illustrated in Figure 5.10. Those shops which are essentially nucleated components of the overall retail system become structured in a series of zonal belts of different threshold values by the same mechanism of rent-paying abilities described in Garner's model. Each belt of functions will again accord to those particular functions diagnostic of various size levels of the city-wide hierarchy. Cutting across this pattern will then be embryonic ribbon-type activities concentrated alongside the main axial

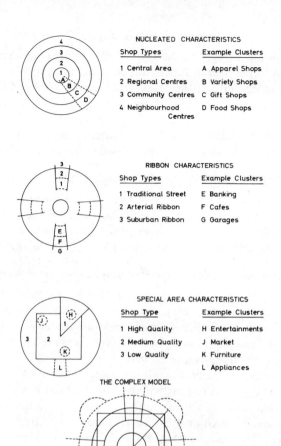

NUCLEATED CHARACTERISTICS

Shop Types		Example Clusters	
1	Central Area	A	Apparel Shops
2	Regional Centres	B	Variety Shops
3	Community Centres	C	Gift Shops
4	Neighbourhood Centres	D	Food Shops

RIBBON CHARACTERISTICS

Shop Types		Example Clusters	
1	Traditional Street	E	Banking
2	Arterial Ribbon	F	Cafes
3	Suburban Ribbon	G	Garages

SPECIAL AREA CHARACTERISTICS

Shop Type		Example Clusters	
1	High Quality	H	Entertainments
2	Medium Quality	J	Market
3	Low Quality	K	Furniture
		L	Appliances

THE COMPLEX MODEL

FIG. 5.10 *A structural model of retail locations inside the core.* The three components of this model can be related to the city-wide classification of business conformations shown in Figure 5.2. The separate locational characteristics that are indicated become blurred in the real world because of the great mixture of activities that are found. Although several commercial functions are incorporated in the examples of retailing clusters, the model really excludes the bulk set of office activities which usually constitute a separate core in the central area. (From Davies, R. L., 'The Retail Pattern of the Central Area of Coventry', *Transactions of the Institute of British Geographers, Occasional Publication No. 1*, 1972, 69–74)

roads; and these might be discriminated into different groupings according to the overall functional emphasis they display. There will tend to be more of the 'traditional street' types of functions close into the core, while those larger space-users and car-oriented service facilities more diagnostic of arterial and suburban ribbons will be found in the frame. Superimposed on both these patterns will be the clusters of specialised retailing activities which appear to be more haphazardly arranged.

There are essentially two different kinds of specialised functional areas that may be defined, however. On the one hand, there are those groupings of business activities which share a common line of trade, or method of business operation, such as is found in entertainments districts and retail markets. On the other hand, there are those groupings of business activities which share a common quality level or status and tend to form 'fashion' streets. In addition, many of the activities which are typical of nucleated and ribbon functions may become sufficiently concentrated together (such as clothes shops in central locations and repair shops along peripheral side streets) that these take on the role of specialised functional areas as well.

It becomes extremely difficult, of course, to distinguish in the real world between those particular, individual shops which reflect on different underlying locational processes. Spatial affinities amongst retail activities grow up through a mixture of varying influences. This means that it is difficult to substantiate in detailed terms the empirical validity of the model we have described.[49] In general terms, however, the most prominent features can be easily recognised, especially in the case of the largest cities such as London. Thus if Oxford Street is taken as an example of where the highest threshold values in nucleated-types of shops occur, then clearly along the Edgware Road there is a decline in threshold values and eventually on the outer edges the nucleated-types of shops give way to ribbon types. Elsewhere around Oxford Street, specialised concentrations of nucleated-types of shops are found, such as in the furniture shops of Tottenham Court Road, the musical and book shops of Charing Cross Road, and the apparel shops of Regent Street and Oxford Street itself. Areal variations in quality levels are apparent with the highest levels occurring perhaps in Bond Street, medium levels in Oxford Street, and a gradual deterioration to lower levels along Tottenham Court Road. In addition, there are of course the specialised entertainments districts which we have mentioned before.

There may be considerable disruption of this overall pattern of retailing activities, however, when central area redevelopment takes place. Not only are many of the ribbon features eradicated, but many of the specialised functional areas become broken up as well, since they tend to be found in the older sections of the central area where there is often a conflict with other land uses and transportation needs. There is currently much debate about the planning proposals to renovate Soho, Covent Garden and Piccadilly in London. The attempts to revitalise the main nucleated shopping facilities of the central area usually lead to an increase in the number of stereotyped chain store operations and a greater uniformity in the quality levels of shops than was found before. All of these kinds of changes tend to suggest that while the planning concepts for the central area as a whole show a strong relationship to the general locational processes at work, the detailed design specifications for the retail core have little regard for those small-scale market forces governing the 'natural' arrangement of shops.

The consensus planning approach in the building of new shopping precincts is to provide a mixture of different types of activities on the grounds that this is usually more attractive to consumers than a segregation of like-kinds of activities. Experience indicates, however, that this is difficult to effect in practice and over a period of time those shops which share a common affinity will gravitate together. A technique called sequence analysis, devised by Athur Getis,[50] may be used to test this. Sequence analysis essentially measures the degree of locational association between like kinds of shops by comparing the actual frequency with which two or more shops are found together against an expected frequency that might be obtained through purely chance occurrences. Although Getis himself suggested that only apparel stores are commonly linked together his case-studies[51] were based on limited samples of shops immediately skirting the peak nodal positions of central areas. An alternative study of Coventry,[52] involving the total number of business establishments to be found, indicates that the shops of each major functional category are more frequently located with each other than they are with those engaged in other lines of trade. These results and the statistical method involved in sequence analysis are shown in Table 5.5.

TABLE 5.5

Store Linkages in Coventry's Central Area

Pair-Wise Occurrences (Store Category)	Ob-served	Ex-pected	Vari-ance	Z value	Levels of Signifi-cance
Food–Food	23	16·16	12·89	1·90	+
Food–Apparel	33	32·31	22·94	0·14	+
Food–Household	16	18·20	14·32	0·58	−
Food–Specialist	20	21·62	16·61	0·34	−
Food–Leisure	19	22·07	16·90	0·75	−
Food–Personal	14	10·92	9·03	1·01	+
Food–Business	9	16·84	13·37	2·14	− *
Apparel–Apparel	108	64·63	41·87	6·70	+ * !
Apparel–Household	43	36·41	25·56	1·18	+
Apparel–Specialist	34	43·24	26·86	1·78	−
Apparel–Leisure	23	44·15	30·34	3·84	− * !
Apparel–Personal	16	21·85	15·95	1·47	−
Apparel–Business	17	33·68	23·82	3·42	− * !
Household–Household	30	20·51	15·92	2·38	+ *
Household–Specialist	25	24·36	18·47	0·15	+
Household–Leisure	25	24·87	18·80	0·03	+
Household–Personal	5	12·31	10·02	2·31	− *
Household–Business	11	18·97	14·86	2·07	− *
Specialist–Specialist	36	28·93	21·45	1·53	+
Specialist–Leisure	23	29·53	21·83	1·40	−
Specialist–Personal	10	14·61	11·63	1·35	−
Specialist–Business	24	22·53	17·27	0·35	+
Leisure–Leisure	45	30·16	22·27	3·14	+ * !
Leisure–Personal	11	14·92	11·83	1·14	−
Leisure–Business	22	23·01	17·54	0·24	−
Personal–Personal	13	7·38	6·35	2·23	+ *
Personal–Business	15	11·38	9·38	1·18	+
Business–Business	40	17·55	13·90	3·34	+ * ·!

Levels of Significance:
     Associations marked with a plus indicate a tendency towards attraction to each other; those with a minus a tendency to repulsion.

Associations with an asterisk are statistically significant at the 5% probability level; those with an exclamation mark at the 1% level.

Method of Analysis:

a. Count the number of times store type A is located next to store type B (for each category of stores)

b. Calculate the expected number of associations of A and $B = \dfrac{2AB}{N}$

   (where N is the total number of stores)

c. To test the statistical significance of any differences between the observed and expected number of associations, compare the variance of the distribution with the variance of the normal curve and consult a table of values for the relevance of Z

$$\sigma^2 = \frac{2AB(2AB + N(C - 1)}{N^2(N - 1)}$$

where C is $(N - A - B)$

$$Z = \frac{\text{Obs} - \text{Exp}}{\sigma^2}$$

where Obs and Exp are the observed and expected number of associations.

Source: Davies, R. L., 'The Retail Pattern of the Central Area of Coventry', *Institute of British Geographers Occasional Publication No. 1* (1973), 1–42; Getis, A. and Getis, J. M., 'Retail Store Spatial Affinities', *Urban Studies*, **5** (1968), 317–32.

Certain particular kinds of shops of course show a much stronger affinity or even repulsion to one another than others do. H. R. Parker[53] has identified as many as twelve factors that account for this:

i. the relative emphasis on daily versus occasional shopping needs on the part of consumers (which leads to the broad grouping tendencies amongst convenience-goods and durable-goods shops described in our model);

ii. physical considerations, where for example certain shops may have similarly large space requirements, and others such as grocers and chemists avoid strong-smelling businesses such as fish and chip shops and public houses;

iii. psychological ties, where banks may be associated together for prestige reasons, though pet shops will tend to avoid proximity to butchers;

iv. links in the hours of trading, so that betting shops and cafés are often found together;

v. degrees of complementarity, as in the case of sweet shops and cinemas, and public houses and fish and chip shops;

vi. degrees of substitutability, which tends to lead to an avoidance of butchers by fishmongers and vice versa;

vii. consumer group orientation, where record shops, boutique and sports outfitters which are catering mainly for the young will become concentrated together;

viii. opportunities for comparisons, as in the case of clothes shops, jewellery shops and furniture shops;

ix. monopoly powers, as for example in the influence of post offices and bus-stops on convenience shops;

x. service links, such as between estate agents;

xi. site considerations, where many shops dependent on comparison shopping prefer corner sites;

xii. pin-money shops, where there is an association between part-time operations such as second-hand shops.

Many of these individual factors and the whole subject of the optimum arrangement of shops is taken up again in Chapter Eight in connection with studies of store location research.

SUMMARY

The business pattern in most westernised cities today reflects the evolution over nearly a hundred years of a wide range of competing activities. Various stages of this evolution, and particularly the periods of more rapid change, are clearly recognisable in different parts of the urban area. The greatest legacy from Victorian times is to be found in the dense concentrations of corner-shops in the inner parts of the city. The first signs of planning control in the inter-war period are conspicuous in the physically detached and spacious parades of the middle parts of the city. The recent trend to mass merchandising techniques is spatially most manifest in the new, outer suburban centres and the redevelopment schemes of the central area of the city. Throughout the whole history of commercial change, however, there have tended to be three common types of locational process at work.

The first concerns the need for most domestic-oriented retail shops to be central to their bulk consumer body. The second concerns the need for many services and specialist businesses to be close to the main arteries of traffic because of a strong dependence on motorised trade. The third concerns the need for certain other kinds of services and specialist businesses to agglomerate together because of the advantages which they can draw from a larger scale economy. These three locational requirements have led to three conspicuous business conformations throughout the city; the compact or nucleated forms of shopping centres proper; string-streets or ribbon developments; and specialised functional areas. They also provide the basis for understanding the detailed site requirements of individual shops inside any one of these business conformations and particularly the structural arrangements of the entire mix of businesses in the main centre or central area of towns. The central area is in fact a composite amalgam of the various kinds of business configurations to be found throughout the rest of the city and constitutes a microcosm of the total urban retail system. Important differences are to be found in the relative status of the central area today between cities in Britain and North America, however, and particularly because of underlying differences in societal conditions and the degree of planning intervention that has been made. These differences and other features reflecting the most recent period of business change are taken up in the next chapter.

REFERENCES

1. See, for example, Carol, H., 'The Hierarchy of Central Functions Within the City', *Annals of the Association of American Geographers*, **50** (1960), 419–38.
2. Davies, R. L., 'Theoretical Frameworks for Urban Planning Shopping Policies', *Proceedings of the P.T.R.C. Conference, Sussex University* (Planning and Transport Research and Computation Co. Ltd., 1973).
3. Berry, B. J. L. and Garrison, W. L. *et al.*, *Studies of Highway Development and Geographic Change* (University of Washington Press, 1959); Davies, R. L., 'Structural Models of Retail Distribution: Analogies

with Settlement and Urban Land Use Theories', *Transactions of the Institute of British Geographers*, **57** (1972), 59–82.

4. Proudfoot, J. J., 'City Retail Structure', *Economic Geography*, **13** (1937), 425–8.

5. Mayer, H. M., 'Patterns and Recent Trends of Chicago's Outlying Business Centres', *Journal of Land and Public Utility Economics*, **18** (1942), 4–16.

6. Berry, B. J. L., 'Commercial Structure and Commercial Blight', *University of Chicago, Dept. of Geography, Research Paper 85* (1963).

7. Fuller descriptions of ribbon developments are contained in Berry, B. J. L., 'Ribbon Developments in the Urban Business Pattern', *Annals of the Association of American Geographers*, **49** (1959), 145–55; Boal, F. W. and Johnson, D. B., 'The Functions of Retail and Service Establishments on Commercial Ribbons', *Canadian Geographer*, **9** (1965), 154–69.

8. See, for example, Cohen, S. B., 'Evaluating Planned Shopping Centres', Chapter 8 in Cohen, S. B. (ed.) *Store Location Research for the Food Industry* (National-American Wholesale Grocers Association, undated), 61–76; Vance, J. E., 'Emerging Patterns of Commercial Structure in American Cities', *Proceedings of the Lund Symposium on Urban Geography, 1960* (University of Lund, 1962).

9. Cohen, S. B. and Lewis, G. K., 'Form and Function in the Geography of Retailing', *Economic Geography*, **53** (1967), 1–42.

10. Parker, H., 'Suburban Shopping Facilities in Liverpool', *Town Planning Review*, **33** (1962), 197–223.

11. Davies, R. L., 'Nucleated and Ribbon Components of the Urban Retail System in Britain', *Town Planning Review*, **45** (1974), 91–111.

12. For example, Weekley, I. G., 'Service Centres in Nottingham', *East Midland Geographer*, **6** (1956), 41–6; Pocock, D. C. D., 'Shopping Patterns in Dundee: Some Observations', *Scottish Geographical Magazine*, **84** (1968), 108–16.

13. For example, Coventry Planning Department, *Shopping in Coventry* (Coventry Corporation, 1964); Edinburgh Planning Department, *Shopping Report 1967* (Edinburgh Royal Burgh, 1967).

14. Carruthers, W. I., 'Service Centres in Greater London', *Town Planning Review*, **33** (1962), 5–31.

15. Smailes, A. E. and Hartley, G., 'Shopping Centres in the Greater London Area', *Transactions of the Institute of British Geographers*, **29** (1961), 201–13. Burns, W., *British Shopping Centres* (Leonard Hill, 1959).

16. Burns, W., *British Shopping Centres* (Leonard Hill, 1959).

17. Thorpe, D., Thomas, C. J. and Kivell, P. T., *Atlas and Statistical Handbook of Major Suburban Shopping Centres* (University of Manchester, Retail Outlets Research Unit, 1971). See also, Thorpe, D. and Kivell, P. T., *Atlas and Statistical Account of the Shopping Centres of Greater London* (University of Manchester, Retail Outlets Research Unit, 1973).

18. Burns, W., *op. cit.*

19. Hoyt, H., 'Land Values in Shopping Centres', *Urban Land*, **28** (1969), 3–12.

20. Berry, B. J. L., 'Commercial Structure and Commercial Blight', *University of Chicago, Dept. of Geography, Research Paper 85* (1963).

21. For a discussion of the use of this approach in shopping models see 'Rent Models', Chapter 4 in National Economic Development Office, *Urban Models in Shopping Studies* (NEDO, 1970). See also, 'Retail Sites and Spatial Affinities', Chapter 2 in Scott, P., *Geography and Retailing* (Hutchinson, 1970).

22. Garner, B. J., 'The Internal Structure of Retail Nucleations', *Northwestern University, Dept. of Geography, Research Series 12* (1966).

23. Garner, B. J., 'Some Reflections on the Notion of Threshold in Central Place Studies', *Annals of the Association of American Geographers*, **57** (1967), 788.

24. Pred, A., 'Business Thoroughfares as Expressions of Urban Negro Culture', *Economic Geography*, **39** (1963), 217–33.

25. Berry, B. J. L., *op. cit.*

26. Garner, B. J., *op. cit.*

27. Davies, R. L., 'Effects of Consumer Income Differences on the Business Provisions of Small Shopping Centres', *Urban Studies*, **5** (1968), 144–64.

28. Parker, H., *op. cit.*, estimated that five-sixths of Liverpool's total shops outside the central area, were concentrated in the inner parts of the city. Contrasts in types of shops between inner and outer areas are described in Leeming, F. A., 'An Experimental Survey of Retail Shopping and Service Facilities in a Part of North Leeds', *Transactions of the Institute of British Geographers*, **26** (1959), 133–52.

29. This is elaborated on in Davies, R. L., 'Structural Models of Retail Distribution: Analogies with Settlement and Urban Land Use Theories', *Transactions of the Institute of British Geographers*, **57** (1972), 59–82.

30. A general review of the literature on boundary delimitation is contained in Murphy, R. E., *The Central Business District* (Longman, 1972).

31. Berry, B. J. L. and Garrison, W. L., *et al., op. cit.*

32. Logan, A., *The Pattern of Service Centres in Warringah Shire, Sydney* (University of Sydney Planning Research Centre, 1968).

33. Scott, P., *op. cit.*

34. See, for example, Seattle City Planning Commission, *Seattle Central Business District: A Land Use Study* (Seattle, 1958).

35. See also the Rate Index used by D. T. Herbert in 'An Approach to the Study of the Town as a Central Place', *Sociological Review*, **9** (1961), 273–92.

36. Murphy, R. E. and Vance, J. E., 'Delimiting the Central Business District', *Economic Geography*, **30** (1954), 197–223; 'A Comparative Study of Nine Central Business Districts', *Economic Geography*, **30** (1954), 301–36.

37. See, for example, Davies, D. H., 'The Hard Core of Cape Town's C.B.D.', *Economic Geography*, **36** (1960), 53–69; Scott, P., 'The Australian C.B.D.', *Economic Geography*, **35** (1959), 290–314.

38. Carter, H., *The Study of Urban Geography* (Edward Arnold, 1972).

39. For example, Bohnert, J. E. and Mattingley, P. F., 'The Delimitation of the C.B.D Through Time', *Economic Geography*, **40** (1964), 337–47; Bowden, M. J., 'Downtown Through Time: Delimitation, Expansion and Internal Growth', *Economic Geography*, **47** (1971), 121–35.

40. Hartenstein, W. and Staack, G., 'Land Use in the Urban Core', in *Urban Core and Inner City, Proceedings of the International Study Week, Amsterdam, 1966* (Brill, 1967), 35–52.

41. Thomas, R. W., 'The Retail Structure of the Central Area', *Institute of British Geographers, Occasional Publication No. 1* (1972), 69–94.

42. Keeble, L., *Principles and Practice of Town and Country Planning* (Estates Gazette, 1961).

43. Buchanan, C. D., *Mixed Blessing* (Hill, 1958).

44. See, for example, Carter, H. and Rowley, G., 'The Morphology of the Central Business District of Cardiff', *Transactions of the Institute of British Geographers*, **38** (1966), 119–34; Diamond, D., 'The Central Business District of Glasgow', *Proceedings of the Lund Symposium on Urban Geography, 1960* (University of Lund, 1962).

45. Horwood, E. M. and Boyce, R. R., *Studies of the Central Business District and Urban Freeway Development* (University of Washington Press, 1959).

46. Goddard, J., 'Multi-variate Analysis of Office Location Patterns in the City Centre: a London Example', *Regional Studies*, **2** (1968), 69–85.

47. Goddard, J., 'Changing Office Location Patterns in the City of London', *Urban Studies*, **4** (1967), 276–86.

48. Davies, R. L., *op. cit.*

49. The model has been found appropriate for describing the planned central area of Coventry, however. Davies, R. L., 'The Retail Pattern of the Central Area of Coventry', *Institute of British Geographers Occasional Publication No. 1* (1973), 1–42.

50. Getis, A., 'A Method for the Study of Sequences in Geography', *Transactions of the Institute of British Geographers*, **42** (1967), 87–92.

51. Getis, A. and Getis, J. M., 'Retail Store Spatial Affinities', *Urban Studies*, **5** (1968), 317–32.

52. Davies, R. L., *op. cit.*

53. Parker, H., *op. cit.*

6 Changes in the Urban Business Pattern

The last chapter was primarily concerned with providing a static assessment of the main features of the urban business pattern. Frequent attention had to be given, however, to the fact that the urban business pattern is continually changing, and in recent years the rate and magnitude of change has been greater than ever before. This warrants some further and more detailed consideration, though shortage of space again compels us to deal predominantly with examples of retail change.

In general, there are two main types of change to be recognised in the city. First, there are those changes which have largely come about through the effects of 'free' market forces, in what we might regard as the normal process of evolution (often described as a general process of decentralisation): these essentially include the relative decline of business facilities in the inner city and the expansion of trade in the suburbs. Secondly, sometimes reinforcing these trends and sometimes working against them, are those more specific changes which have been deliberately effected by planning: these are most in evidence in the form of inner city redevelopment schemes and the morphology of new types of outlying shopping centres.

The basic causes of decentralisation and the concurrent need for increasing planning controls are some fundamental changes in the nature of consumer demands and the methods of business supply. In broad terms, these may be summarised as:

1. Changes in the spatial composition of consumers. The continuing growth of the population as a whole has been accompanied by massive shifts in the locational pattern of different socio-economic groups. In general, the younger, richer and more mobile sections of society have migrated to the suburbs to create

157

new, large sources of demand in areas where few, if any, shopping facilities had previously existed. The older, poorer and less mobile sections have tended to concentrate within the inner city, where their overall lower levels of purchasing power are insufficient to support the surfeit of shopping facilities that remain.

2. Changes in shopping habits and consumer tastes. Such diverse factors as the growth of female employment and car ownership, and the increasing use of deep freezers and other domestic appliances, have combined to produce some major changes in the life-styles of consumers, particularly in the suburbs, and to alter the traditional patterns and profiles of shopping behaviour. Most noticeably, there has been a reduction in frequent, daily trips to small local centres and much greater emphasis on single, weekly bulk-buying trips to the largest centres available. At the same time, there has been a growing demand for more convenience and comfort in shopping which newer rather than older centres can obviously better provide.

3. Changes in the scale-economies of businesses. Not only has there been an increase in the corporate sizes of the multiple chain groups of companies but, as we have seen, there has also been an increase in the floorspace sizes of individual stores. This has led to some major changes in locational requirements, with the main need being an improvement in conditions of accessibility, both for the satisfaction of customers and for efficiency in servicing. In addition, the lower rents and larger sites to be found in the suburbs have obviously become increasingly attractive to those stores less dependent on a highly centralised location.

4. Changes in business interaction and channels of distribution. To a considerable extent, there has been an overall decline in the dependency of retail establishments on the wholesaling facilities that were once so heavily concentrated in and around the central area. So too, the growth in mobility of the population and improvements in the methods of goods deliveries have led to a weakening of those linkages that formally created clusters of specialisation in city centres. The consequence has been a gradual erosion of the traditional hierarchical organisation of business transactions throughout the city and the growth of separate networks of activity scattered throughout the suburbs.[1]

In considering the cumulative effects of these changes, however, some important differences must again be stressed between those conditions which have been experienced in North America and those in Britain and the rest of Europe. Generally speaking, the pressures towards retail decentralisation have been altogether much greater and more effective in North America than elsewhere.[2] Against the background of a relatively 'free' market economy and the absence of a strong body of state and local government planning laws, a tremendous number of new, and sometimes extremely large, suburban shopping centres have been built. At the same time, there has been a very rapid deterioration of shopping facilities in the inner city and a considerable erosion of the former status of the central area. In Britain, in contrast, much stricter and nationally co-ordinated planning policies have attempted to curtail the worst effects of decentralisation, although at the expense of providing only limited amounts of new suburban developments, many of which have been no more than expansion schemes of traditional village centres. An emphasis has been put instead on the redevelopment of the central area and other inner city shopping facilities and a continued concentration of resources on the old (and some might argue outmoded) elements of the urban retail system. In other European countries, there has tended to be a mixture of the two kinds of trends observed in North America and Britain.

CHANGES IN THE NORTH AMERICAN CITY

There are, of course, several special cultural and physical circumstances which help to explain the vast scale of decentralisation in the North American city. Of most importance, perhaps, are the immense social upheavals that have followed from successive waves of migrants. In the United States especially, the post-war influx of large groups of Southern Negroes and Puerto Ricans, had the dual effect of both promoting rapid residential changes within the city itself and intensifying a so-called 'flight' to the suburbs of the white middle-class population. This led to dramatic alterations in the traditional pattern and characteristics of trade areas to which the retail system inevitably responded. A number of more specific factors further encouraged the trend: the enormous amount of land available for new shopping centre developments; the almost total dependence on the motor car for all shopping purposes; a vigorous economic climate conducive to massive, speculative retailing investments; relatively few 'bureaucratic' or corporate planning constraints, permitting such things as extended opening hours and the widespread use of 'store buggies'; the incidence of many unincorporated townships[3] on the periphery of cities where land-use controls have traditionally been weak and in some cases virtually non-existent. At the same time, in North America, there has always been a great readiness on the part of the population as a whole to initiate and participate in change, and while this is difficult to identify in precise terms, has been reflected in the early development and adoption of mass-merchandising techniques.

The Growth of New Suburban Shopping Centres

The new suburban shopping centres in North America are described as being both planned and unplanned. The term 'planned' centre has a slightly different connotation to that used in Britain, however. For the most part, it refers to a complex of shops which are owned and managed as one unit[4] and does not necessarily mean that it has been especially influenced by public planning land-use controls. Indeed, there is often found next to a planned centre an unplanned complex of shops or a new suburban ribbon development. It is with the characteristics of planned centres that we will be particularly concerned in this section. Their most distinctive features include a highly co-ordinated layout or design, an almost complete emphasis on retail provisions to the exclusion of other commercial services, wide expanses of car parking, and a site which is nearly always physically divorced and sometimes quite remote from the residential areas they serve.

The origins of the planned centre can be traced back to the beginning of the century. Simmons claims that the first fully recognisable planned centre was Roland Park, built in Baltimore in 1907;[5] while Kelly suggests that the first truly suburban or 'out-of-town' planned centre was Country Club Plaza, built on the outskirts of Kansas City in 1923.[6] The main period of their growth has been in the last two decades, however, during which more than 10,000 assorted centres have been developed in the USA alone.[7] These now account for approximately thirty-seven per cent of total retail trade.[8]

In the last chapter, in connection with Brian Berry's classification of the urban business pattern of Chicago, there was some discussion of the extent to which the new planned centres may be seen to constitute a hierarchy like that found amongst older unplanned centres. It was suggested that while their functional roles had become much more blurred, there was much more of a distinct tier structure of sizes by virtue of some common floorspace standards which have been adopted. This is borne out in a separate and nation-wide survey conducted by the Urban Land Institute of the USA which recognises three main categories of centres.[9] First, there are a set of regional shopping centres, with floorspace sizes of more than 400,000 square feet and sometimes reaching over one million square feet. These usually have a minimum site area of forty acres and space for about 4,000 cars. The major tenant is a department store (and there may be up to three of these), and the catchment area typically contains 100–250,000 people. Secondly, there are community shopping centres with average floorspace sizes of 100–150,000 square feet. These have site areas of 10–30 acres and space for about 1,300 cars. The major tenant is more likely to be a 'junior' department store or variety store and the catchment area typically contains 20–100,000 people. Thirdly, there are neighbourhood shopping centres with average floorspace sizes of 30–40,000 square feet. These have site areas of 4–10 acres and space for about 360 cars. The major tenant will usually be a supermarket and the catchment area typically contains 7–20,000 people. In addition, there are a number of free-standing superstores, including discount houses (such as K-Mart and Korvette), department stores (especially Sears Roebuck), and giant supermarkets (from chains like Kroger, Stop and Shop, A and P, etc.).

It is the planned regional shopping centres which form the most spectacular element of the new suburban hierarchy. These rival the size and status of the central areas of the largest metropolises on which they have had a tremendous, competitive effect. There were estimated to be nearly 300 in existence in the USA in 1968, and no signs have yet been seen that a saturation level has been reached.[10] Table 6.1 indicates some projected growth in numbers up to 1978 for selected examples of metropolitan areas. During this period of continued expansion, there will be three particular criteria involved in determining their relative success: the locations of the new regional shopping centres; their layout and design; and the mix of the tenants to be brought in.

TABLE 6.1

Projected Growth in Households, Income and New Regional Shopping Centres for Selected U.S. Metropolitan Areas 1968–1978

Metro Areas	Additional Households by 1978	Disposable Incomes by 1978	No. of New Centres by 1978
New York-N.E. Jersey	650,000	$8,450m	9
Los Angeles-Orange Co.	837,000	$11,676m	12
Chicago-Gary	403,000	$5,400m	6
Washington D.C.	340,000	$5,304m	6
Miami-Ft. Lauderdale	263,750	$2,717m	4
Philadelphia	208,000	$2,454m	3
San Francisco-Oakland	285,000	$3,848m	5
Seattle-Tacoma	240,000	$3,060m	4
Detroit	200,000	$2,670m	3
Atlanta	175,000	$1,968m	2
Boston	149,250	$1,940m	2
Houston	150,000	$1,650m	2
Minneapolis-St. Paul	132,000	$1,634m	2

Source: Compiled from Hoyt, H., 'Land Values in Shopping Centres', *Urban Land*, **28**, July-August (1969), 3–12.

Hitherto, most of the locations sought for new regional shopping centres have been 'greenfield' sites close to expressways. Frequently the single most successful locations have been those at the intersections of outer ring-roads and major radial routes. A typical example is the Yorkdale Centre in Toronto which was built in 1965 and is widely quoted as a 'model' for many subsequent developments. This was built at the junction of the east-west Highway 401 (forming the outer ring-road of Toronto) and the north-south Spadina expressway, joining the suburbs to the inner city. In a broader context, this location was well placed at the general boundary between a well-populated inner suburban area and a rapidly expanding outer suburban area. Such prime locations are becoming increasingly more difficult to obtain, however, and many future developments are now having to be planned in anticipation of expressway systems not yet built. These will continue to perpetuate the outward sprawl of shopping centres in the wave-like motion shown in Figure 6.1. A significant by-product of this is that whereas regional shopping centres previously competed with the central area and led to its decline, increasingly they are competing amongst themselves and it will be those developed earlier in the inner suburbs which will suffer most as a result.

There have been some considerable changes in the layout and design aspects of planned regional shopping centres during the last two decades. Most noticeable has been the trend from 'open air' centres with several scattered units, involving a great deal of varied pedestrian flows, to the modern enclosed centres with their controlled atmospheric environments and rigid alignment of shops along just one or two central malls. Increasingly, there has been a tendency for the newest centres to adopt certain standardised forms.[11] The smaller ones have tended to approximate a 'dumb-bell' shape, where a single straight mall links up two major and outer attractor stores (usually department stores). The larger ones have tended to assume an 'L' shape or 'T' shape of the kind illustrated in Figure 6.2. A single straight mall is seen in this case to be too long and generally unattractive to the shopper; and the protrusion of further malls can link up other major attractor stores such as giant supermarkets or variety stores. In addition, there have been a number of minor adjustments to the widths of malls, mainly in respect of making them narrower than in the older centres in order to encourage more cross-shopping. So far there has been little development of two-storey suburban shopping centres, although most servicing is now done underground. Some trend to multi-storey car parking may be perceived, however, for many of the surface

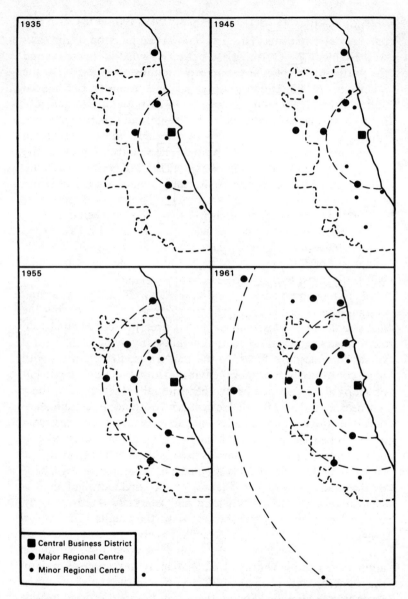

FIG. 6.1 *The growth of regional shopping centres in the Chicago metropolitan area.* (After Simmons, J., 'The Changing Pattern of Retail Location', *University of Chicago, Department of Geography, Research Paper No. 92*, 1964)

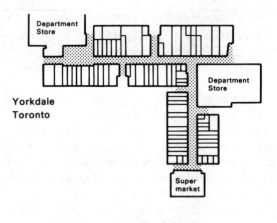

**Yorkdale
Toronto**

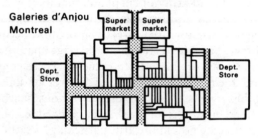

**Galeries d'Anjou
Montreal**

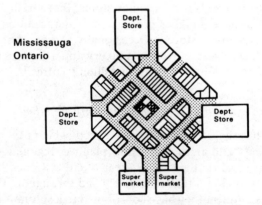

**Mississauga
Ontario**

FIG. 6.2 *Examples of conventional layouts for large 'out-of-town' regional shopping centres.* Yorkdale illustrates the L shape, Galeries d'Anjou the T shape and Mississauga a diamond shape, sometimes described as the 'super anchor complex'. (Adapted from Capital and Counties Property Co. Ltd., *Design for Shopping*, London, 1970)

car parks (generally at 5·5 car spaces per 1,000 square feet of retail floorspace) have now become so vast that they incur considerable inconvenience in walking for the average American customer.[12]

The types of retail firms that become the tenants of regional shopping centres are critical factors involved in getting a new development properly established. Most important of all are the department stores, which will normally occupy about fifty per cent of the total floorspace and command forty-five per cent of the total trade. Very often, in fact, it is the department stores themselves (with headquarters in the central area) which are the property developers and managers of the new shopping centres. These attract a broad array of small and mainly specialist shops that are arranged in uniform sizes of units with uniform levels of rent. There is usually little direct competition between these stores and few convenience functions or large space-users (such as appliance stores) are allowed to come in. These consequently tend to find their way to unplanned centres or link up with service establishments along suburban ribbons.[13] There is an increasing trend, however, for the smaller planned regional centres especially to become geared towards particular kinds of customer groups. Thus the centres in low income areas will frequently exhibit a large number of discount stores; those in high income areas tend to have a higher proportion of the traditional downtown and prestige stores. Occasionally, some centres have become so specialised in women's luxury apparel stores that they have come to be known as High Fashion Centres.[14]

Effects on the Central Area and Inner City Retailing

It is easy to exaggerate the adverse effects which new suburban developments and particularly the planned regional shopping centres have had on the central areas of cities. Generally speaking, there is no doubt that collectively and throughout the North American continent they have contributed to a substantial overall decline. However, the extent of the decline, especially in terms of relative sales performance, has varied considerably amongst different types of cities.[15] The most serious repercussions have been felt within the largest metropolitan cities when many of the smaller and more self-contained places have suffered relatively little at all. So, too, the period of most marked decline occurred in the late 1950s and 1960s, since when there has tended to be a much more static situation with some revival of trade in certain particular cases.

These features are particularly well-illustrated in the cities of the Mid-West, which have always been at the forefront of new suburban developments. During the inter-censal period of 1954 to 1963 the percentage share of total retail trade commanded by CBDs of all metropolitan cities fell from sixteen to ten.[16] Over the same period, the percentage share commanded by the suburbs rose from thirty-one to forty-six. Of the individual stores within the CBDs, the hardest hit were the department stores of which the share of trade plummeted from fifty per cent to twenty-six per cent.[17] Figure 6.3 indicates the differential rate

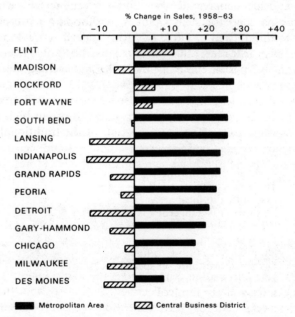

FIG. 6.3 *The decline of the CBD and growth of suburban retail sales in mid-western cities of the USA, 1958–63.* (After Federal Reserve Bank of Chicago, 'Retailing—Rapid Growth in the Suburbs', *Business Conditions*, May, 1966, 12–16)

at which various cities were affected. The CBDs of the medium-sized cities, such as Chicago, Detroit and Milwaukee, experienced the earliest decline. These were subsequently followed by the CBDs of the medium-sized cities, such as Lansing, Indianapolis and Grand Rapids. The CBDs of the smallest cities, nevertheless, those not classified as metropolitan areas, maintained their momentum throughout the period.

A number of consumer surveys have been undertaken to provide further documentary evidence of these trends and also elucidate some of the more specific reasons behind them. One recent survey in Pittsburgh showed that the average proportion of all shopping trips made by the residents of Allegheny County which focused on the central area declined from twenty per cent in 1958 to 11·6 per cent in 1970.[18] Over the same period, the average proportion of all shopping trips which went to suburban shopping centres increased from 22·1 per cent to 54·7 per cent. The reasons cited for such changes in shopping patterns were similar to those listed in Table 6.2. Although these tend to reflect on consumer attitudes, other surveys have dealt much more with the characteristics of the consumers themselves. Thus a survey

TABLE 6.2

*Reasons for Not Shopping in the
Central Area of Seattle, Washington*

Parking lots are full	23%
Don't like downtown	22%
Too expensive	17%
Less traffic in local areas	17%
Downtown is dangerous	16%
Free parking in local areas	16%
Local shopping is good	14%
Shopping areas close to home	12%
Go downtown only on special occasions	10%
Downtown is congested	6%
Inconvenience involved	4%

The percentage figures refer to the number of people who cited each reason. They total more than 100 because of multiple responses.

Source: Smith, A., 'The Future of Downtown Retailing', *Urban Land*, **31**, No. 11 (1972), 3–10.

conducted in Cincinnatti showed that even as early as 1959 some fundamental differences in the types of consumers served by the central area and suburban centres had already emerged.[19] For example, whereas forty-three per cent of shoppers in the central area had incomes of less than $4,000 only twenty-one per cent of shoppers in suburban centres did; again, while eighty-five per cent of central area shoppers were shopping alone, forty-two per cent of suburban shoppers were accompanied by some other member of the family.

What has essentially happened in the largest cities is that the central area has lost the bulk of its 'external' market and increasingly become dependent on an 'internal' market.[20] While this has so far tended to comprise mainly the poor, elderly and coloured ethnic groups, there are three other sources of continuing support who are likely to become of much greater importance in the future. These include the office workforce, visiting tourists and businessmen, and a growing number of higher-income, central-area residents.[21] It is largely due to these particular groups, in fact, that the general trend in sales decline has recently been off-set and in several cities, such as Denver and Seattle, there has been a notable recovery. In other cities, however, the support generated by these groups has tended to lead to a segregation of the central area into two distinct parts; a growth area of new specialised shops catering mainly to fashion demands; and a deteriorating area made up of the older remnants of retail trade. This is conspicuous in Chicago in the contrast found between shopping facilities around North Michigan Avenue and those in the traditional downtown area of the Loop.

Further improvements in the relative status of the central area have occurred from redevelopment schemes. Substantial programmes have been implemented in cities such as Hartford, Boston and Baltimore. In Chicago, a massive face-lift has recently been proposed for the Loop area while the Marshall Field (department store) Company is spearheading a new six-storey shopping centre to be called the Water Tower Plaza along North Michigan Avenue.[22] This will be integrated with new office and apartment complexes to provide an additional three million square feet of land use by 1975. Redevelopment schemes have also been increasingly undertaken in the downtown areas of satellite cities and the large, inner suburbs of metropolitan areas. In New York, more emphasis has so far been given to redeveloping the subsidiary centres of Newark, Brooklyn and Jamaica than the main core of Manhattan.[23] At the same time, an entirely new central area has been proposed for the outer suburban areas of Nassau County which currently have numerous scattered shopping centres but no real focus of mixed commercial activities.

The need for redevelopment is often more pressing for the older regional shopping centres of a metropolitan area than the central area itself. This is because the combined effects of competition from new centres and population change in the surrounding residential areas have led to a more permanent and irreversible loss of trade. Table 6.3 compares the trends in land values experienced in two traditional outlying centres of Chicago with those in the middle of the central area. The centre at 63rd Avenue and Halsted Street is the second largest in the metropolitan area and caters predominantly for a Negro population on the South Side. Evanston is a formerly prominent fashion centre geared to higher-income residents of the North Shore. While land values in the central area have shown a marked recovery, there continues to be a sustained decline in the two outlying centres. Ford City is a new development seriously affecting 63rd and Halsted, and Evergreen Plaza and Old Orchard are new developments drawing trade away from Evanston.

The most visually depressing evidence of decline is to be seen in the smaller centres and ribbon developments of the inner city, however. These are the victims of a more general process of blight or decay which recent population changes and the competition of new centres have really only intensified. Brian Berry has suggested that there are four main kinds of blight affecting the older and weaker elements of the retail system.[24] First, there is an economic blight, which essentially involves the closure of large numbers of businesses because of a reduction in the amount of trade area or purchasing power support. Secondly, there is physical blight, which simply refers to the structural deterioration of buildings, primarily because of their age but also because of an inability to maintain them. Thirdly, there is functional blight, which mainly pertains to the obsolescence of small, family

businesses as a result of the impact of mass-merchandising techniques and the growth of automobile shopping. Fourthly, there
is frictional blight, which encompasses a wide range of adverse
environmental effects created by such problems as traffic congestion, litter accumulation and vandalism of vacant properties.
The combined result of all these conditions, of course, is the
formation of the commercial slum.

Extensive slum clearance programmes have now been undertaken in most North American cities, although much work
remains to be done. While most people agree on the necessity
for such programmes, however, there has been considerable

TABLE 6.3

*Changes in Shopping Centre Land Values
in the Chicago Metropolitan Area*

1. *Examples of Peak Land Values per Front Foot in Traditional Centres.*

	State St., W. Side Madison-Washington (Central Area)	63rd and Halsted St. (Outlying Centre)	Church-Orrington Evanston (Outlying Centre)
1929	$22,000	$10,000	$4,500
1933	14,000	6,500	4,000
1940	10,000	10,000	3,000
1952	17,000	9,000	3,500
1960	17,500	5,500	3,500
1967	22,000	3,000	3,200

2. *Examples of Land Values per Acre in New Planned Shopping Centres.*

	Old Orchard	Evergreen Plaza	Ford City
1929	$4,000	$5,000	$3,000
1933	2,250	2,250	1,000
1940	800	1,500	600
1952	2,000	3,000	3,000
1960	50,000	50,000	26,000
1967	152,000	130,680	109,000

Source: Hoyt, H., 'Land Values in Shopping Centres', *Urban Land*,
28, July-August (1969), 3–12.

controversy about the way in which they are conducted. The main issue concerns the fate of the small, marginal businessman who finds it difficult to re-locate. High rents usually prevent him from entering a new planned centre in the same area and he is either forced to move to some different locality altogether or go into liquidation. It has been estimated that over 100,000 small businesses have been dislocated through urban renewal schemes in the United States since 1950, and of these about a third have never started up again.[25] The question to be asked is whether this represents an excessive rate of liquidation induced by slum clearance itself, or whether, given time most of these businesses might never have survived anyway.

One answer has been provided in a detailed case-study of the effects of urban renewal in the Hyde Park-Kenwood district of Chicago[26] (see Figure 6.4). This considered the consequences that followed from 641 business displacements in the late 1950s. Two hundred and seven businesses were immediately liquidated; a further 201 businesses subsequently became liquidated after they had moved to a new location; a total of 233 businesses survived into the mid-1960s, although only eighty-three of these had relocated in the same area. While this may seem at first sight to be a staggering rate of failures, it was in fact about the same as had been predicted to occur if no renewal programme had been carried out. Moreover, comparisons drawn with neighbouring areas unaffected by clearance schemes suggested that the number of failures recorded was lower than experienced elsewhere. Part of the reason for this is that the very act of clearance prevented new speculative businesses from opening up, and past trends had indicated that thirty-one per cent of these normally folded within two years. The general conclusion of the study, therefore, was that in purely numerical terms the rate of liquidation promoted by urban renewal did not seem excessive.

Some concern was nevertheless expressed in the study that forced displacements of this kind were far more detrimental to the weaker firms than the stronger ones. Initially, no compensation was received by any of the businesses though this was later rectified by federal legislation. It proved especially difficult for the marginal businessman to find a viable new location. The first new planned shopping centre to be built in the area (the

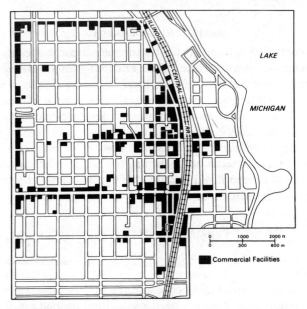

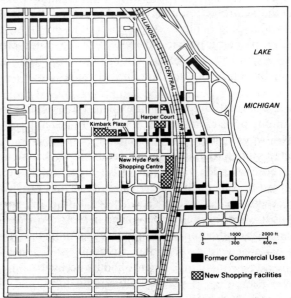

FIG. 6.4 *The effects of urban renewal on the business pattern of Hyde Park-Kenwood in south Chicago*. Above: the business pattern in 1954; below: the business pattern in 1967. (After Berry, B. J. L., Parsons, S. J. and Platt, R. H., *The Impact of Urban Renewal on Small Business: The Hyde Park-Kenwood Case*, Centre for Urban Studies, University of Chicago, 1968)

Hyde Park Centre) tended to discriminate against all the local businesses in favour of the multiple chain groups. In view of this, the more solvent of the local businesses then banded together to form their own centre called Kimbark Plaza. This still left the marginal businessman with few opportunities until the University of Chicago initiated a community development project to subsidise a third centre known as Harper Court. Although this offered rents at twenty-two per cent below normal levels, by the time it was finally built most of the businesses for which it was intended had long since disappeared.

CONCENTRATION VERSUS DECENTRALISATION IN BRITAIN

There is a strong contrast between recent changes in the urban business pattern of Britain and those we have described for North America. The main difference lies in the limited amount of sub-urban development that has been allowed to take place in Britain and the relative protection afforded to the central area and other inner city shopping centres. A general criticism might be that whereas lax planning policies in the North-American city have permitted a spatial excess of growth and decline, strict planning policies in Britain have had the effect of maintaining the *status quo*.

There are several factors which explain the evolution of such strict planning policies in Britain, of course. In general, the central area has always held a more dominant position over the rest of the retail system than its counterpart in North America. There has also been a much richer historical legacy of buildings to be preserved and a much greater mixture of non-retailing land uses to be controlled. More specifically, during the formative years of post-war suburban development in North America, many central areas and other inner shopping centres in Britain remained severely damaged from war-time bombing and some recon-struction and new retail investments had by necessity to be made. There was also a lag in pressures for retail locational change. As late as the mid-1950s, shopping habits in Britain had still not been revolutionised either by the impact of the automobile or mass-merchandising techniques and most retailing businesses wanted to stay where they were.

During the last decade, however, market conditions have changed substantially and there has been a clamour of demand for more suburban developments to be allowed which has been expressed in a wide range of applications for planning permission to build discount stores, hypermarkets and various sizes of shopping centres in predominantly 'green-field' sites. So far, the bulk of these applications have been refused. A major debate continues, nevertheless, as to the overall desirability of following policies of concentration rather than decentralisation.[27] There are three main issues involved:

a. Economic Considerations

Most planners tend to argue that the competitive trading effects of new suburban shopping facilities will lead to the same relative decline in the status of the central area and other inner city business complexes that has been experienced in North America. They feel they have a much greater moral obligation to prevent such decline because of the vast amount of public money which has been invested in post-war redevelopment schemes. Against this, many sections of the business community claim that rents and congestion costs have now become so high in traditional locations that inefficient trading practices are being supported, ultimately leading to unnecessary price increases for the consumer.

b. Environmental Considerations

Planners are always suspicious of any development that may be seen to contribute to urban sprawl. They are particularly reluctant to allow new suburban shopping facilities to enter green belt areas on the grounds that these will erode their essential rural character. However, green belt areas are not always uniformly attractive. It has been suggested that new suburban shopping facilities could occupy derelict sites and contribute to a visual upgrading of the landscape. So too, in a wider context, they might act as small growth points in areas of economic and environmental decline.

conc^ of shpg area = comfort to shoppers.

c. Social Considerations

Many planners feel that decentralisation will lead to two different standards in shopping provisions. Most of the benefits which are likely to accrue from suburban developments will go to a car-oriented middle-class population. The poorer sections of society, particularly the elderly, will remain dependent on the traditional types of shopping centre which are likely to become impoverished and severely run-down. The general argument against this is that different standards in shopping provision already exist within the retail system and, although attention needs to be given to the requirements of minority groups, there is no reason why the majority should be deprived of a greater choice. There is a pressing need especially to alleviate many of the discomforts of shopping in the central area which, despite some improvements through redevelopment schemes, continues to be grossly overcrowded and atmospherically polluted.

These opposing viewpoints have often been exaggerated, however, and there has tended to be an oversimplification of the likely consequences of new suburban developments. There is a vast difference, for example, between the potential impact of a large 'out-of-town' regional centre (of the North-American kind) and a small 'edge-of-town' discount store. Considerable controversy has particularly surrounded hypermarkets,[28] although these can vary in size from 50,000 to over 250,000 square feet. A recent study of the possible effects of a new hypermarket outside Sunderland[29] concluded that, while many neighbouring local centres would suffer a rapid decline, the central area would lose only three per cent of its total trade and 4·45 per cent of its durable-goods trade. Nevertheless, this proposal was refused planning permission, along with more than thirty other applications for a wide variety of schemes in the same location. The planning department opted to build a conventional type of neighbourhood shopping centre instead.

It is largely because of the emotional reaction which a hypermarket generates (particularly from the small, independent traders) that all proposals for new suburban developments over 100,000 square feet (formerly 50,000 square feet) must be submitted for inspection by the Department of the Environment.[30] The basic idea behind this is to provide a more equitable system of assessment throughout the country as a whole.[31] The general effect, however, has been to promote an even stronger and more united body of planning opposition to most forms of new sub-urban shopping facilities.[32] The major exceptions have tended to be the smaller versions of the free-standing superstores which are geared to convenience rather than durable-goods trade. Between January, 1972 and April, 1974, nevertheless, only three applications for such superstores were approved by the Department of the Environment.

There is no other country in Western Europe which has sought to contain the process of decentralisation to the same degree as in Britain. We noted in Chapter Three that a vast number of hypermarkets have been built, particularly in France and Germany, and several new outlying regional shopping centres of the kind found in North America have recently been introduced. The principal forerunner of these is Parly Deux, which was opened on the outskirts of Versailles in 1969.[33] Sweden has also deliberately encouraged the development of various sizes of suburban shopping centre although these have been more tightly controlled in their locations and are usually integrated in new planned residential schemes.[34]

THE EMPHASIS ON CENTRAL AREA REDEVELOPMENT

Britain stands at the forefront of other countries, however, in terms of its central-area redevelopment schemes. Although we are primarily interested here in changes in the retail sector, it is important to remember that these are usually part of a wider programme of modernisation involving all types of land use. This comprehensive approach to central-area redevelopment was heavily stressed in a series of planning guide-lines prepared for local authorities by a joint working-party of the Ministry of Housing and Local Government and Ministry of Transport in 1962.[35] While these guide-lines never became a statutory policy, they tended to serve as the main blue-print for central-area redevelopment schemes throughout the 1960s.[36] The key feature was the use of a set of sketch maps to identify the main problems and objectives involved. Two examples of these, representing the first and final stages of a hypothetical programme, are shown in Figures 6.5 and 6.6. The principal considerations are: the separation of vehicles from pedestrians and an improvement in traffic circulation; the conservation of buildings of historical and aesthetic importance; and the segregation of the major land-uses of shops, offices and commercial services.

The Growth of Precinct Shopping Schemes

The most conspicuous change in the retail sector of the central area in recent years has been the development of the precinct or pedestrianised zone. The earliest innovators of this were the post-war New Towns and those cities largely reconstructed after the blitz. Crawley claims to have built the first single pedestrianised street; Coventry claims to have built the first fully-pedestrianised shopping complex. The precinct concept was rapidly adopted in other towns and cities during the late 1950s and became as significant an influence on central-area retail planning in Britain as it was on the new types of suburban shopping centres emerging in North America. Indeed, the precinct concept ultimately flourished in the 1960s as the cornerstone of new shopping developments that are best described as the 'in-town' equivalents of the North-American 'out-of-town' centres.

As in the North-American suburban developments, the new types of central-area shopping centres in Britain vary considerably in size. Some are no more than small convenience centres; others are extremely large and specialised centres. So far, however, there has been no attempt to work out a classification of size. This is likely to prove extremely difficult, since many of the centres are really temporary features of more extensive redevelopment schemes. Considerable similarities exist, nevertheless, between the new 'regional' shopping centres of the largest cities in Britain and those in the outlying suburbs of the North-American metropolis. Some comparative statistics for selected examples are given in Table 6.4.

TABLE 6.4

Characteristics of New Regional Shopping Centres

	Site Area (Acres)	Floor-space (Sq. Ft.)	No. of Shop Units	No. of Car Spaces
Examples of New 'In-Town' Centres in Britain				
Large Centres				
Victoria Centre, Nottingham	14	580,000	88	1,670
Broadmarsh Centre, Nottingham	13	485,000	90	1,600
Whitgift Centre, Croydon	12	464,000	200	1,600
Under Construction:				
Eldon Square, Newcastle	9·5	684,000	120	1,700
Arndale Centre, Manchester	16	1,000,000	200	—
Small Centres				
Merrion Centre, Leeds	9·4	170,000	120	1,200
Butts Centre, Reading	4·4	300,000	105	800
Main Centre, Blackburn	—	350,000	132	1,740
Examples of New 'Out-of-Town' Centres in N. America				
Northland Centre, Detroit	162	985,000	122	10,500
Yorkdale Centre, Toronto	72	1,250,000	100	6,500
Tyson's Corner, Washington	84	1,000,000	105	6,000
Montgomery Mall, Washington	55	750,000	56	4,500
Cross County, New York	77	750,000	60	6,500

Most of the new central-area shopping centres in Britain are the result of a joint venture between the city planning department and a large property development company. The planning department maintains overall control of the scheme, and especially in terms of its locational relationship to the existing retail pattern and its integration with other features of the redevelopment programme; but the detailed design aspects, and particularly the internal layout of shops, are left for the property developer to decide. The centre then becomes managed as an integrated unit in much the same way as it is in the planned suburban developments in North America.

The precise location selected for an 'in-town' centre is just as crucial a determinant of success as it is in the case of the 'out-of-town' centre. The choice of location is usually more

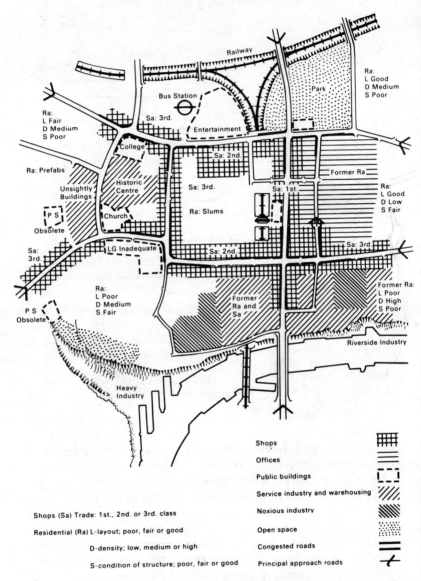

Railway

Park

Ra:
L Good
D Medium
S Poor

Bus Station

Ra:
L Fair
D Medium
S Poor

Sa: 3rd.

Entertainment

College

Sa: 2nd.

Ra: Prefabs

Unsightly
Buildings

Historic
Centre

Sa: 3rd.

Sa: 1st.

Former Ra

Ra:
L Good
D Low
S Fair

Church

Ra: Slums

P S
Obsolete

Sa:
3rd.

LG Inadequate

Sa: 2nd.

Sa: 3rd.

Ra:
L Poor
D Medium
S Fair

Former
Ra and
Sa

Former Ra:
L Poor
D High
S Poor

P S
Obsolete

Riverside Industry

Heavy
Industry

Shops	⊞
Offices	≣
Public buildings	[⌐¬]
Service industry and warehousing	⫽⫽
Noxious industry	⧄⧄
Open space	∴∴
Congested roads	═
Principal approach roads	⟊

Shops (Sa) Trade: 1st., 2nd. or 3rd. class

Residential (Ra) L-layout; poor, fair or good

D-density; low, medium or high

S-condition of structure; poor, fair or good

FIG. 6.5 *The identification of planning problems and requirements in the central area.* (This is a simplified version of a more detailed example in Ministry of Housing and Local Government and Ministry of Transport, *Town Centres: Approach to Renewal*, HMSO, 1962)

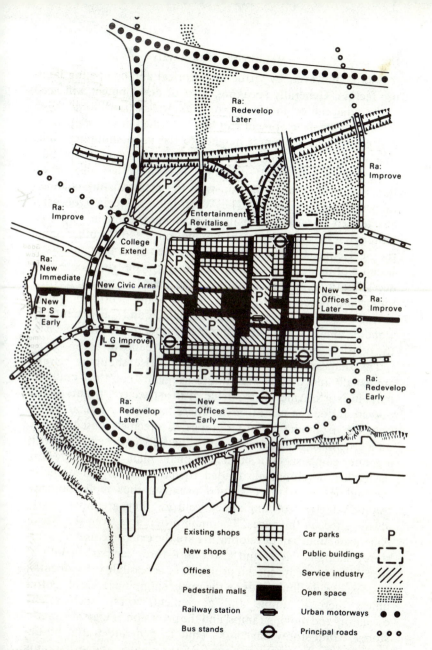

Ra:
Redevelop
Later

Ra:
Improve

Ra:
Improve

P

Entertainment
Revitalise

College
Extend

Ra:
New
Immediate

New Civic Area

New
P S
Early

P

L G Improve

P

P

P

P

P

New
Offices
Later

Ra:
Improve

P

Ra:
Redevelop
Early

P

Ra:
Redevelop
Later

New
Offices
Early

Existing shops	⊞	Car parks	P
New shops	⫽	Public buildings	⬛
Offices	≡	Service industry	⫽⫽
Pedestrian malls	■	Open space	░
Railway station	⊟	Urban motorways	● ●
Bus stands	⊖	Principal roads	○ ○ ○

FIG. 6.6 *The final blue-print for the new form of the central area.*
Other intermediate stages deal with the phasing of particular land-use
categories. (After Ministry of Housing and Local Government and
Ministry of Transport, *Town Centres: Approach to Renewal*, HMSO,
1962)

restricted, however, by virtue of historical and competing land-use factors. Generally speaking, a small development will need to be adjacent or in close proximity to the traditional High Street; a large development can be established in a more peripheral position as a counter magnet to the main shopping node. In both cases, however, nearness to car parks and major bus-stops is obviously highly desirable. Experience has also shown that it is preferable to link up with the main existing channels of pedestrian circulation. The Waterdale Centre in Doncaster has tended to suffer from its lack of integration in this way, although it is very close to the bus station.[37] On the other hand, the St. George Centre in Preston has been extremely successful because of its deliberate siting on a major pedestrian route. The accessibility or approachability of the main entrance is further important. Some centres, such as the Main Centre in Derby, Tricorn Centre in Portsmouth and Elephant and Castle Centre in London, almost seek to deter shoppers rather than attract them by the constrictions and placements of their main entrance.

The shapes and forms of the new British shopping centres are usually much more varied and irregular than their counterparts in North America by virtue of the space constraints which operate inside the central area. There has been a similar trend, however, from the 'open-air' types of precincts based largely on a cruciform or square design to the fully enclosed types with a greater emphasis on a single, dominant mall.[38] So, too, where the earlier developments tended to have the largest stores in the middle (as in the case of Coventry), thus replicating the traditional types of unplanned centres, they are now nearly always sited on the edges. The main differences from the North American suburban developments are the extensive use of multi-storey shopping levels and also multi-storey car parks. Both of these features create special problems of accessibility. Frequently, customer trade diminishes on the upper shopping levels of centres unless there is ample and convenient access, such as by escalators and moving ramps, and the provision of major attractor stores. Multi-storey car parks tend to generate traffic bottle-necks (in peak shopping hours) at their entry and exit points and involve difficulties in stair climbing when there is a shortage of lifts. In general, there is usually a lower provision of car-parking spaces than in North-American centres (about 2–3 spaces per 1,000 square feet of retail floorspace), although bus stations and concourses are increasingly integrated into the larger schemes (such as the Bull Ring Centre in Birmingham and the Victoria Centre in Nottingham). A further feature of some schemes is the addition of large blocks of flats.

The tenant mix of the new 'regional' shopping centres is dominated once again by the department stores. Unlike the North-American centres, however, these occupy proportionately much less floorspace, and compete with other large magnets such as indoor markets and variety stores. Most of the smaller units are occupied by the national chains, although these frequently trade under new store names. Thus in the Victoria Centre in Nottingham, which is currently the largest centre in Britain and is shown in Figure 6.8, the Burton Tailoring Group is represented by a store called The Orange Hand and John Temple by The Leg Inn. There tends to be a much greater range of different types of store than in the North-American centres, and particularly of service facilities such as cafés and public houses. Largely as a result of this, there is less distinct orientation to special consumer groups. Some recent trends towards customer differentiation are to be seen in the twin developments of the Birmingham Centre and Bull Ring, nevertheless, where the former is geared much more to a middle-class of consumer and the latter to a lower-class. Certain centres, too, such as the Merrion Centre in Leeds, have emerged as a focus of entertainment and hence cater predominantly for the young.

Other Aspects of Redevelopment

Little study has yet been made of the repercussions which follow from the development of new 'in-town' shopping centres and particularly those of a 'regional' kind. It is obvious, however, that the largest ones may lead to substantial changes not only in the composition of retail trade but also in the entire fabric of central area land-uses. The majority of them are built within the decaying frame on sites which were formerly occupied by a wide mixture of commercial activities. Their immediate effect is therefore both to increase the overall amount of specialised retail floorspace to be found and to physically enlarge the core area of shopping.

This is well-illustrated in the case of Nottingham. The Broadmarsh centre which has recently been opened on the southern extremity of the central area adds, together with the already well-established Victoria Centre on the northern extremity, a total of more than a million square feet of new retail floorspace (Figure 6.7). The major artery linking the two centres (now pedestrianised) extends for almost three-quarters of a mile; and this is by no means the only principal shopping street. Indeed, until the advent of the two planned centres, most growth in the core area of shopping within the central area had followed an east-west direction rather than the north-south axis which is now being planned.[39]

The development of such large 'regional' shopping centres usually leads to a major shift in the 'centre-of-gravity' of retail trade. It is hoped that this will be minimised in Nottingham by the creation of two opposite poles of attraction. However, the Victoria Centre (Figure 6.8), initially had the effect of depressing sales and rents in the traditional nodal position of the market square, and several vacant premises appeared following the movement of many businesses into the new centre itself (including the department store of Jessops). The situation has recently improved but could well deteriorate again with the completion of the Broadmarsh Centre, although there are considerable doubts about the long-term success of this second venture which has the cooperative society as its major tenant. Most local businessmen consider that the initial decline in the market-square area was a temporary phenomenon, and that it is the areas to the east and west which will suffer a more serious and permanent loss of retail trade.[40]

The pedestrianisation of traditional shopping streets is one way of combating the competitiveness of new shopping centres. Until very recently, however, this was often bitterly opposed by many of the smaller shopkeepers. It was judged that motorised traffic not only formed an important source of potential customers in itself, but that it leant an atmosphere of 'busyness' to a street and hence contributed to its overall attractiveness. Experience has shown, however, that when the main High Streets in particular are pedestrianised then more crowds tend to be generated and the sales of individual businesses actually increase. Some notable examples are London Street in Norwich, Northumberland Street in Newcastle and Oxford Street in London.

Pedestrianisation is usually accompanied by several other measures of environmental improvement, of course. Typically, these include the provision of seats, intermittent clusters of shrubbery, and the modernisation of shop-fronts. There may also be some changes in the position of lighting fixtures and the nature of pavement surfaces. In conservation areas, local authorities have been able to furnish improvement grants to help individual businesses pay for the costs of cleaning their buildings; and in certain circumstances, they have assisted in major structural alterations to buildings of historical significance. In some cities, such as Coventry, there has even been a physical relocation of the more important historical buildings to combine them in restricted access or pedestrianised streets.

There are several problems associated with the traditional shopping streets, however, that are not easily solved. Perhaps the most important of these is the difficulty involved in the servicing of stores. There is usually little space at the rear entrances of stores to accommodate the larger types of vehicles now needed in goods deliveries; and while it is possible to use the front entrances, this is clearly undesirable in terms of the inconvenience to customers. Many of the traditional shopping streets are also extremely long, and have grown up along former tram lines and bus routes. Although it is still possible to maintain public transport services along these streets (when they are pedestrianised), the population has increasingly come to rely on car-borne shopping and will likely be increasingly deterred from walking excessive distances to and from peripherally-located car parks. The general exposure of these streets to weather hazards is a further problem that may become a more critical consideration in the future. The variety of sizes and architectural styles of the stores to be found makes it extremely difficult to provide any large or consistent canopies over wide sections of the streets. Taken together, these problems really raise serious questions about the long-term viability of many of the traditional shopping

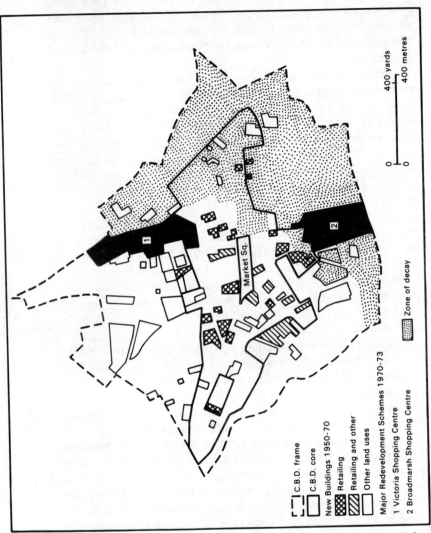

FIG. 6.7 *Post-war retailing development in the central area of Nottingham.* (After Giggs, J. A., 'Retail Change and Decentralisation in the Nottingham Metropolitan Community', *Geographia Polonica*, **24**, 1972, 173–88)

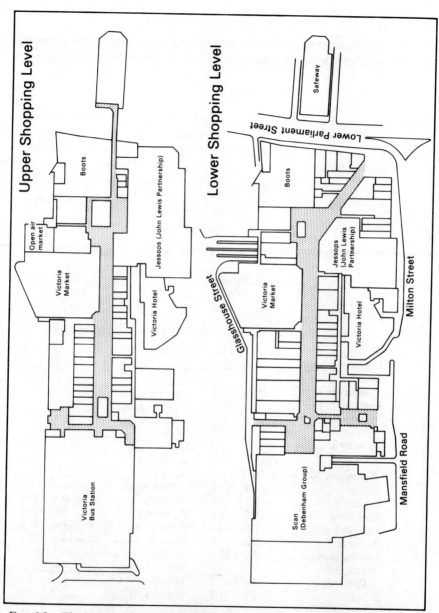

FIG. 6.8 *The layout of the Victoria Shopping Centre in Nottingham.* The Victoria centre is a multi-level complex having three levels of parking and service access below the main shopping levels and 464 flats above them. The total letable area of the development is 984,000 square feet of which the eighty-eight stores occupy 632,000 square feet and the market a further 120,000 square feet. (Based on floor plans of Capital and Counties Property Co. Ltd.)

streets, especially given a continued growth in the new types of enclosed shopping centres.

THE EXTENT OF DECENTRALISATION IN BRITAIN

Although we have stressed in earlier sections that there has been much less decentralisation of retail trade in Britain compared to other countries, there has of course been a certain amount especially in terms of convenience trade. There have been the same broad shifts in population distribution from the inner areas of the city to the suburbs, as Table 6.5 indicates, and these have

TABLE 6.5

Population Shifts in Britain's Metropolitan Areas 1961–71

	% Changes Inner Area	% Changes Outer Area		% Changes Inner Area	% Changes Outer Area
Total Population Over 1 Million			*Population 250,000–499,000*		
Birmingham	−8·8	12·7	Blackpool	−1·2	16·5
Leeds/Bradford	−2·2	6·4	Bournemouth	−0·6	16·7
Liverpool/			Brighton	1·8	9·8
Birkenhead	−16·1	15·9	Chatham/		
London	−7·7	15·2	Gillingham/		
Manchester/			Rochester	15·9	32·9
Salford	−17·7	7·9	Derby	3·1	6·8
Newcastle/			Hull	−6·1	23·2
Gateshead	−15·1	4·1	Mansfield	8·2	9·8
Population 500,000–1 Million			Newport/		
Bristol	−2·9	31·1	Pontypool	0	1·7
Cardiff/Rhondda	−4·5	12·4	Norwich	0·5	29·6
Coventry	5·7	18·5	Plymouth	3·9	18·0
Leicester	−1·5	33·7	Portsmouth	−8·4	35·8
Teesside	5·6	11·6	Preston	−14·1	23·1
Nottingham	−3·9	15·6	Reading	10·1	47·5
Sheffield/			Southampton	4·8	29·4
Rotherham	−3·4	17·3	Swansea/Neath	1·7	3·9
Stoke	−4·4	11·1	Wigan/Leigh	2·0	21·9

Source: Kivell, P. T., 'Retailing in Non-Central Locations', *Institute of British Geographers Occasional Publication No. 1* (1972), 49–58.

been accompanied by an outward spread of predominantly small types of shopping centres. At the same time, many larger outlying centres that represent the former nuclei of villages or towns subsumed into a wider metropolitan area have often grown at a faster rate in recent years than the central area itself.[41] Generally speaking, however, retail trade has not expanded as rapidly in the suburbs as the population has. Giggs found in Nottingham that while the population of the outer parts of the city grew by 33·6 per cent from 1951 to 1968, the number of retail outlets provided grew by only 9·8 per cent.[42] Over the same period the average number of people served by each shop increased from 82 to 103, although within the inner city the corresponding figures were 51 and 53. Clearly, such trends need to be considered against the background of changes in consumer-shopping patterns and developments in mass-merchandising techniques. Nevertheless, the broad weight of the evidence suggests that the overall imbalance between retail supply and population demand in the suburbs has tended to get worse rather than better during the last decade.

Emerging Types of New Suburban Shopping Centres

We have indicated that there are essentially two main elements to the new suburban retail system in Britain. On the one hand, there is a set of what we might regard as modern, purpose-built shopping centres that have been predominantly built in conjunction with new housing areas. On the other hand, there is a set of much older or traditional shopping centres that have recently become re-vitalised because of their location within the outer margins of a metropolis. Neither of the two sets of shopping centres really operates independently or in isolation from the retail system to be found in inner areas, however. They effectively form an extension of the city-wide hierarchy previously described, as Table 6.6 suggests.

Our main interest here is with the modern types of suburban shopping centres which are extremely difficult to classify in terms other than size.[43] This is because they tend to exhibit a wide variety of shapes or forms (ranging from a single dominant store to a complex of numerous small outlets); they

TABLE 6.6

A Classification of New Types of Shopping Centres in Britain

Centres in New Housing Areas on 'Greenfield' Sites	Centres in Old Housing Areas on Redeveloped Sites

New regional centres
   e.g. Brent Cross, London
	Redeveloped regional centres
	   e.g. Croydon, London

New sub-regional centres
   or large district centres
Centres of new towns
   e.g. Washington, Co. Durham
Centres of new suburbs
   e.g. Seacroft, Leeds
	Redeveloped sub-regional centres
	   or expanded district centres
	Centres of old towns
	   e.g. South Shields, Co. Durham
	Centres of old suburbs
	   e.g. Cross Gates, Leeds

New district centres
Centres of new estates
   e.g. Bell Green, Coventry
	Redeveloped district centres
	Centres of old estates
	   e.g. Hillfields, Coventry

New neighbourhood centres
Centres of new estates
   e.g. Willenhall, Coventry
	Redeveloped neighbourhood centres
	Centres of old estates
	   e.g. Benwell, Newcastle

Free-standing superstores
   e.g. Fine Fare, Aberdeen
	Free-standing discount stores
	   e.g. Former Co-op premises

occupy a number of different types of locations (ranging from 'greenfield' sites in a proper sense to sites in the middle of densely populated communities); they engage in a wide assortment of different functions (without the clear-cut distinctions between convenience trade and specialised trade to be found in the more traditional centres). There is also a general problem of semantics regarding these centres, for they are frequently described as being 'out-of-town' or as 'edge-of-town' centres, when few really ever extend beyond the built-up parts of the city.[44]

There is but one example of a new outlying regional shopping centre in Britain: the Brent Cross scheme in North London. This was finally opened in 1976 after a series of planning objections and revisions that date back to 1963. The centre occupies a location at the junction of the North Circular Road and the A.41, which is a spur of the M.1. The site is a 'greenfield' one to the extent that it was formerly an area of open space and allotments between two industrial estates, but it is ringed on all sides by large residential tracts. The centre approximates to a dumb-bell shape, and its two levels provide approximately 775,000 square feet of retail floorspace. There are two department stores, five other major attractor stores and seventy-seven smaller units. 3,500 car-parking spaces will be eventually realised, the majority of them at surface level.

The two types of sub-regional shopping centres referred to in Table 6.6 reflect on an entirely new level or size-order of centres to be found in the urban hierarchy of Britain. They are sometimes described as the equivalent of district centres, but their influence in fact extends over a much wider territorial area. They serve not only the local populations of the new towns or new suburbs in which they are located, but also act as 'out-of-town' centres for the older parts of a metropolitan area. Their nearest parallel perhaps is the 'shopping goods' centre which Berry recognised in Chicago[45] (and which we reported in Chapter Five).

A good example in the case of the New Towns is the main centre for Washington, which was opened in November, 1973. This has been deliberately conceived as an 'out-of-town' centre for the southern part of the Tyne and Wear conurbation, for places like Gateshead, Jarrow and Sunderland are less than five miles away. Figure 6.9 indicates its convenient location alongside a major expressway system and the enormous amount of car-parking spaces which have been made available. There are currently about 3,000 car-parking spaces in fact, although these are intended to serve a complex of office and social facilities as well. The final plan calls for a total of 7,000 car-parking spaces, which is more than will be built for the whole of the central area of Newcastle! The main attractor store at present is a Woolco development, which in itself provides 104,000 square feet of retail floorspace. This is physically separate from, but adjacent to, an enclosed area of sixty-eight smaller shops arranged on two storeys; with the upper storey primarily devoted to business services, such as building societies and banks, and the lower storey to purely retailing functions.

Examples of similar kinds of sub-regional shopping centres

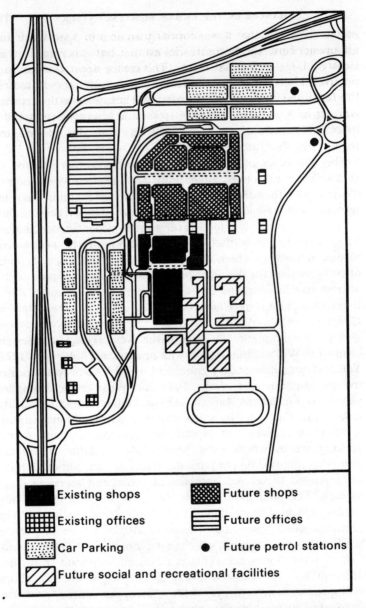

■ Existing shops	▨ Future shops
▦ Existing offices	▤ Future offices
▢ Car Parking	● Future petrol stations
▨ Future social and recreational facilities	

FIG. 6.9 *The site and layout of the main shopping centre of Washington new town.* (From source material provided by Washington Development Corporation)

within the middle of new suburbs include the Yate Centre in Gloucestershire, the Seacroft Centre in Leeds and the Cowley Centre in Oxford. Those like the Cowley Centre which are relatively close to the central area of a city resemble most closely the form and function of conventional district centres.[46] They tend to have an open precinct type of layout and cater for a higher proportion of walking as opposed to car-borne shopping trips. They are usually dominated by a department or large variety store, however, and may contain as many as 100 smaller shops. The more conventional district centres rely on supermarkets or small variety stores as their main magnets and typically contain about fifty smaller shops. Neighbourhood centres tend to be laid out as a single mall of shops (though an increasing number of these are enclosed) and they cater almost exclusively for the housing estates in which they are built. Supermarkets are again the main attractor stores, supported by an average of 20–30 smaller shops.

The final category of new centres comprises a miscellaneous group of free-standing superstores. These are generally found on the outer margins of the city, in what may be regarded as 'off-centre' locations. They occupy sites alongside the major radial routes or ring-roads of cities and may be some distance away from residential areas. Various examples include the Fine Fare superstore on the outskirts of Aberdeen (which is 40,000 square feet in floorspace size); the Gem superstore on the outskirts of Nottingham (84,000 square feet); the Co-operative Society superstore on the outskirts of Birkenhead (70,000 square feet); and a large number of Asda stores scattered throughout the North-East. All of these essentially rely on car-borne shopping from wide parts of the city.

SUMMARY

Britain stands virtually alone amongst the westernised countries of the world in its heavily restrictive planning controls over the decentralisation of retail trade. While this forbearance in the face of considerable pressure may be seen by foreign eyes as reflecting the 'stiff upper lip' the irony of the situation is that retailing is the only major land-use category in the distributive trades and entire tertiary sector which has been treated in this way. Most other activities, such as wholesaling and head-quarters offices, have instead been deliberately encouraged to disperse and indeed in many individual cases have been given government subsidies as inducements to re-locate. Even industry, with its vast claims on site resources and local infrastructures, has never faced such massive resistance to its encroachment on suburban land. No-one, of course, would wish to advocate a repetition of the mistakes of uncontrolled expansion too fre-quently experienced in North America over the last two decades, and there is a clear responsibility towards preserving the relative economic health of the central areas of our cities. There is a strong case, however, for a more enlightened planning policy particularly towards the convenience trades. It is not beyond the bounds of reason or imagination to provide suitable sites for moderate-sized 'edge-of-town' centres which could readily be integrated into the hierarchical system of a new structure plan. The danger of the current, rather reactionary, planning stance is that monopoly powers are becoming increasingly en-trenched amongst the major central-area investors (including the local authorities themselves). Meanwhile, the British housewife continues to spend more time and effort on her shopping chores and under more arduous conditions than any of her con-temporaries in the advanced economies.

REFERENCES

1. Allpass, J., 'Change in the Structure of Urban Centres', *Journal of the American Institute of Planners* (1968), 170–3.

2. Cox, E. and Erickson, L. G., *Retail Decentralisation* (Bureau of Business and Economic Research, Michigan State University, 1967).

3. The unincorporated township represents a community which does not come under the jurisdiction of either the city or county local governments and is essentially independent in the way it conducts its zoning practices.

4. A commonly accepted definition of the planned shopping centre is: 'A group of commercial establishments planned, developed, owned and managed as a unit, with off-street parking provided on the property, and related in location, size and type of shops to the trade area that the unit serves—generally in an outlying or suburban area.'

J. R. McKeever, 'Shopping Centres Restudied', *Urban Land Institute, Technical Bulletin No. 30* (1957).

5. Simmons, J., 'The Changing Pattern of Retail Location', *University of Chicago, Dept. of Geography, Research Paper No. 92* (1964).

6. Kelley, E., *Locating Planned Regional Shopping Centres* (Eno Foundation for Traffic Control, Connecticut, 1956).

7. Hoyt, H., 'Land Values in Shopping Centres: The U.S. Metropolitan Areas with Greatest Total Prospective Growth in Retail Sales in 1967–78', *Urban Land*, **28**, No. 7 (1969), 3–12.

8. Capital and Counties Property Co. Ltd., *Design for Shopping* (London, 1970).

9. McKeever, J. R., *op. cit.*

10. Hoyt, H., *op. cit.*

11. National Economic Development Office, Committee for the Distributive Trades, *The Future Pattern of Shopping* (HMSO, 1971).

12. Jones, C. S., *Regional Shopping Centres: Their Location, Planning and Design* (Business Books Ltd., 1969).

13. Simmons, J., *op. cit.*

14. See, for example, Drachman, R. P., 'Emerging Types of Shopping Centres', *Urban Land*, **21**, No. 3 (1962); Raeburn, A. and Jenkins, G. M., 'High Fashion Centres', *Urban Land*, **24**, No. 12 (1965).

15. Variations in the amount of CBD sales according to differences in urban characteristics were the subject of a special study by Boyce, R. R. and Clark, W. A. V., 'Selected Spatial Variables and Central Business District Retail Sales', *Papers and Proceedings of the Regional Science Association*, **11** (1963), 167–93.

16. Federal Reserve Bank of Chicago, 'Retailing—Rapid Growth in the Suburbs', *Business Conditions*, May (1966), 12–16.

17. The category of trade which has suffered most are apparel goods, particularly female clothing. See Russwurm, L. H., 'The Central Business District Retail Sales Mix, 1948–58', *Annals of the Association of American Geographers*, **54** (1964), 524–36.

18. Smith, A., 'The Future of Downtown Retailing', *Urban Land*, **31**, No. 11 (1972), 1–10.

19. Sternlieb, G., 'The Future of Retailing in the Downtown Core', *Journal of the American Institute of Planners*, **29** (1963), 102–11.

20. Vance, J. E., 'Focus on Downtown' in Bourne, L. S. (ed.), *Internal Structure of the City* (Oxford University Press, 1971).

21. Smith, A., *op. cit.*

22. Marshall Field and Company, *Annual Report* (Chicago, 1971).

23. Regional Plan Association, *The Second Regional Plan: A Draft for Discussion* (New York, 1968).

24. Berry, B. J. L., 'Commercial Structure and Commercial Blight', *University of Chicago, Dept. of Geography, Research Paper No. 85* (1963).

25. Berry, B. J. L., Parsons, S. J. and Platt, R. H., *The Impact of*

Urban Renewal on Small Business: The Hyde Park-Kenwood Case (Centre for Urban Studies, University of Chicago, 1968).

26. Berry, B. J. L., *et al., op. cit.*

27. There are numerous articles which deal with different aspects of the debate. A wide range of viewpoints is contained in a special issue of *Built Environment*, **2**, No. 2 (1973). See also, Thorpe, D. and Kivell, P. T., 'The Decentralisation of Shopping', *Distribution Briefing*, **1**, No. 1 (1971), 1–13; Sainsbury, T. A. D., 'Retail Store Location', *Estates Gazette*, **224**, November (1972), 803–5; Freeman, H. B., 'The Case for the High Street', *Estates Gazette*, **221**, March (1972), 1501–3.

28. Hillman, M., 'In the Market Place: The Hypermarket Debate', *New Society*, **21**, Sept. 21st (1972).

29. Sunderland Corporation, *A Hypermarket Survey* (1971).

30. Department of the Environment, 'Out-of-Town Shops and Shopping Centres', Development Control Policy Note No. 13.

31. There is an extremely interesting and valuable record of the public enquiry held by the Department of the Environment for five applications for new shopping developments outside Bristol. Bristol City Planning Department, *Cribbs Causeway Out-of-Town Shopping Centre Enquiry: A Report of the Proceedings* (1972).

32. The opinion column 'Pragma' states in reference to hypermarkets that 'Planners almost to a man have set their hearts against these forms of development.' 'Planners versus Shopping Centres', *Journal of the Royal Town Planning Institute*, **58** (1972), 244.

33. Smith, B. V., 'Retail Planning in France: The Changing Pattern of French Retailing', *Town Planning Review*, **44** (1973), 279–306.

34. Jones, C. S., *op. cit.*, 'Multiple Shops Federation', *Shopping Centres in North-West Europe* (London, 1967).

35. Ministry of Housing and Local Government and Ministry of Transport, *Town Centres: Approach to Renewal* (HMSO, 1962).

36. For a summary of some of the major redevelopment schemes in British cities, see Holliday, J. (ed.), *City Centre Redevelopment* (Charles Knight, 1973).

37. National Economic Development Office, Committee for the Distributive Trades, *op. cit.*

38. For some detailed examples of the layouts of enclosed shopping centres, see Darlow, C., *Enclosed Shopping Centres* (Architectural Press, 1972).

39. Giggs, J. A., 'Retail Change and Decentralisation in the Nottingham Metropolitan Community', *Geographia Polonica*, **24** (1972), 173–88.

40. 'The Victoria Centre, Nottingham: A Special Report', *The Times*, February 28th (1973).

41. Schiller, R. K., 'The Growth of Shops and Offices in the Outer Metropolitan Area, 1963–68', University of Reading, Department of Geography, Discussion Paper No. 6 (1970).

42. Giggs, J. A., *op. cit.*

43. Some general and alternative descriptions of new suburban

shopping centres are given in Hillier, T. J., *The Growth and Development of Out-of-Town Shopping Centres in the U.K.* (Bradford University, Management Centre, 1970); Kivell, P. T., 'Retailing in Non-Central Locations', *Institute of British Geographers Occasional Publication No. 1* (1972), 49–58.

44. Thorpe, D. and Kivell, P. T., 'The Decentralisation of Shopping', *Distribution Briefing*, **1**, No. 1 (1971), 1–13.

45. Berry, B. J. L., 'Commercial Structure and Commercial Blight', *University of Chicago, Department of Geography, Research Paper No. 85* (1963).

46. For a detailed case-study of this centre, see Bacon, R. W., *The Cowley Shopping Centre* (HMSO, 1968).

7 Consumer Behaviour and Space Preferences in Shopping

It was emphasised in the early chapters of this book that marketing geography is as much concerned with the demand for various goods and services as it is with their supply. That most of our attention has so far focused on the supply side is really a reflection on the overall state of the literature to be found. There have tended to be many more studies of the locational characteristics of shops and shopping centres than there have of the behavioural patterns of the consumers they serve.

The interest shown on the demand side and with consumer behaviour in particular, however, has seemed to follow a clear sequence of development. Simply put, this has involved a shift in emphasis from the more general to the more specific: from studies conducted at a regional scale level of enquiry to those concerned with the greater complexity of urban shopping trips; from studies dealing with the population as a whole to those concerned with particular kinds of consumer reference groups; from studies aimed at elucidating the prevailing regularities of shopping trips to those concerned much more with the variability that is found. In a theoretical context, this has meant a shift in emphasis away from central place theory and general interaction theory as the most appropriate frameworks for describing and explaining the broader aspects of consumer behaviour towards a series of more micro-theories dealing with the space preferences of the individual.

In following these trends, we will be concerned in this chapter only with the journeys that take place to shopping centres and will leave consideration of shop-to-shop movements or patterns of circulation inside shopping centres to a later chapter on store location research. We will also be primarily concerned with the characteristics of domestic shopping trips rather than with the full spectrum of business or commercial trips. There is insufficient space to deal with such trips as those to garages, building supply merchants, cash-and-carry wholesalers, entertainment centres and the like.

STUDIES OF AGGREGATE PATTERNS OF MOVEMENT

The bulk of the traditional work on consumer behaviour has been concerned with describing the overall numbers, distances and directions of alternative kinds of shopping trips. These are often crudely distinguished in terms such as convenience shopping, comparison shopping and specialty shopping, or trips for convenience-goods versus durable-goods, or food versus non-food goods, etc. The main point of interest is the differential use made of individual shops or shopping centres for any or all of these types of goods. This is associated in part with the delimitation of trade areas and in part with the testing of central place theory to see to what extent consumers functionally utilise a hierarchical system of shops and shopping centres in their aggregate patterns of movement.

The Delimitation of Trade Areas

Although we have made repeated reference to the term trade area, there is in fact considerable confusion as to what this properly means.[1] We noted in Chapter Five, for example, that there are really two ways in which the size of a trade area may be defined. It is possible to interpret size in terms of the amount of trade that may be involved (in the sense of the volume of customer support that a centre commands), or alternatively in terms of its areal or territorial extent (in which case this will refer to the maximum reach of the customer support that is drawn).

Further differences are apparent in the methods used to delimit trade areas and the uses to which they are ultimately put. To help clarify the situation at this stage, we might initially discriminate between three categories of trade areas: what we will call potential trade areas, probable trade areas, and actual trade areas. Potential trade areas are those which are often delimited on maps in a crude and rather subjective way to indicate the possible, though largely unknown, areas from which trade will be conceivably drawn to a series of centres. Such trade areas are essentially drawn on the basis of experience or by working to certain rules of thumb, such as a half-mile radius to indicate the normal limit for a trade area of a small neighbourhood shopping centre. Alternatively, they may be calculated from a break-point type of gravity model (such as is described in Chapter Two). Probable trade areas are those which indicate with more certainty the amount of trade that may be generated in different parts of the surrounding territory of centres. These are often worked out through more rigorous kinds of gravity models (such as the Huff model described in Chapter Two) and plotted on maps in the form of a series of contours of probability values for consumers visiting alternative centres. Actual trade areas are those which refer to the known patterns of use of centres because these are based on customer surveys. A much more precise set of boundaries can therefore be drawn on maps to indicate both the amount of trade and maximum reach of the trade areas of alternative centres.

Three different forms of the actual trade areas may be described, however: what we will call general trade areas, composite trade areas, and proportional trade areas. These are illustrated in Figure 7.1.

1. General trade areas are the simplest kinds of actual trade areas and are represented on maps by a single boundary line. They may be used to indicate either the maximum reach of a trade area's extent (or the range of its goods in terms of central place theory) or alternatively the main source area from which most trade is gained. They are usually derived from 'pavement' surveys conducted in a focal position inside a centre, or shop, and which involve a limited questionnaire concerned primarily with eliciting the home origins of customers.[2] Such trade areas are similar in kind to those based on the frequency of bus services or the deliveries of certain goods and are often used in planning to provide a broad regional context for studies of the central area or other major centres.

2. Composite trade areas refer to a series of separate boundary lines which are superimposed to represent the multiple functional role of most shopping centres. The separate boundary lines may refer to individual categories of goods or collective categories such as convenience-goods and durable-goods. They may again be used to indicate either the maximum reach of a trade area's extent or alternatively the main source areas from which most trade is gained. They tend to be derived from 'home-interview' surveys, however, where more detailed information can be gained about the different centres used for different shopping purposes.[3] Such trade areas are often usefully employed in conjunction with studies based on central place theory to demonstrate the nesting arrangement of smaller trade areas inside larger ones in relation to a hierarchy of shopping centres.

3. Proportional trade areas are those where a series of gradational boundary lines are drawn on maps to indicate more precisely the relative numbers of consumers visiting any centre or the relative amount of trade available in different parts of a surrounding territory. They therefore resemble in form the probable trade areas although there is usually less regularity in

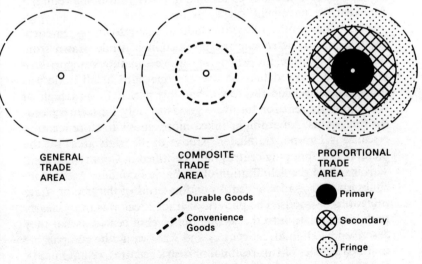

FIG. 7.1 *The three main types of 'actual' or known trade areas.* An explanation of each of these is given in the text.

the interval scales between the boundaries reflecting diminishing trade. The proportions of trade commonly refer to arbitrary categories that have been found meaningful in particular case-studies. Thus Applebaum,[4] for example, has defined a primary trade zone as one where fifty to seventy per cent of the population may be expected to patronise a particular store; the secondary trade zone as one where twenty to thirty per cent of the population may be expected to be customers; and the fringe zone as one where ten to twenty per cent of the population may be expected to be customers. In planning applications, a distinction is often drawn between that trade which comes from the city proper and that which emanates from the suburbs. These trade areas may be derived from both 'pavement' and 'home-interview' surveys, although the latter is more suitable if data on expenditure patterns is required.

Although these basic differences exist between the three types of actual trade areas, it is of course quite possible and common in practice to combine them together. A typical example in planning is the use of composite and proportional trade areas to indicate the relative amount of convenience- versus durable-goods shopping which is conducted in district shopping centres.[5] An extensive 'pavement' survey by Bengtsson[6] of 4,000 shoppers in the main centre of Mariestad, a small town in Sweden, enabled him to determine the proportion of trade drawn from inside and outside the town for twelve separate categories of goods. This showed that on average one-third of all trade was drawn from outside the town, but this varied from a high of sixty-four per cent for furniture goods to only thirteen per cent for food items. An example linked more closely to store-location research is Thorpe and Nader's study[7] of the trade areas for the hierarchy of shopping centres they identified in County Durham. This involved the delimitation of primary, secondary and fringe-zones for four grades of centres and in terms of thirteen separate categories of goods. The pattern of trade areas was most clearly revealed in relation to the second tier level of centres (what they described as High Street centres and what would be comparable to the categories of sub-regional or district centres we have used). Here the primary zone had a maximum reach of two miles; the secondary zone extended from two to four miles; and the fringe extended from four to eight miles. These contained respectively seventy, twenty and ten per cent of the non-food custom of High Street shopping centres. The general trade area they demarcated for the main source of custom lay at about three miles from each of these centres.

The Functional Use of Centres

Most of the theoretical interest in the characteristics of actual trade areas has focused less on the precise form which these take than on what they reveal about the functional use of centres. In a strict interpretation of central place theory, all trade areas should be hexagonal in shape and equal in areal extent for the same types of goods. No-one really expects to be able to identify a system of equal-sized hexagons in the real world landscape, however, without recourse to serious distortions or complex transformations of the data itself.[8]

The main question addressed in connection with central place theory, therefore, has been whether there is sufficient evidence from the recurrent travel patterns of the population to indicate a systematic use of the various levels of a hierarchy of centres. A common approach towards tackling this has been to plot as a series of flow lines or desire lines the movements of a sample of (home-interviewed) consumers for a wide selection of goods and services. A typical example is the study conducted by Berry and others[9] into the functional use of the hierarchy of centres in western Iowa, the structural characteristics of which we described in Chapter Four. A selection of the maps they compiled is shown in Figure 7.2.

If we examine the case of food shopping first, it can be clearly seen that all of the people living in the urban areas make use of the store provisions within their own locality. The people in the rural areas either go to the nearest village available or alternatively to a nearby town or city. In the case of the movements for dry-cleaning services, however, the absence of these functions within the villages compels a much greater orientation to the towns and cities and a consequent increase in journey lengths. A pattern of dominance and dependence is established which becomes further pronounced in the case of clothes shop-

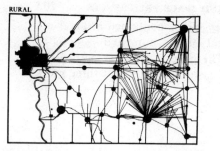
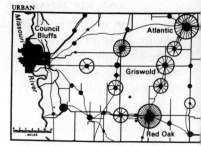

Movements for foodstuffs

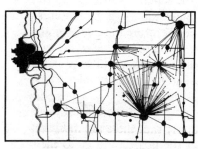
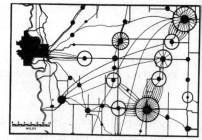

Movements for dry cleaning

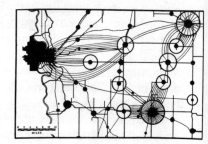

Movements for clothing

FIG. 7.2 *The choice of centres for various shopping purposes in western Iowa.* The cartwheel appearance of the circles represents the movements of the urban residents within their own settlements; the flows between the circles represent the movements of urban residents to other settlements; the other desire lines represent the movements of the rural residents. (After Berry, B. J. L., Barnum, H. G. and Tennant, R. J., 'Retail Location and Consumer Behaviour', *Papers of the Regional Science Association*, **9**, 1962, 65–106)

ping. Here, the absence of an effective choice within the towns (except for work-clothes) leads to a concentration of both urban and rural trips on the two cities (Atlantic or Red Oak) or alternatively the regional capital of Council Bluffs. If we were to go on and deal with the case of a luxury item we would likely find that all of the trips were concentrated on Council Bluffs alone.

The evidence provided by this kind of study, however, suggests that the systematic use of the hierarchy of centres is wholly dictated by what is available. The orderliness in the patterns of movement is a direct result of the presence or absence of certain goods or services at successive levels of centres. Since the hierarchy itself is a well-defined one in an area with few constraints on travel, what appear to be some striking results are perhaps only to be expected. In many, less idealistic situations, the patterns of movement become considerably blurred.

There are two features within this study which hint at some of the difficulties experienced elsewhere. First, it can be seen in the case of food shopping particularly that there are instances where consumers do not always visit the nearest centre to them in the way a strict interpretation of central place theory suggests they should.[10] Secondly, and linked to this, consumers do not always visit that class of centre for which a good or service is deemed to be most typical.[11] This leads to an overlapping of trade areas and a breakdown of the nesting arrangement of smaller, lower-order trade areas inside larger, higher-order ones. Such variability in shopping for the same kinds of goods and services is particularly conspicuous inside the city. It arises of course because of the multi-purpose functions which are often involved and also because of the increased mobility of consumers which allows them a greater ease of access to alternative choices of centres.

It is this variability in shopping which has led many researchers to be extremely critical of central place theory as a basis for explaining the broader aspects of consumer behaviour and to prefer instead the more flexible approach of general interaction theory. Such criticism, however, needs to be carefully considered against the background conditions in which various studies have been conducted and the way in which central place theory has itself been interpreted. There are major differences to be found, for example, between those conditions prevailing in Britain and other countries again, and between those studies which have dealt with the theory in a literal sense and those which have treated it much more freely.

There are three particular considerations to be borne in mind.

1. We have stated that most studies have made only a crude distinction between various kinds of trip purposes. In testing the postulate of central place theory that consumers will always visit a nearest centre that offers a required good or service, a much clearer definition of what is meant by a 'required' good or service must be given.[12] It is not sufficient to characterise all food trips as being the same, for there are obvious differences between the requirements to be met in a major bulk-purchasing trip and a minor small-purchasing trip. If they were the same, then all trips should strictly speaking terminate at a local corner-store which, of course, rarely happens. The requirements to be met include not only the main type of good or service, but the opportunity to select from a range of like kinds of products in certain congenial store surroundings. It is necessary, in fact, to interpret the requirements much more in terms of satisficer criteria,[13] which notion then remains compatible with central place theory to the extent that consumers will always be seen to visit the nearest centre at which a required level of satisfaction may be achieved.

2. Few studies have bothered to discriminate between types of shopping trips in the same way as between varying types of retailing sub-systems. It will be remembered that the hierarchy of shopping centres in urban areas is but one component part of the overall system of retailing provisions. In testing the postulate of central place theory that consumers will utilise each structural level in the hierarchy for different goods and services, therefore, much more care and attention needs to be given to ensure that an appropriate combination of trips are used.[14] Many trips for services, such as dry-cleaning, washing or hairdressing, are oriented towards ribbon developments rather than centres; and many trips for specialist needs, such as furniture, domestic appliances and even clothes are oriented towards specialised functional areas. These will obviously incur very different patterns of movement from those which are solely linked to centres in a

proper sense and may seriously affect an objective assessment as to how a hierarchy is used.

3. Generally speaking, there is much more variability in patterns of movement within North America than in Britain, partly because of the greater amount of car-borne shopping to be found and partly because of the greater choice in shopping opportunities available. In Britain, the bulk of the population still conducts its shopping by walking and bus travel and the planned provision of shopping centres is rigidly geared to this. The fact that the British housewife is still constrained to using either the small centre in her immediate locality or alternatively the central area means that there is a clear-cut distinction between minor trips and major trips and those for convenience-goods and durable-goods. Increasingly, there is also a deliberate planning policy of concentrating the population in small, physically separate neighbourhood units which are then served individually by neighbourhood centres and collectively by district centres. This is tending to strengthen rather than diminish a consumer-functional identification of the hierarchy of centres.

These three features are well-illustrated in a case-study of daily shopping trips in Coventry, which were recorded in a city-wide diary survey conducted in 1969 (Table 7.1).[15] An example of the patterns of movement for food and other 'convenience' items on a Friday is shown in Figure 7.3. The first point to note is that there is a clear distinction between those trips which focus on local centres and those which are oriented to the central area. The extent to which this reflects on major trips versus minor trips or bulk-purchasing versus small-purchasing trips is concealed, however, by the way that all trips have been classified as the same. Whichever type of centre a consumer has selected, nevertheless, it is nearly always that type of centre which is nearest to him. There is very little cross-travel through the city such that a consumer in one area uses the centre of another area. If his shopping requirements can be satisfied in a district centre he invariably visits the closest one to him; if he can only obtain satisfaction from a very large centre, he invariably visits Coventry's central area rather than one in another town. Where external movements do occur, such as to Leamington or Birmingham, they are predominantly by higher-income consumers who seek higher quality provisions

TABLE 7.1

*Number of Daily Shopping Trips Recorded from
the Diary Survey of Housewives in Coventry*

	Trips to a 1st Centre	*Link Trips to a 2nd Centre*	*Separate Trips on Same Days*	TOTAL *All Trips*
MONDAY	363	47	21	431
TUESDAY	413	90	20	523
WEDNESDAY	418	62	21	501
THURSDAY	390	80	30	500
FRIDAY	445	106	47	598
SATURDAY	414	116	38	568
	2,443	501	177	3,121
Mean Frequency	5·0	1·0	0·4	6·4

Source: Davies, R. L., 'Patterns and Profiles of Consumer Behaviour', *University of Newcastle, Department of Geography, Research Series No. 10* (1973).

than Coventry can supply. The second point to note is that there is very little interaction with those ribbon developments which extend from the inner parts of the city and mainly in a northerly direction. This can be seen more clearly from the trade-area map of Figure 7.4 which generalises on the total of a full week's shopping for both convenience- and durable-goods. The empty areas in the middle of the map broadly correspond to where the ribbons occur (see also Figure 5.1) whereas the empty areas on the outskirts indicate an absence of residential occupance. The final point to note is that the trade areas which have been compiled tend to suggest a clear relationship to the three main structural levels of the hierarchy of centres (the central area, district centres and local centres); but that the nesting pattern of smaller trade areas inside larger ones is best realised in the newer, outer parts of the city which have been rigidly planned, such as in the Bell Green area to the north-east.

THE STRUCTURE OF URBAN SHOPPING TRIPS

In recent years, there has been an enormous increase in information available on urban shopping trips. A large number of assorted surveys have been undertaken not only for specifically geographical purposes but for use in transportation, planning and marketing research as well.[16] The majority of them concern rather localised problems and present a static picture which is

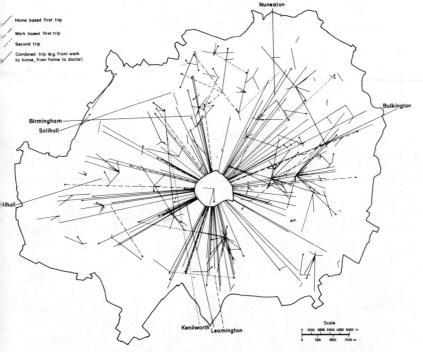

FIG. 7.3 *Directions of shopping trips for food and other 'convenience' goods on a Friday in Coventry.* The continuous lines reflect home-based primary trips; the larger pecked lines reflect work-based primary trips; the smaller pecked lines reflect various types of secondary trips undertaken on the same day; all the lines emanating from small dots indicate the shopping trips were combined with some other journey purpose. (From Davies, R. L., 'Patterns and Profiles of Consumer Behaviour', *University of Newcastle, Department of Geography, Research Series No. 10*, 1973)

rapidly out-dated; nevertheless, collectively, they provide a useful
general insight into the prevailing characteristics of the journey
to shop in modern times. In this section we will focus our attention primarily on the structure of urban shopping trips in Britain
and particularly on the findings of the Coventry diary survey and
a comprehensive 'home-interviewed' survey conducted in
Watford at about the same time by the Building Research
Establishment.[17] A summary of the daily profiles of shopping
in Coventry for a sample of 487 predominantly adult female
shoppers is given in Figures 7.5 and 7.6.

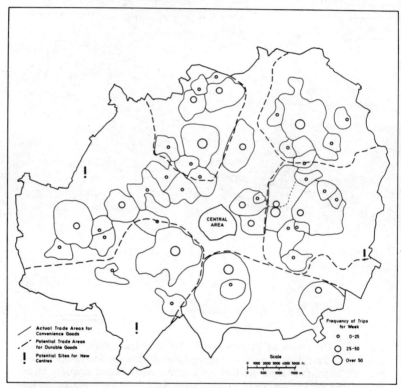

FIG. 7.4   *Trade areas for nucleated shopping centres in Coventry*. Based
on the total numbers of trips for convenience- and durable-goods
recorded in a diary survey of one week's shopping in September, 1969.
(From Davies, R. L., 'Patterns and Profiles of Consumer Behaviour',
*University of Newcastle, Department of Geography, Research Series No.
10*, 1973)

a. Trip Frequencies

Average figures concerning the frequency of shopping in Britain have varied according to the way in which trips may be classified. In general, there is usually one major expedition during the week (for bulk-buying and specialist needs) and between three and four subsidiary trips (for mainly convenience items). Any one single trip may include visits to a second shopping centre, however, so the actual number of journeys made during the week may be as many as five or six. Friday is usually the single most important day for adult female shopping, although Saturday often generates the greatest amount of traffic and trade (and particularly in the main centres of towns), and Monday generally exhibits the least. The habitual routine of daily shopping which many women still cling to in Britain has largely disappeared in North America where there is usually only one or two trips in total per week.

b. Trip Origins and Terminations

By far the greatest number of all shopping trips still begin and end at home. The Watford survey indicated that only about one-fifth of all trips are linked to places other than the home; and this is confirmed in the Coventry survey where rather more actually ended at home rather than began there. The concentration of home-based trips reaches its highest peak on Saturday, of course, when as many as ninety per cent of all trips will be home-based. This situation is again rather different from that in North America where many more trips are bound up with journeys to or from work places, recreational centres, medical centres and the like.

c. Travel Modes

Despite the growth in car ownership, between fifty-five per cent and sixty-five per cent of all shopping trips are still made on foot, 15–25 per cent by bus, only 10–15 per cent by car and 5–10 per cent by other means. These weekly averages conceal important differences on Friday and Saturday, however, and for trips which

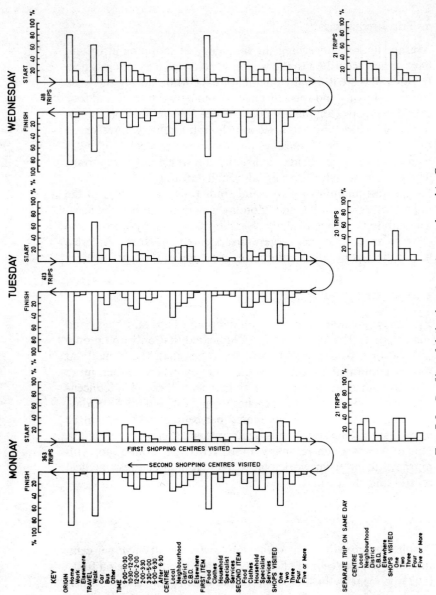

FIG. 7.5 *Profiles of daily shopping trips conducted in Coventry.*

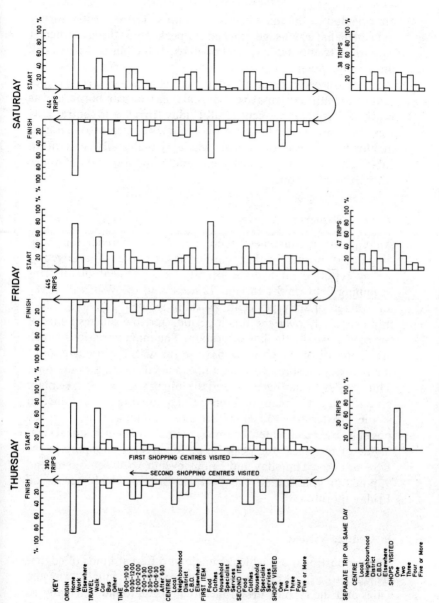

Fig. 7.6 Profiles of daily shopping trips conducted in Coventry (continued).

are oriented to the main centres of towns. The Coventry survey indicated that car usage reached its peak on Saturday, when it comprised twenty-two per cent of all trips, and bus travel its peak on Friday, when it comprised thirty per cent of all trips. The Watford survey in turn indicated that as much as forty-five per cent of all Saturday trips to the central area were car-borne, and as much as forty-two per cent of all Friday trips to the central area were bus-borne. Such figures provide a stark contrast to the norms in North America, of course, where virtually all trips within suburban areas are made by car and well over half of those within the city proper.

d. Time Sequences

Amongst most consumers, there is a clear preference for shopping in the morning rather than in the afternoon. The Coventry survey reported an average of fifty-nine per cent of all trips beginning between 9 a.m. and 12 noon and the Watford survey an average of sixty per cent. Working women, of course, shop more regularly over the lunch period; and the quietest time of the day is usually the late afternoon. The main variations which are found through the week have to do with the occurrence of the half-day closure of shops, the extended opening hours on a Thursday or Friday evening, and the longer trips which take place on Saturday. The main difference to be noted in North America is the greater prevalence of evening shopping. This is made possible by much later opening hours, frequently on several nights of the week: the peak hours for grocery shopping in the USA are on a Thursday and Friday evening between 6 p.m. and 9 p.m., in contrast to the peak in Britain which occurs on Friday morning.

e. Centres Visited

The proportional use which is made of different kinds of centres depends to a large extent on the nature of individual towns and cities and the type of urban hierarchy to be found. Virtually all consumers use the main centre or central area at some time or another but, whereas in small towns as many as eighty per cent of all consumers may be described as regular users of the main centre, in large metropolitan cities there may only be thirty per cent. In Watford, fifty-two per cent of consumers were described as regular users of the main centre, but nearly all these used their local area facilities for convenience items as well. The diary survey in Coventry recorded that, on average throughout the week, there was a fairly even split between trips oriented towards all four shopping areas—the main centre, district centres, neighbourhood centres and small parades. Most use is made of the main centre on a Friday and Saturday, of course, especially for bulk grocery purchases and specialised needs, and relatively more reliance is placed on local facilities at the beginning of the week. In North America, there tends to be less use both of the main centre and the smaller centres, and instead a much greater use of the middle range of centres and particularly the new forms of community and regional level centres.

f. Goods Sought

We have already noted that there are considerable difficulties involved in properly distinguishing between the nature of goods and services sought on shopping trips, at least in so far as these reflect on the main purposes of trips. The Coventry survey attempted to disentangle the priorities assigned to different types of goods and services and found that food items constituted the first priority in almost eighty per cent of shopping trips. This varied, however, from ninety-one per cent of trips to small, local centres to sixty per cent of trips to the central area. Food items also formed the most common second priority, though less dominantly so, and one quarter of all trips had apparel goods as the second priority. Household goods, specialised goods, and a category of general services each accounted for about ten per cent of all trips when these were stated to be the second priority. Clearly, these priorities vary across the week, however, so that much more equivalence in weight may be given to a wide range of items on Saturday whereas food needs will more completely dominate the composition of shopping on Friday. In North America, there tends to be much less mixing of the different shopping functions, particularly between food and durable-goods shopping. This is primarily because of a greater incidence of one-stop shopping for food needs in predominantly free-standing supermarkets.

g. Shops Patronised

The number of shops visited is often a good guide to the differential use made of a hierarchy of centres. In Coventry, the average number of shops visited in local parades, neighbourhood centres, district centres and the central area increased steadily from 1·86, 2·37, 2·82 to 3·31. Overall, for a total of 7,800 shops visited (and where purchases were made) during the course of one week, the average number of shops visited was 2·65 for primary trips, 1·91 for link trips (to a second centre) and 2·05 for secondary trips (conducted on the same day). More shops are visited on Friday and Saturday than other days in the week, of course. Nineteen per cent of consumers on a Saturday and fifteen per cent of consumers on a Friday in Coventry made purchases from five or more stores compared to only five per cent and six per cent on a Monday and Thursday, when there are in any case much fewer numbers of trips. In North America, the average number of shops visited will generally be much lower, partly because of the greater incidence of one-stop shopping cited above, but also because of the prevalence of larger shop units and, particularly, variety stores and department stores.

h. Trip Lengths and Duration

The distances that consumers journey and the time they expend on shopping are obviously dictated by the types of centre they visit and the mode of travel they employ. More than fifty per cent of all trips are no more than a half-mile in length representing the normal limits for walking to local shopping facilities. The average distances covered on motorised trips to the main centre will depend on the sizes of individual towns, but in Coventry it is almost two-and-a-half miles for the case of durable-goods. The time spent on different trips is more difficult to generalise about. The actual journey to a local centre by walking may incur as much time as the journey to the main centre by car, but the time spent on the business of shopping will vary according to whether minor or major purchases are to be made. The Coventry study indicated that on average one hour and eighteen minutes was spent on convenience shopping (including the journey time) and two hours and twenty-four minutes on durable-goods shopping. In North America, the greater mobility of consumers and the wider spacing of centres means, of course, that much greater distances are travelled and the time spent on the business of shopping is likely to be higher since there are fewer numbers of trips and more emphasis on bulk-purchasing.

VARIATIONS AND CHANGES IN CONSUMER BEHAVIOUR

The effects of broad cultural differences on patterns and profiles of consumer behaviour have been the subject of a number of specialised studies dealing particularly with the use of a hierarchy of shopping centres at the regional scale level of enquiry. Thus Murdie[18] has provided an interesting comparison of the shopping habits of Old Order Mennonites and 'modern' Canadians in Ontario, where it was shown that the former remain much more dependent on the nearest centres to them (principally because of their continued reliance on the horse and buggy for transportation) whereas the latter travel much greater distances and make much greater use of the larger centres and regional capital. Similarly, Ray[19] has found significant differences in the distances and directions in which French Canadians and British Canadians travel to shops. Further variations are to be found within any one society, particularly in the context of urban shopping trips. These may be considered both in terms of the effects of socio-economic differences amongst the population and of the continued changes taking place in life-styles and opportunities for shopping.

Effects of Differences in Socio-Economic Conditions

Most attention has focused on the variability in consumer behaviour that may be seen in relation to different age groupings, household sizes and social classes amongst the population.[20]

There have been a number of conflicting claims, however, as to which of these is the single most important factor, particularly in determining the variability in frequency of trips. Such discrepancies arise because of differences in the samples of consumers which are studied, the types of areas from which they are drawn, the way in which the trips are classified, etc. There is generally little consistency between one case-study and another; hence it is extremely difficult to draw universal conclusions.

The average weekly trip frequencies recorded for different socio-economic groupings amongst the adult female shoppers of Coventry are listed in Table 7.2. These indicate that all three factors have virtually an equivalent influence. In general the greatest numbers of trips are made by women from the lower

TABLE 7.2

Mean Frequencies of Weekly Shopping Trips for Different Socio-Economic Groupings in Coventry

	Trips to a 1st Centre	Link Trips to a 2nd Centre	Separate Trips on Same Days	TOTAL All Trips
SOCIAL CLASS*				
census class 2	4·7	0·5	0·4	5·6
census class 3	4·8	0·7	0·4	6·0
census class 4	5·1	1·0	0·4	6·5
census class 5	5·1	1·1	0·3	6·5
AGE GROUP*				
21–35 years	5·0	1·1	0·4	6·5
36–50 years	5·1	1·0	0·4	6·6
51–65 years	4·9	1·2	0·3	6·4
over 66 years	4·8	0·7	0·1	5·7
HOUSEHOLD SIZE*				
1 person	4·6	0·7	0·0	5·3
2 persons	4·8	0·8	0·3	6·0
3 persons	5·0	1·0	0·2	6·3
4 persons	5·2	1·1	0·5	6·9
5 persons	5·3	1·4	0·6	7·4

Excluded are the small samples for social class 1, females under 21 years of age and household units with more than 5 persons.

social classes, the younger age groups and the larger household size groups; the lowest numbers of trips are made by women from the higher social classes, the older age groups and the smaller household size groups. If on balance household size may be seen to have slightly more effect, age and social class become more pronounced in other aspects of shopping. In the Coventry study age was found to be more influential on the origins and destinations of trips, and also the types of goods that were sought. Social class was found to be more influential on the modes of travel, types of centres visited and the average length of trips.

The relative importance of each of these factors, but particularly social class, nevertheless, needs to be considered against the differences in residential location of different sections of the population.[21] Broadly speaking, the lower social classes tend to be concentrated in the inner parts of the city where there is a high incidence of shops that are close to home; the higher social classes, on the other hand, tend to be widely distributed throughout the suburbs where the opposite conditions apply. The longer trips in more variable directions which are usually exhibited by the higher social classes, therefore, are not necessarily always a direct reflection of class attributes (such as their greater mobility) but are often quite simply an expression of locational constraints.

This problem formed the basis to a detailed case-study of shopping patterns in two areas in Leeds.[22] Here, an attempt was made to isolate the effects of social class differences from the normal locational constraints by selecting two areas which, while markedly distinct in terms of the income levels and employment structures of their populations, were very similar in terms of their distance from the main centre, their proximity to major roads and the local retailing facilities that were found within them. A straightforward comparison of the distances and directions of various kinds of shopping movements indicated that considerable variations still occurred. In short, the sample consumers from the lower social class area were found to be much more dependent either on their local facilities or on the main centre of Leeds, whereas those from the higher social class area visited a wide range of centres not only in other parts of the city but also outside. An example of the differences in their patterns of movement is given in Figure 7.7.

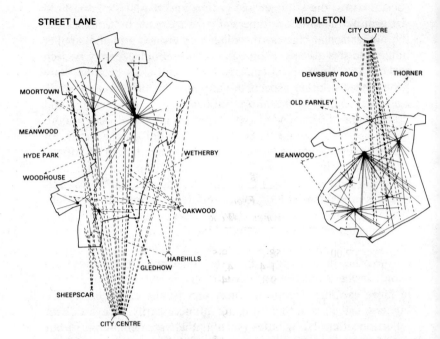

FIG. 7.7 *Variable patterns of shopping trips for groceries in two areas of Leeds.* Street Lane constitutes a high-income area on the northern side of the city and Middleton a low-income area on the southern side. (After Davies, R. L., 'Effects of Consumer Income Differences on Shopping Movement Behaviour', *Tijdschrift voor Economische en Sociale Geografie*, **60**, 1968, 111–21)

Changes in Life-Styles and Opportunities

Consumer behaviour, like the retail system itself, is continually changing and, at the individual household level, slight changes in domestic circumstances can often have a major impact on the entire pattern of shopping. Perhaps the two most obvious examples of this are the acquisition of a car and a housewife obtaining a job. The general growth in car ownership and female employment in recent years has led to massive changes not only in modes of travel and the origins of trips, but to the whole frequency of shopping, the times and days of the week when most

of it is conducted, the types of centres visited and even the shops
patronised. Some indication of this is given in Table 7.3.

The acquisition of a car, unlike a housewife obtaining a job,
however, does not always lead to an immediate change in shopping habits. The change is often a gradual one as a husband
slowly begins to relinquish his hold over the new asset or slowly

TABLE 7.3

*Examples of Variable Trip Structure Characteristics for
Different Origins and Modes of Travel*

| | % From | | % By | | |
	Home	Work	Walking	Car	Bus
TIME STARTED					
Before 12.00	68·8	9·5	55·4	55·3	63·6
12–2.00	11·4	43·9	21·9	11·5	12·6
After 2.00	19·8	44·6	22·7	33·2	23·8
1ST CENTRE VISITED					
Local	22·7	19·2	29·8	14·6	3·7
Neighbourhood	23·1	22·1	30·5	18·6	4·6
District	27·6	19·5	30·0	25·1	15·4
CBD	26·6	38·9	9·7	41·7	76·3
1ST GOOD SOUGHT					
Food	72·6	83·4	89·0	64·7	61·7
Apparel	11·4	5·7	2·9	13·5	21·0
Other Goods	9·1	7·1	3·9	14·4	11·3
Services	6·9	3·8	4·2	7·3	5·9
SHOPS PATRONISED					
One	23·6	35·4	29·1	30·3	18·4
Two–Three	48·5	51·3	53·2	41·5	42·5
Over Three	27·9	13·2	17·7	28·3	39·1
TRIP LENGTH					
Under ½ mile	62·8	45·7	89·5	34·1	12·8
½–1 mile	9·5	15·6	5·3	16·2	9·1
1–2 miles	14·2	22·9	2·9	20·0	43·6
Over 2 miles	13·5	15·8	2·3	29·7	34·5

Source: Abbreviated from Davies, R. L., 'Patterns and Profiles of
Consumer Behaviour', *University of Newcastle, Dept. of
Geography, Research Series No. 10* (1973).

becomes embroiled in the business of shopping itself! The Watford study cited previously found that consumers themselves rarely gave the acquisition of a car as a reason for their own recent changes in shopping habits. Much more influential on immediate changes were particular events in the family cycle: getting married, the birth of a child, the giving up as well as obtaining a job, etc.

Changes in residential location are frequently cited in American studies as another major cause of immediate changes in shopping habits.[23] The lower levels of mobility in this respect in Britain make it much less of an obvious factor. However, certain changes have been noted especially in connection with those people forced into a new environment through redevelopment schemes, though these changes are often made with some reluctance. Nader[24] found in north Durham, for example, that the newcomers to estates frequently return to their former localities for many goods and services, and particularly for such things as hairdressing and children's clothes for which there are strong store loyalties.

In North America, vast changes in shopping habits have also resulted from the enormous changes in the spatial pattern of the retail system. In Britain, there is clearly no parallel to this though certain developments may be seen to have had both a general and a localised effect. The growth of the supermarket and spread of multiple firms have obviously contributed to the trend for weekly instead of daily shopping trips. Those few types of 'out-of-town' centres and superstores which have been built have tended to change quite dramatically the nature of shopping amongst those consumers fortunate to be near them.

The specific appeal which the new suburban developments have for the British housewife has been closely examined by David Thorpe and his associates. Several case-studies of customer profiles have been undertaken particularly for the new Woolco stores.[25] Generally, the customers of these stores tend to be younger, have larger families and higher incomes than those who continue to patronise the smaller, traditional stores. Virtually all trips to the Woolco store at the Hampshire centre are made by car and substantial expenditures are made on mainly bulk purchase orders (an average of £3·24 for food and £3·12 for non-food in 1971). Most custom is drawn on a Saturday morning, but the next most busy period is between 5 p.m. and 8 p.m. on a Friday evening. Attitudes towards the stores have been canvassed, and while these are difficult to measure in precise terms, the general reaction amongst the store-goers has clearly been favourable. The principal reasons given for visiting the stores have mainly related to the parking provisions available and the size and layout of the stores.

A recent study by David Rogers[26] has also attempted to assess in more detail the changes in shopping habits that immediately follow from the opening of a new superstore. Extensive diary surveys were conducted in Bretton, Peterborough for the two-week period immediately before as well as after the opening of a large Sainsbury's. The results indicated some major changes both in terms of patterns of movement and in the structural characteristics of trips. The new store led to a marked growth in the amount of bulk food purchasing within the suburbs at the expense of the city centre, but its greatest competitive effect was felt by the existing supermarkets rather than the corner stores. There was a large growth in single-stop shopping; and the proportion of car usage for bulk food purchasing trips throughout the suburbs increased from thirty per cent of all trips to fifty-four per cent.

PERCEPTION STUDIES AND THE COGNITIVE-BEHAVIOURAL APPROACH

Perhaps the most important conceptual outcome of the various case-studies into variations and changes in consumer behaviour is the emphasis which has been given to the space preferences of the individual.[27] These are not fully accounted for in central place theory or general interaction theory which tend to assume that all consumers will act in a rational and generally similar way. In practice, each individual behaves according to his own satisfying criteria which may include the fulfilment of deep-seated psychological needs as well as social and/or economic objectives.[28] Considerable differences in behaviour between one individual and another may be seen because of differences in personality traits, differences in states of knowledge about the facilities available, differences in tastes and aspirations and so on. Collectively, different groups of individuals have different perceptions about the way in which they can or would like to behave in relation to the opportunities they are confronted with.

These subjective rather than objective aspects about the decision-making process involved in shopping have formed a major focal area of recent research into consumer behaviour. As yet, it is difficult to identify some distinctive threads amongst a large number of assorted studies. Garner,[29] however, has proposed a general research strategy for this cognitive-behavioural approach which we will adopt as a framework to consider some representative examples of the type of work being conducted.

Garner's strategy refers in specific terms to the images or value judgements which different individuals have of the urban retail system. He suggests there are four broad problems requiring investigation. First, the nature of the images themselves need to be examined and measured in terms of people's attitudes towards shops and shopping centres. Secondly, the relationship between different images and different types of consumers needs to be explored in more detail, involving more in-depth studies of individual motivations. Thirdly, the relationship between different images and the objective facts of the urban retail system need to be considered, and here the main aim would be to ascertain what parts of the system are really known. Fourthly, much more understanding is necessary of the mechanism by which different images arise and mainly because of the continual adjustment that is made from increasing experience and the provision of new opportunities.

The first of these problems has been directly pursued by Garner himself.[30] In a detailed case-study of female attitudes to women's clothing stores in Bristol, he sought to demonstrate the practical utility of a measuring technique called the semantic differential. This enables the qualitative aspects of stores to be differentiated according to a gradational scale of values (usually seven) between two semantic opposites (such as good and bad, clean and dirty, etc.). The technique was used by seventeen students to rank ten stores according to twenty-seven different criteria judged to be indicative of quality status. In ranking the total points scored by each shop, three clear classes of quality emerged. Closer scrutiny of the profiles of the scores led to some re-alignment of the classes, with the main differences reflecting on chain stores, boutiques and the more conservative or traditional stores. The same technique has been used by Bruce[31] on a wider range of stores to see which ones are generally considered the most friendly or unfriendly, the most honest or dishonest, the most attractive or ugly and so on. Some examples of the results obtained are shown in Figure 7.8. Likewise,

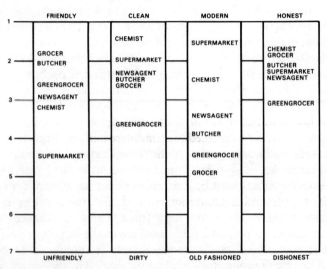

FIG. 7.8   *Selected examples of consumer impressions of shops.* The positions on the scales of the bar graphs for different types of shops indicate the degree to which they are held to be friendly or unfriendly etc. (After Bruce, A. J., 'Housewife Attitudes Towards Shops and Shopping', *Proceedings of the Architectural Psychology Conference*, Kingston Polytechnic, 1970)

Downs[32] has extended the technique for measuring consumer attitudes towards an entire shopping centre. The specific objective of this study, however, was to identify what sorts of criteria are most important in contributing to a centre's image. Eight sets of criteria were identified, four concerned with the characteristics of the shops found, namely the quality of the service, prices, the hours of shopping and the range of the shops, and four concerned with the structure and function of the centre as a whole, its layout and design, internal pedestrian circulation, visual appearance and traffic conditions.

Each of these studies also went some way to addressing the second problem, that of relating different types of images to different types of consumers. Thus Bruce found that housewives from the higher social classes were more prone to rate supermarkets as unfriendly than those from the lower social classes. Younger housewives tended to rate greengrocers more dirty than older housewives. However, as yet little in-depth study has been made in the way Garner recommends or in the way various marketing practitioners have linked different images of brand products to different types of customers. Various kinds of studies have dealt with the motivations for trips but largely outside the scope of perception research. Thus Stone[33] has distinguished between types of consumers using chain stores or small independent stores as those who are economic (or price-conscious) types, personalising (habit-bound or knowing-the-staff) types, ethical (supports the 'little' man) types, and apathetic (any store will do) types. In the Coventry diary survey, a detailed record was kept by consumers about the reasons for each of their trips and a factor analysis of the sum total of these revealed six sets of motivations: those where the choice of a centre was made predominantly because of the attractions of the shops; those where the choice was simply for convenience sake; those where a conscious evaluation between the costs and benefits of alternatives was made; those where it was known that a special good could be obtained; those where it was known that shopping would be enjoyable; and those where some search or investigation was thought likely to be fruitful. An attempt to relate these sets of motivations to different types of socio-economic households, however, proved rather inconclusive.

The third problem concerning the consumer's knowledge of the retail system has been more actively studied in North America than Britain. Horton and Reynolds[34] have promulgated the notions of individual action spaces and individual activity spaces to distinguish those parts of the retail environment familiar to the consumer from the actual distribution of facilities that may be found. The action space refers in precise terms to those facilities which a consumer may have some knowledge of and may potentially interact with according to his personal preferences. The activity space refers to those facilities which he regularly visits on a day-to-day or weekly basis. Horton and Reynolds' primary interest lay with the action spaces which they viewed from a dynamic rather than static perspective. In conceptualising the process through which an action space develops for the recent in-migrant to an urban area, they suggested three main stages may be recognised. In the initial stage, the action space would be distance-biased because most knowledge about shopping opportunities would be limited to the home environment and the journey to work. In the second stage, the action space would become areally expanded as a result of 'community socialisation' and the information gained from neighbours and work colleagues. In the third stage, the action space would reach a state of spatial equilibrium where shopping has in fact become routinised or habitual, or the activity space has become equivalent to the individual's perception of the opportunities available. In applying these ideas to sample consumers in Cedar Rapids, Iowa, clear differences in levels of familiarity were found to occur.

The underlying premise in Horton and Reynolds' work is that the continual changes taking place in consumer behaviour may be viewed essentially as a learning process. Learning models, of a mathematical probabilistic kind and borrowed for the most part from psychology, have been frequently mentioned elsewhere as the best means for dealing with the fourth of our major problems, the general understanding of how consumer images arise. Golledge has developed this work most fully and suggests four alternative kinds of learning models that might be applied.[35] The first are called the 'concept identification' models which attempt to simulate the trial and error behaviour through which consumers progress from an initial search period to one of habituary routines. The second are called the 'paired associate' models where scaling techniques can be used to trace the way consumers select between pairs of alternative choices in centres to visit.[36] The third are called the 'interactance-process' models, which include the family of gravity models as well as gaming models and Markov models, and deal essentially with establishing the probabilities of choice through a competitive process.[37] The fourth are called the 'avoidance-conditioning' models which incorporate linear difference equations to represent the outcome of rewards or setbacks in visiting alternative centres.

SUMMARY

The subject of consumer behaviour is an extremely complicated one and geographers have really only just begun to scratch the surface as far as their understanding of the detailed composition of individual shopping trips is concerned. A fairly comprehensive picture of the aggregate patterns of shopping trips has been built up in recent years, but even here there remain some difficult problems to overcome, particularly in properly distinguishing the different categories or purposes of shopping trips. There is considerable confusion over the degree to which central place theory continues to provide an appropriate framework for explaining the modern patterns of shopping trips, and mainly because there has been a glib acceptance on the part of British researchers that the findings reported in the American literature are applicable to their own situation. In fact, considerable differences in consumer behaviour are to be found between Britain and North America and most evidence in this country suggests that the bulk of the population still behaves in a rigidly routinised and deterministic way. This is primarily because the strict planning controls which are enforced over the retail system have virtually eliminated any real choice in opportunities for shopping except in a systematic use of the hierarchy of centres. Other theories are clearly necessary, however, for explaining the variability in consumer behaviour amongst small groups or individuals and particularly in terms of the way they themselves perceive their opportunities. In this respect, a much closer link needs to be forged with the marketing literature, for marketing experts have now accumulated a wealth of information and insight into the characteristics of purchasing behaviour. There are strong parallels to be drawn between the decision processes involved in purchasing behaviour and movement behaviour, with the same requirement for a deeper understanding of the socio-psychological factors affecting people's motivations. How far the field of marketing geography should become embroiled with such aspatial considerations, nevertheless, will doubtless become a topic for debate.

REFERENCES

1. Gist, R.E., *Retailing: Concepts and Decisions* (Wiley, 1968).
2. A general description of how to undertake these kinds of surveys is contained in Applebaum, W. and Spears, R. F., 'How to Measure a Store Trade Area', Chapter 23 in Kornblau, C., *Guide to Store Location Research: With Emphasis on Supermarkets* (Addison-Wesley, 1968).
3. A detailed example of the questionnaires used in a 'home-interview' survey is contained in Ward, S., 'A Study of a Shopping Centre', Chapter 8 in Adler, M. K., *Leading Cases in Market Research* (Business Books Ltd., 1971).
4. Applebaum, W., 'Advanced Methods for Measuring Store Trade Areas and Market Penetration', Chapter 24 in Kornblau, C., *op. cit.*
5. See, for example, Birmingham Corporation, Planning Department, *City of Birmingham Structure Plan, Report of Survey on Shopping* (1973).
6. Bengtsson, R., 'The Structure of Retail Trade in a Small Swedish Town', *Lund Studies in Geography, Series B*, **24** (1962), 297–312.
7. Thorpe, D. and Nader, G. A., 'Customer Movement and Shopping Centre Structure', *Regional Studies*, **1** (1967), 173–91.
8. Some attempts have in fact been made to abstract trade areas to a hexagonal form. See, for example, Skinner, G. W., 'Marketing and Social Structure in Rural China', *Journal of Asian Studies*, **24** (1964), 3–43, 195–228, 363–99.
9. Berry, B. J. L., Barnum, H. G. and Tennant, R. J., 'Retail Location and Consumer Behaviour', *Papers of the Regional Science Association*, **9** (1962), 65–106.
10. For a detailed investigation of this postulate, see, Clark, W. A. V., 'Consumer Travel Patterns and the Concept of Range', *Annals of the Association of American Geographers*, **58** (1968), 386–96.
11. For a detailed investigation of this postulate, see, Johnston, R. J. and Rimmer, P. J., 'A Note on Consumer Behaviour in an Urban Hierarchy', *Journal of Regional Science*, **7** (1967), 161–6.
12. Davies, R. L., 'Patterns and Profiles of Consumer Behaviour', *University of Newcastle, Department of Geography, Research Series No. 10* (1973).
13. Pred, A., 'Behaviour and Location: Foundations for a Geographic and Dynamic Location Theory', *Lund Studies in Geography, Series B*, **27** (1967).
14. Johnston, R. J. and Kissling, C. C., 'Establishment Use Patterns Within Central Places', *Australian Geographical Studies*, **9** (1971), 116–32.

15. Davies, R. L., *op. cit.*

16. See, for example, the different perspectives taken in a series of case studies on Stevenage, Bunker, R. C., *Travel and Land Use in Stevenage* (Dept. of Transportation and Environmental Planning, University of Birmingham, 1966); Madge, J., *Shopping Survey for the Research Institute for Consumer Affairs* (London, 1969); Stevenage Development Corporation, *Stevenage Household, Shopping and Transportation Survey* (1966).

17. Daws, L. F. and Bruce, A. J., *Shopping in Watford* (Building Research Establishment, Garston, 1971).

18. Murdie, R. A., 'Cultural Differences in Consumer Travel', *Economic Geography*, **41** (1965), 211–33.

19. Ray, D. M., 'Cultural Differences in Consumer Travel Behaviour in Eastern Ontario', *Canadian Geographer*, **11** (1967), 143–56.

20. See, for example, Ambrose, P., 'An Analysis of Intra-Urban Shopping Patterns', *Town Planning Review*, **39** (1968), 327–34; Nader, G. A., 'Socio-Economic Status and Consumer Behaviour', *Urban Studies*, **6** (1969), 235–45; Royal Commission on Local Government in England and Wales, *Community Attitudes Survey* (HMSO, 1969).

21. Horton, F. E., 'Location Factors as Determinants of Consumer Attraction to Retail Firms', *Annals of the Association of American Geographers*, **58**, 787–807; Marble, D. F., 'Transport Inputs at Urban Residential Sites', *Papers of the Regional Science Association*, **5**, 253–66.

22. Davies, R. L., 'Effects of Consumer Income Differences on Shopping Movement Behaviour', *Tijdschrift voor Economische en Sociale Geografie*, **60** (1968), 111–21.

23. See, for example, Horton, F. E. and Reynolds, D. R., 'An Investigation of Individual Action Spaces: A Progress Report', *Proceedings of the American Association of Geographers*, **1** (1969), 70–5.

24. Nader, G. A., 'Private Housing Estates: The Effect of Previous Residence on Workplace and Shopping Activities', *Town Planning Review*, **39** (1968), 65–74.

25. See, for example, Thorpe, D. and Kivell, P. T., 'Woolco: Thornaby' and 'The Hampshire Centre: Bournemouth', *Manchester University Business School, Retail Outlets Research Unit*, Reports No. 3 and 6 (1971 and 1972).

26. Rogers, D. G., 'Bretton, Peterborough: The Impact of a Large Edge of Town Supermarket', *Manchester University Business School, Retail Outlets Unit*, Report No. 9 (1974).

27. For a summary of the various factors affecting space preferences, see Huff, D. L., 'A Topographical Model of Consumer Space Preferences', *Papers of the Regional Science Association*, **6** (1960), 159–74.

28. Harvey, D., 'Conceptual and Measurement Problems in the Cognitive-Behavioural Approach to Location Theory', in Cox, K. R. and Golledge, R. G. (eds.), 'Behavioural Problems in Geography: A Symposium', *Northwestern University, Dept. of Geography, Research Series 17* (1969).

29. Garner, B. J., 'Towards a Better Understanding of Shopping Patterns', in *Geographical Essays in Honour of K. C. Edwards* (Nottingham University, 1970).

30. Garner, B. J., 'The Analysis of Qualitative Data in Urban Geography: the Example of Shop Quality', Proceedings of the Institute of British Geographers' Urban Study Group Conference, Salford University (1968).

31. Bruce, A. J., 'Housewife Attitudes Towards Shops and Shopping', Proceedings of the Architectural Psychology Conference, Kingston Polytechnic (1970).

32. Downs, R. M., 'The Cognitive Structure of an Urban Shopping Centre', *Environment and Behaviour*, 2 (1970), 13–39.

33. Stone, G. P., 'City Shoppers and Urban Identification', *American Journal of Sociology*, 60 (1954), 36–45.

34. Horton, F. E. and Reynolds, D. R., 'Effects of Urban Spatial Structure on Individual Behaviour', *Economic Geography*, 47 (1971), 36–48.

35. Golledge, R. G., 'The Geographical Relevance of Some Learning Theories' in Cox, K. R. and Golledge, R. G. (eds.), *op. cit.* See also, Golledge, R. G., 'Conceptualizing the Market Decision Process', *Journal of Regional Science*, 7 (1967), 239–58; Golledge, R. G. and Brown, L. A., 'Search, Learning, and the Market Decision Process', *Geografiska Annaler*, 49 (1967), 116–24.

36. For an application of this technique, see Rushton, G., 'The Scaling of Locational Preferences' in Cox, K. R. and Golledge, R. G. (eds.), *op. cit.*

37. For an application of gaming models, see Marble, D. F., 'A Theoretical Exploration of Individual Travel Behaviour', in Garrison, W. L. and Marble, D. F. (eds.), 'Quantitative Geography, Part I', *Northwestern University, Research Series No. 13* (1967).

8 Forecasting and Allocation Techniques

A detailed understanding of consumer behaviour and the way it is changing is fundamental to the basic requirement of retail planning, that of projecting the future level and character of demand for shopping provisions. In essence, the retail planner is confronted with two related problems. First, he has to determine what the size capacities of individual shops and shopping centres can and should be at some particular point in time. Secondly, he has to arrange these in such a way that for any particular situation there will be some measure of protection given to the existing elements of the system but that there will also be an overall improvement in relative economic health or efficiency. These have to be dealt with against the background of changes in consumer preferences and new forms of business organisation. In recent years, a large body of technical literature has emerged—especially in reference to British conditions—that provides a comprehensive choice in techniques that may be used. This chapter takes stock of the most common types of techniques and provides a critical assessment of their relative strengths and weaknesses.

THE MAIN TYPES OF TECHNIQUES

There are three main types of forecasting techniques in use: ratio methods, regression equations and general interaction models.[1] The allocation procedures that relate to these are less distinct as a separate body of techniques and refer for the most part to the way in which the forecasting techniques are applied. The most common form of application is through a hierarchical arrangement of centres of the kind we have already described. In dealing with the forecasting techniques, careful attention needs to be given to their scale level of relevance and the particular circumstances to which they are best suited. Like all other projection techniques, too, those used for forecasting in retailing are highly susceptible to the vagaries of broad changes in economic conditions, changes in political attitudes and also changes in the tastes or social mores of society. They therefore need to be employed conservatively and with a good deal of subjective interpretation of the results. The results themselves can only be taken as broad guide-lines for future development rather than detailed blue-prints to be strictly adhered to.

Ratio Methods

The size criterion of most importance to the retail planner is the amount of future floorspace to be provided. Although he may be equally interested in the potential sales and composition of shops he has much less direct control on these (though much more information is available about sales and the composition of shops—mainly from the Censuses of Distribution—than there is about floorspace). At some point in virtually all projection exercises, therefore, some form of ratio between these variables has to be employed.[2] This is also true in the case of translating the floorspace standards to be adopted in the future to individual shop-unit sizes and the rents or rates that are subsequently charged. Generally speaking, this involves undertaking a small survey of existing relationships and using some arbitrary standards about the most desirable forms that these might henceforth take. For example, if the average shop-unit size in a small centre is now 1,250 square feet, the average for a new development in 1981 might be taken as 2,500 square feet; if the average rent per shop is now £1·50 per square foot, then a reasoned assumption would be that these will rise to £2·00 per square foot in 1981.

The use of ratios as a general methodology for forecasting the size capacities of smaller centres in urban areas, however,

was first explicitly demonstrated by Diamond and Gibb in connection with their work on Cumbernauld New Town.[3] The basis
to their approach is that the strong relationship that currently
exists between population size and sales levels can be simply
extrapolated through to a future time period. A sales-per-head
figure can be calculated from the Census of Distribution for
several categories of retailing and, when these are multiplied by
the anticipated number of people, the total sales expected in
the future time period is obtained. A sales-per-square-foot figure
can then be calculated from a sample survey of individual firms
and grossed up to yield an expected global floorspace requirement.
A detailed example of the procedure for a hypothetical suburban
centre (which also has a small number of existing shops) is shown
in Table 8.1.

Certain modifications can be introduced into the initial calculations of the sales-per-head figures in dealing with centres in
differing situations. Thus while it may be sufficient to use census
statistics for local authorities in the case of convenience-trades
in a dominant town centre, it would be preferable to use expenditure data (from the Family Expenditure Survey) in relation to
a wider trade area population for the case of durable-trades in
a more competitive environment. In the special case of a new
town's main centre, Diamond and Gibb found it necessary to
make a wide range of comparative assessments of towns in order
to determine some threshold levels of sales commensurate with
different levels of population growth. This involved examining
the average sales performance of 100 towns with populations
between 25,000 and 100,000 and then deriving some weighted
means for the projected population sizes of Cumbernauld.

Such a step-by-step approach to retail forecasting has been
extensively employed in local planning and particularly for
estimating the future size capacity of the central area.[4] It has also
been used in a broader regional context, although it is generally
better suited to the case of a single centre rather than a whole
system of competing centres. The relationship between sales and
population size is more difficult to specify in precise terms when
there is a series of overlapping trade areas rather than discrete
ones. Where several centres have been considered, such as in the
first study of the potential effects of an 'out-of-town' regional

TABLE 8.1

Forecasting a Suburban Centre's Size by a simple Ratio Method

	1	2	3	4	5	6	7
Type of Business	Population	Sales Per Head £	(1×2) Total Sales £000s	Sales Per Sq. Ft.	(3÷4) Gross Area 000s Sq. Ft.	Area Existing Shops 000s Sq. Ft.	(5−6) Area to be Provided 000s Sq. Ft.
Grocers and Other Foods, etc.	23,000	77	1,770	38	46·6		
Tobacconists, Newsagents, etc.	23,000	17	392	32	12·2		
Chemists and Photographic	23,000	6	138	30	4·6		
TOTAL CONVENIENCE	23,000	100	2,300		63·4	14·4	49·0
Apparel Goods	50,000	26	1,300	26	50·0		
Household Goods	50,000	19	950	20	47·5		
Specialised Goods	50,000	5	250	20	12·5		
General Stores	50,000	20	1,000	40	25·0		
Cars, etc.	50,000	11	550	30	18·3		
Catering	50,000	10	500	20	25·0		
TOTAL DURABLES	50,000	91	4,500		178·3	5·2	173·1

Source: Diamond, D. R. and Gibb, E. G., 'Development of New Shopping Centres: Area Estimation', Scottish Journal of Political Economy, 9 (1962), 130–46.

shopping centre at Haydock Park,[5] the various centres have been first distinguished in terms of hierarchical status, and then separate trade areas for each hierarchical size-order worked out through a Reilly breakpoint model. Future changes in these trade areas then have to be subjectively assessed, however, and usually on the basis of past trends in population growth, knowledge of pending transportation improvements, new building applications and so on. While some degree of subjective assessment is desirable, the amount involved in this type of application seems to be excessive. Generally speaking, the use of ratio methods in any event is best suited to short-term rather than long-term forecasting. This is due to the assumptions concerning the consistency of sales-figures-per-head of population.

Regression Equations

The close relationship that exists between sales and population size (and also other variables such as floorspace and numbers of shops) may also be described in terms of a simple regression equation.[6] If sales are taken as the dependent variable and population size the independent variable, then Y (sales) $= a + bX$ (population size). The values for a and b are determined empirically for any particular situation. This can be illustrated by reference to Figure 8.1. The scatter of points in the graph represent the correspondence in sales and population sizes for a hypothetical series of neighbourhoods within a city. When such a scatter is highly concentrated in a thin band it indicates a very strong relationship (or correlation) between the two variables; when it is widely dispersed, it indicates the relationship is much weaker. The regression line which is fitted to the scatter effectively represents the mean of the average variation between the points. The value of a is then taken as the intercept position on the Y axis from where the regression line begins: the value of b refers to the angle of the slope, or the increment that is realised on the Y axis for a given change in X. Once the values for a and b are known, the equation can be used to forecast an expected sales figure for any new population size.

In practice, the values for a and b are normally calculated as:

$$a = \frac{(\Sigma Y)(\Sigma X^2) - (\Sigma X)(\Sigma XY)}{N\Sigma X^2 - (\Sigma X)^2}$$

$$b = \frac{N\Sigma XY - (\Sigma X)(\Sigma Y)}{N\Sigma X^2 - (\Sigma X)^2}$$

where Y is an abbreviation for sales in a series of centres X_j
   X is an abbreviation for population sizes in a series of areas Y_i
   N is the total number of cases (for which there must be an equal number of i's and j's)

It is also useful to provide a measure of the relative scatter of points about the regression line in order to indicate the reliability of the regression model for forecasting purposes. This can be achieved by calculating the standard error of the estimate of

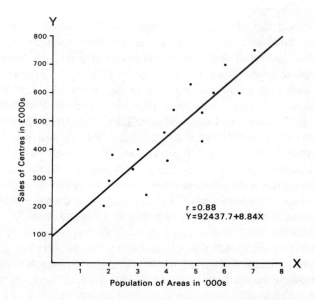

FIG. 8.1   *A Hypothetical diagram and regression line.* Each dot indicates the number of people resident in an area and the corresponding sales achieved in the area's centre. The regression line shows the average increase in sales to be found for a given increase in population size. Thus a new centre in an area of 8,000 population size would be expected to attain approximately £800,000 in sales.

Y on X, which is analogous to the standard deviation. The standard error of estimate effectively shows the reliability of the sample used in the exercise to predict the relationships between two wider universes of sales and population.

$$Syx = \sqrt{\frac{\Sigma(Y - Y_{est})^2}{N}} \quad \text{or} \quad S^2yx = \frac{\Sigma Y^2 - a\Sigma Y - b\Sigma XY}{N}$$

When two lines are drawn on a graph at parallel intervals to the regression line, indicating equivalently the 1st and 2nd standard deviations, then confidence limits are established to show that 99·7 per cent and ninety-five per cent of all points respectively are contained within these bands. Such confidence limits may be used in a case-study application to indicate the upper and lower estimates for a series of alternative projections about future retailing conditions.

Despite the objectivity and precision contained in this technique, however, relatively little use has been made of regression models for retail planning purposes in Britain. An interesting exception is the work undertaken by IBM Ltd. for forecasting the potential shopping capacity of Skelmersdale New Town.[7] Here a regression model was applied to the same step-by-step approach utilised by Diamond and Gibb in their study of Cumbernauld. Census data were collected for seven main retail trade groups and seventeen sub-groups and for a total of 317 towns with population sizes between 20,000 and 100,000. Confidence limits at the ninety-five per cent level were used to provide an upper and lower estimate of sales according to whether Skelmersdale would emerge as a strong regional shopping centre or a relatively weak one. The average sales figure expected for a future population of 80,000 was calculated as £16,406,000 per annum; but this could rise to £22,217,000 under favourable circumstances or be as low as £10,630,000. Such a large difference in these potential outcomes depended on whether the new town centre was built up rapidly or slowly, whether a policy for a dominant town centre or relatively weak one was adopted, and whether the Haydock Park 'out-of-town' centre was to be developed or not. In terms of what could be foreseen at the time, the average figure was accepted as the best one to work from but this referred to the town as a whole and further figures for the town centre versus other local facilities were required. From the 317 comparative towns examined, it was found that about sixty per cent of total retail trade was concentrated in the town centre. When this was converted by ratio methods into floor-space needs for Skelmersdale it meant that 401,000 square feet had to be provided for the town centre and 219,000 square feet for the smaller centres elsewhere.

This simple type of regression analysis can be modified in two ways. First, a whole series of similar kinds of structural equations can be specified for several different retailing variables and these applied to varying consumer conditions in different parts of the city. Secondly, more than one independent variable can be used to explain the dependent variable, such that a multiple regression model is produced. Both of these modifications require some refined data, or data that are not commonly available; but they have been fairly extensively developed in the USA.

Berry's study[8] of the business pattern in Chicago illustrates a particularly detailed application of a chain of structural equations that become translated into linked sets of regression models. These were formulated in respect to the shopping requirements that may be expected to occur in high and low income areas of the city and according to whether planned or unplanned centres are considered. Table 8.2 lists a variety of the models that were calibrated against known conditions in 1961. The r^2 which is recorded here refers to the coefficient of determination, a statistic which may be used to indicate the relative amount of variation in the dependent variable explained by the independent variable. Thus in the examples of the unplanned centres, fifty-nine per cent of the variation in numbers of establishments between centres and sixty-seven per cent of the variation in floorspace are explained by the variation in trade area population sizes.

Berry also sought to expand certain of these models into multiple regression equations. This was achieved by using coarser trade areas within the city to include a variable on income as well as population size. The calibrated model for the total number of establishments within the city worked out as $E = -3471 + 13 \cdot 35\,P + 41 \cdot 76\,I$ and for the total floorspace found $G = -16,974,173 + 29,338\,P + 176,664\,I$. An indication of

TABLE 8.2

Regression Equations for Nucleated Centres in Chicago

	Se	r^2
1. Unplanned Centres in High-Income Areas		
$B = -201·8 + 32·48 \log \$$	9·0	0·51
$\log E = 1·111 + 0·020 B$	0·057	0·92
$\log F = 3·268 + 1·043 \log E$	0·183	0·87
$E = 89·09 + 0·00496 P$	34·0	0·59
$G = 85,064 + 1·667 P$	94,000	0·67
2. Unplanned Centres in Low-Income Areas		
$\log E = 1·242 + 0·018 B$	0·101	0·69
$\log G = 3·145 + 1·126 \log E$	0·2	0·82
$\log E = 0·332 + 0·303 \log P$	0·16	0·27
$\log G = 2·938 + 0·461 \log P$	0·18	0·34
3. Planned Centres		
$B = -83 + 14·848 \log \$$	—	0·41
$\log E = 0·843 + 0·0263 B$	—	0·90
$\log G = 3·261 + 1·2567 \log E$	—	0·85

where   B = number of different functions in a centre
        E = number of establishments in a centre
        G = ground floorspace occupied by retailing
        $ = total sales of all establishments
        P = population served by a centre

Source: Berry, B. J. L., 'Commercial Structure and Commercial Blight', *University of Chicago, Dept. of Geography, Research Paper No. 85* (1963).

the relative accuracy of these models is given in Table 8.3. Other multiple regression models used for the purpose of forecasting levels of retail employment in cities such as Baltimore and New York have included a variable on relative accessibility.[9]

Regression models, both of a simple and refined kind, are again best suited to the urban scale level of enquiry where the trade areas around centres are relatively discrete. They are more powerful as forecasting techniques than the ratio methods since they provide a quantitative assessment of their relative reliability and accuracy in prediction. Difficulties are often experienced, however, in collecting the most appropriate data and particularly in the case of the future situation. There are also certain statistical limitations which preclude their widespread use, namely the theoretical assumptions regarding linearity in the data and independence between the variables.[10] While tests for independence between the variables are in fact commonly ignored, many studies transform the data into a logarithmic scale in order to reduce any skewness that may be observed.

General Interaction Models

General interaction models differ from the regression and ratio techniques in three important respects. First, they attempt to simulate much more closely the actual flows of expenditure or movements of groups of consumers to a variety of shopping centres. Secondly, they allow for the effects of competition between shopping centres to be taken into account and hence are applicable to situations where there are strongly overlapping trade areas. Thirdly, they are much more flexible mathematically, such that they can be relatively easily manipulated to suit a variety of problems. While the interaction models are seen to be more 'behavioural', however, they deal essentially with aggregate volumes of trips and these are assumed to decline or decay in

TABLE 8.3

Retail Floorspace as a Function of Population and Income

Zone	Actual G	Predicted G	Residual
1	10,248	11,908	−1,660
2	9,401	7,915	1,485
3	16,007	14,484	1,522
4	8,695	10,705	−2,010
5	14,003	17,363	−3,360
6	7,155	7,871	−716
7	18,008	16,091	1,916
8	17,473	14,383	3,089
9	8,244	8,927	−683
10	5,939	5,521	417

Source: Berry, B. J. L., 'Commercial Structure and Commercial Blight', *University of Chicago, Dept. of Geography, Research Paper No. 85* (1963).

direct proportion to the relative attractions of centres and in-versely to the distances that have to be travelled. This theoretical premise is best realised at a sub-regional or regional scale level of enquiry and hence interaction models are more appropriate for forecasting the size capacities of larger centres rather than of smaller ones and in a rural rather than specifically urban context.

The primary objective in most case-study applications, more-over, has been not so much to forecast the future size capacities of individual centres but rather to assess the consequences of new or enlarged centres (with a pre-determined size) on the rest of the retail system. In Britain, in particular, the most common type of problem addressed has been the impact which a new 'out-of-town' regional shopping centre or hypermarket will have on the traditional forms of shopping centres.[11] Here the model is really used in an allocational way since it seeks to re-distribute an antici-pated set of expenditure flows to a new set of retailing circum-stances; and the precise form of these circumstances may be dictated by alternative strategy designs.[12]

We have already indicated in Chapter 2 that the main type of operational model in use is some derivative of the Lakshmanan-Hansen model.[13] The first application of this in Britain was the second study made by Manchester University's Department of Town Planning to assess the likely impact of the proposed 'out-of-town' regional shopping centre at Haydock Park.[14] An outline of this will serve to demonstrate the procedures involved in apply-ing the model and will also provide a useful comparison to the step-by-step approach adopted in the first Haydock Park study. The objectives remained the same, namely to assess the future pattern of shopping amongst large centres in the North-West given three alternative planning policies: the development of a very large 'out-of-town' regional shopping centre at Haydock Park, a less attractive centre in the same location, or no 'out-of-town' centre at all. The form of the model adopted was:

$$S_j = \sum_{i=1}^{n} C_i \frac{F_j^\beta/d_{ij}^\alpha}{\sum_{j=1}^{m} (F_j^\beta/d_{ij}^\alpha)} \qquad ; \Sigma S_j = \Sigma C_i$$

where S_j = durable-goods sales in a centre j (or the sum total of
        expenditures on durable-goods in this centre)
   C_i = the expenditure available for durable-goods shopping
        in an area i
   F_j = a measure of the attractiveness of a centre j, inter-
        preted as an index of the composition of stores found
   d_{ij} = the driving time between the centroid of an area i and
        a centre j
  α, β = structural parameters determined from the calibration
        exercise
    n = the total number of consumer areas
   m = the total number of shopping centres considered

(a simplified example of the calculations involved is given in Table 2.2, p. 35).

The most difficult variable to define in the model is the attraction variable, for this reflects on the imagery of a shopping centre which cannot be adequately measured in numerical terms. The Manchester University team attempted to use an index of the mix of shops as a best approximation. This was made up from the number of variety stores to be found in a shopping centre (V), the number of department stores (D), the number of selected chain stores (C) and the presence or absence of a market (M). The figures used for calibrating the model were obtained from field surveys and directories for a total of forty-seven shopping centres and weighted in a formula $F = 2V + 3D + C + M$. The attraction factor was also raised to a power function on the grounds that the larger shopping centres tend to have an extra level of attraction beyond their greater size because of the increase in choice of goods and the benefits of scale economies.

The expenditure available in each of the 244 local authority areas was obtained by multiplying the known population by the average regional expenditure figures on durable-goods recorded in the Family Expenditure Survey. The deterrence factor on travel was interpreted as a time constraint and measured by taking the shortest road distances between the centroids of areas and shopping centres. In those cases where there were intra-zonal trips (to a shopping centre within the same area), mean distances were calculated and multiplied by an average driving speed of twenty miles per hour. The source for the sales figures used to test the relative efficiency of the model was the 1961 Census of Distribution. This gave details on the central area durable-goods sales of twenty-five towns, but estimates had to be made for the central areas of a further twenty-two towns for which only town-wide statistics were available. Some attempt was also made to take into account the special effects of the holiday trade on sales recorded in the coastal towns.

The model was calibrated through trial and error methods where different values for α were input in steps of 0·1 from 2·0 to 3·5 and β in steps of 0·05 from 0·50 to 5·00. For each pair of possible combinations of values an estimated sales figure was compared to the known sales and a 'goodness-of-fit' measured by a correlation coefficient and chi-square statistic. The optimum values selected as providing the best fit after 150 computer runs were for $\alpha = 3·0$ and $\beta = 2·6$.

Once the model had been tested and found acceptable in this way, each variable had to be reconstructed for the predictive year of 1971. The expenditure figures were derived from national and regional forecasts; the future hierarchical status of each centre was assessed subjectively from knowledge of recent trends and redevelopment schemes that were known to be in the 'pipeline'; the travel times were re-calculated to take account of transportation improvements and particularly the opening of the M6. While the α exponent was held constant, the β exponent was reduced to allow for an increase of trade in the medium-sized centres at the expense of the largest ones. A series of predicted sales at each centre was then calculated according to the three alternative assumptions regarding the Haydock Park shopping proposal. An indication of the results obtained is given in Table 8.4. A comparison of these with the results obtained in the first Haydock Park study reveals a close agreement for the 'status quo' policy of no new development, but considerable divergence for the other two policies, sufficient at any rate to lead to different conclusions and recommendations.

This study has since stimulated a flurry of research activity into gravity models and there have been a large number of further case-study applications to different parts of Britain. Broadly speaking, there have been three main lines of development within the methodology. First, a number of attempts have been made to improve the rigour of the Lakshmanan-Hansen model, mainly

TABLE 8.4

Predicted Sales for Selected Centres in the North West, 1971
(where 1961 sales = 100)

	No Haydock Centre	Small Haydock Centre	Large Haydock Centre
Wigan	1·68	1·28	0·88
Chorley	1·27	1·21	1·08
St. Helen's	1·31	1·11	0·87
Leigh	1·25	1·14	0·94
Manchester	1·38	1·33	1·21
Warrington	1·78	1·53	1·14
Northwich	1·60	1·50	1·20

Source: Manchester University, Dept. of Town Planning, *Regional Shopping Centres in North-West England, Part Two* (1966).

through alternative interpretations of the variables and a greater disaggregation of the data. Secondly, it has been seriously questioned as to whether the deterrence factor should be treated simply as a distance constraint or whether it might not be more suitably defined in terms of a series of intervening opportunities. Thirdly, concern over the model's limited relevance to the detailed composition of urban shopping trips has led a group of researchers at the Building Research Establishment to attempt to accommodate the individual preferences of consumers and add a stronger behavioural element to the whole approach.

Some examples of the different ways in which the basic Lakshmanan-Hansen model has been formulated are given in Table 8.5. Clearly, the most preferred indices used to measure attraction have been the size criteria of sales and floorspace, and for the deterrence factor either straight-line distances or travelling times. The precise choice has largely depended on the data available and the time and cost constraints under which a study has been conducted. Dissatisfaction with the coarseness of these indices has led some researchers to add weighted 'scores' to the attraction variable and friction coefficients to the deterrence factor.[15] The weighted 'scores' have included such considerations

TABLE 8.5

The Inputs for Alternative Retail Potential Models

Area	Attraction Variable	Deterrence Variable	Attraction Parameter	Deterrence Parameter
Haydock	functional index	travel time	3·00	2·60
Leicestershire	floorspace	airline distance	1·60	0·95
Lewisham	sales	airline distance	—	1·10
Notts/Derby	sales	travel time	1·30	2·40
Oxford	sales	airline distance	0·95	0·20
Severnside	sales	airline distance	0·92	0·91
South Beds.	floorspace	travel time	—	1·30
Teesside	floorspace	airline distance	1·38	2·36
E. Midlands	sales	airline distance	0·905	0·19

Based on: Batty, M. and Saether, A., 'A Note on the Design of Shopping Models', *Journal of the Royal Town Planning Institute*, **58** (1972), 303–6.

as the amount of car-parking provision available, the amount of local service employment to be found, the presence or absence of certain magnet stores in different shopping centres, etc.; the friction coefficients have included differences in congestion levels along different types of routes, the time spent on parking or waiting for public transport facilities, the disruption caused by road improvements, and so on. Several studies have also dis-aggregated the model to deal with different categories of retail trade, such as between convenience-goods and durable-goods, and different modes in transport used, mainly car-borne shopping as opposed to that by public transport.[16] Little agreement has been found in the parameter values obtained since these tend to reflect on the particular conditions in retail opportunities and levels of mobility in each area of study. Many of the studies listed in Table 8.5 have also been undertaken for the specific purpose of investigating the scope of application of this type of gravity model. Thus the Lewisham study was concerned with testing the model in a conurbation setting,[17] where no assumptions could be made about dealing with a 'closed' system; the South Bedfordshire study[18] showed how the retail potential model can be easily incorporated into a wider model of land-use change based on the Lowry type of approach.

The intervening-opportunities model provides an alternative conceptual viewpoint of the constraints involved in consumer choice of shopping centres to visit.[19] It is formulated in probability terms such that the probability of any shopping centre being selected is seen to depend less on the distance which may have to be travelled and more on the number of suitable attractions presented elsewhere. Mathematically, it is comprised of two components, one dealing with the possibility that consumers will opt to shop close at home, the other that they will select a centre some distance away. These are formulated in reverse order as:

the probability of trips going behind a centre $j = e^{-\sum\limits_{h}^{j} A_j}$

the probability of trips terminating before the centre

$j = -\sum\limits_{h}^{j-1} A_j$

When these two parts are brought together, the probability of trips actually ending in the designated centre j itself may be calculated:

$$T_{ij} = KC_i\left(e^{-\sum\limits_{h}^{j-1} A_j} - e^{-\sum\limits_{h}^{j} A_j}\right)$$

where K = a constant
C_i = the number of trips originating from an area i
A_j = the attractiveness of a centre j
e = the base of the Napierian logarithmic scale

While this type of model is attractive in conceptual terms, however, it is extremely difficult to apply in practice. This is because it is almost impossible to differentiate the relative importance of several intervening opportunities without recourse to some measurement of the distances between them. Once the distance variable is incorporated, of course, the model reverts to the traditional gravity form.

The type of model being developed at the Building Research Establishment is equally concerned with providing a better explanation for the choice of shopping centres but attempts to simulate much more fully the actual decision-making process that consumers go through.[20] The model is currently limited to the case of food shopping but also includes a choice over modes of travel. It works on the simple premise that consumers 'trade-off' the relative costs and benefits involved in visiting alternative centres, but according to their own perceptions of the attractiveness of each centre and the effort that will be incurred in visiting them. The relative benefit involved in obtaining a good g at a centre s is represented as $A(s, g)$; the relative cost involved in visiting a centre s over a distance d and by a travel mode m is represented as $E(m, d, s)$. Every consumer may then be seen to give a rating of the various alternative courses of action open to him according to:

$$R(s, g, m) = A(s, g)/E(m, d, s)$$

The actual choice which he makes, in terms of s and m for any good g, will be determined by the largest R. Under the circumstances in which the model is applied, each value of R may also be interpreted as an indication of the relative amenity or 'convenience' of a centre. These can be grossed up to provide a more general picture of consumer preferences. Clearly, this approach adds an important new dimension to the methodology of interaction models, especially in providing an avenue for dealing with more localised intra-urban trips. To date, however, it has had little empirical testing, although some preliminary studies using the Watford diary survey data have pointed to encouraging results.

PROBLEMS IN THE APPLICATION OF INTERACTION MODELS

The retail potential model, of the Lakshmanan-Hansen form, is rapidly emerging as the most preferred technique for forecasting purposes in Britain and some further discussion is warranted. There are a number of technical problems involved in its application, some of which derive from the shortcomings of the data, and some from the choice of the areal units and nodes. There are also certain difficulties involved in calibrating the model and these raise important questions concerning its conceptual validity. As in the case of central place theory and the use of the hierarchy as a design framework for the spatial control of shops and shopping centres, there have been many practitioners who have misused general interaction theory and applied gravity models to situations where their relevance is weak.

The Variable Inputs

While most studies have tended to use either floorspace or sales as an index of attraction, neither of these criteria is really satisfactory. Floorspace is particularly insensitive to the changes in methods of business organisation, although for certain centres the physical size of particular schemes in the pipeline may be known; sales have been criticised on the basis that this is the variable which is usually to be predicted, although the model in fact redistributes such data through a series of competing centres. Both variables lack a true reflection on the qualitative aspects of a centre's attractiveness and both refer to the total composition of shops and related service establishments without distinguishing those particular businesses which provide the main drawing capacity for domestic shopping trips. In this respect, they share the same limitation of most indices of centrality used in descriptive hierarchy studies. The various attempts made to disaggregate these variables, however, are difficult to justify on the grounds that detailed indices of attraction are difficult to replicate in the future state. It is also questionable in philosophic terms whether models intended to provide broad guide-lines for development should be designed to provide some highly specific results. The ultimate choice in attraction variables is therefore largely a matter of individual preference; and for most general statistics there is such a high correlation between them at the regional scale level of enquiry that this preference is mainly guided by what is available.[21]

A high correlation also exists between the most common indices of travel deterrence, namely travel times and airline distances. In this case, however, airline distance is clearly a much simpler variable to deal with and measure. The advantage of a time index is that it is much more sensitive to varying accessibility conditions, and changes in accessibility conditions are perhaps the most crucial consideration in this type of forecasting. The desirability of having an index related to accessibility, nevertheless, needs to be carefully weighed against the problem of compound errors that occur when arbitrary travelling speeds must inevitably be assumed. A special problem exists in relation to the deterrence factor in areas where consumers choose their own localised facilities (i.e. the intra-zonal shopping trips). There is no generally accepted rule of thumb here and various researchers have used an arbitrary distance measurement of one kilometre or half the radius of each area, or alternatively a mean travelling time calculated from various points in the middle or periphery of areas to the nodes of the shopping centres.

Compared to the attraction and deterrence variables, relatively little attention has been given to the best ways of obtaining appropriate input data for the expenditures of consumers. This is mainly because there is really no alternative to the general figures of the Family Expenditure Survey. Much more research could be done, however, in drawing together the limited information about expenditures available in scattered surveys, if only to provide a more reasonable basis for taking account of variations in spending patterns. The estimation of future expenditures is particularly dubious. Assumptions have to be made about anticipated growth rates in income and consumption and these obviously become easily upset by unexpected changes in economic conditions. (Many studies, for example the East Midlands' study,[22] have assumed an annual growth rate in domestic product of three per cent up to 1981, which is clearly no longer to be tenable.) This kind of problem is not unique to the gravity model, however, and is a feature of all types of projection techniques. The susceptibility of the gravity model is that it incorporates several variables that must each be independently forecast before their combined interrelationships are also worked through.

The Areal Units

The size, shape and number of the areal units utilised in a study are important considerations in that they can seriously affect the amount and type of interaction to be simulated by a model.[23] The main objective should always be to select a zoning system which allows for the maximum volume and diversity of flows as is practically possible. The model is of little use if virtually all interaction is represented by intra-zonal trips, for then a series of discrete trade areas will have been specified and the researcher might as well use regression techniques.

It is difficult to recommend an ideal type of zoning system, however. On the one hand, it is desirable to have a large number of very small areas of irregular shape in order to approximate the realities of conditions on the ground. On the other hand, the problems involved in acquiring data at this scale suggest it is preferable to deal with a small number of large areas of similar shape. In practice, some form of compromise has to be made and most researchers have utilised the census areas of wards, parishes, enumeration districts and entire local authorities. The 1971 Census data will shortly be available in grid square form and this will provide an improved and consistent basis for the selection of areas.

The areas need not necessarily be uniform in size, for they are best related to the actual distribution of population to be found. Thus large areas should be used where the population is sparse and small areas where the population is dense. Some conformity to a rounded or compact shape is necessary, however, since distance measurements taken from the centroids of areas can be severely distorted by irregular (and especially elongated) boundaries. The precise number of areas selected will often be governed by time and cost constraints and the computer facilities available for processing the data. The East Midlands' study used a total of 374 areas and 106 shopping centres. The Lewisham study dealt more modestly with sixty-two areas and ten shopping centres.

A related problem to the choice of the zoning system is the problem of defining the overall spatial limits to the area of study. Since most studies make the assumption that the $\Sigma Ei = \Sigma Sj$, it is desirable to try to close-off the area of study with as little interaction taking place across the boundary as possible. There are three established methods for dealing with these external flows (Figure 8.2). First, it is possible to subtract from the total amount of sales and expenditures incurred in the study area those flows which cross the boundary when these can be reasonably estimated. In some situations, outgoing flows may in fact almost counter-balance the incoming flows. Secondly, where the external flows are more substantial, a series of broader zones may be demarcated around the periphery of the study area and the flows into and out of these areas calculated separately. Some further boundary beyond this transitional belt will then have to be defined, however. Thirdly, a whole series of rings or belts may be drawn around the study area, with or without the coarser zones, and the flows into and out of these included in the calibration exercise.[24] When the results of the model indicate that any further increase in the width or the number of these belts does not make an appreciable difference, the study area can be finally closed-off. The East Midlands' study utilised two such belts at twenty-five kilometre distances apart, and this extended their zoning system to include 850 areas.

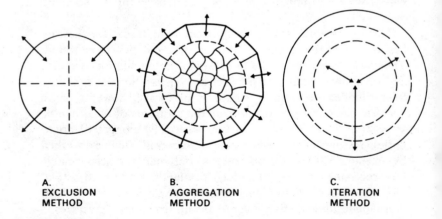

A.
EXCLUSION
METHOD

B.
AGGREGATION
METHOD

C.
ITERATION
METHOD

FIG. 8.2   *Methods for determining the spatial limits of an interaction study area.* These are explained in the text. (After Davies, R. L., 'Problems of Variable Selection and Measurement', Chapter Two in *Gravity Models in Town Planning*, Lanchester Polytechnic, Coventry, 1969)

Calibration

The calibration exercise is essentially concerned with finding the values for the parameters in a model. This can be achieved in two ways: either internally within the model or externally to it. The internal method requires some form of iterative search procedure, either on a trial and error basis where different values are repeatedly examined and the most plausible ones accepted, or by a systematic search where an optimum solution is obtained by successive modest changes programmed to converge on the closest possible fit. The fit which is normally made, however, involves predicted sales to actual sales and while correlation coefficients and chi-square statistics may indicate that these are often exceedingly close they do not necessarily indicate a similar closeness of fit in the detailed pattern of expenditure flows. The total of the predicted sales could be derived from expenditure flows from a variety of directions. This problem in interpretation is compounded by the fact that, when two parameters are used in a model, more than one optimal solution may be found for their values.[25] Furthermore, a perfect fit in sales terms will occur when $\alpha = 1$ and $\beta = 0$. This has been described as a bogus calibration,[26] for in such a case the predicted sales would be simply a function of the attraction variable used and unaffected by the deterrence factor.

The so-called external method of calibration attempts to get round these problems by establishing values for the parameters from trip distribution data collected in surveys that are not necessarily directly a part of the study. The data are often taken from traffic surveys which contain an element of shopping trips. The values for the parameters are usually obtained by comparing an estimated mean trip length to the average that has been recorded. Batty and Saether[27] have explored this approach in detail, however, and again found that multiple solutions for the parameters are possible when α and β are used together, although the danger of a bogus calibration is much reduced. An example of the alternative solutions possible in a case-study of shopping in southern Norway is shown in Figure 8.3. Batty and Saether have therefore recommended that only single parameter models should be used in future, and this is perhaps desirable in any event since the parameter on the attraction variable is not really properly understood. For the case of the single parameter model, they have developed a special fast calibration technique to reduce the time and costs involved in the whole calibration exercise.[28]

Statistical evidence has recently been provided by Openshaw,[29] however, that suggests that even the single parameter models have a trivial solution though this is often hidden and more difficult to recognise. Openshaw has therefore claimed that none of the existing types of gravity models in operation are suitable for forecasting purposes in terms of the data which is input to them. He argues that extensive diary surveys should be undertaken on the grounds that a valid calibration can only be achieved on the evidence of actual expenditure flows. While the inclusion of this type

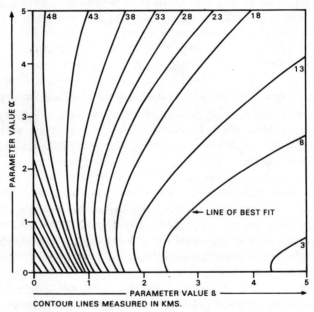

FIG. 8.3 *Contour lines representing the response surface yielded in a calibration exercise.* The model assumes a mean trip length of eight kilometres. The predicted contour line of best-fit cuts across a wide range of values for the parameters indicating that a variety of combinations of values can be used to derive the best-fit. (After Batty, M. and Saether, A., 'A Note on the Design of Shopping Models', *Journal of the Royal Town Planning Institute*, **58** (1972), 303–6)

of data would be extremely informative, nevertheless, it would require a massive investment and research effort to collect it for a meaningful sample of consumers at the regional scale level of enquiry. More fundamentally, it is doubtful whether the detailed records of actual expenditure flows would confirm the theoretical tenets of the models being applied.[30] The data would in a sense be too refined for what the models are attempting to show and would, in any event, be impossible to replicate for a future situation since the values obtained for the parameters would inevitably change. This is because the main effect of a new hyper-market or 'out-of-town' centre, or even a central-area redevelop-ment scheme, will be to promote radically different forms of consumer behaviour. There can be little justification for building a model which is extremely sensitive to past or present conditions when it is known that these will substantially change.

SUMMARY

Forecasting the future level of demand for any land-use activity is an extremely difficult undertaking, and in retail planning the normal problems to be encountered are exacerbated by some serious deficiencies in the amount and kind of data required and the increasing pace of change experienced in consumer behaviour. For example, there are no comprehensive data on incomes or expenditure for small areas; the current trend to car-borne shop-ping and bulk weekly purchases can either be slowed down or quickened according to a variety of political decisions regarding the development of new suburban centres or parking policies in existing central areas. Although these special problems exist, how-ever, they have sometimes been over-exaggerated and used as a convenient excuse for a casual approach to forecasting. Given that there are such uncertainties, a number of assumptions have to be made and a whole series of alternative possible outcomes predicted for the future. The actual programming or implementa-tion of any proposals will in themselves need to be phased over a certain length of time, and this usually gives considerable scope for monitoring the way in which a preferred course of action is kept in tune with emerging conditions. There is available a wide range of techniques for the actual mechanics of forecasting in a variety of retail situations. Of the three main sets of techniques we have reviewed here the ratio methods are most applicable to the urban scale and are best used for predicting the sizes of individual town centres in a relatively isolated environment; regression equations are more suited to an intra-urban scale and are particularly appropriate for dealing with the entire system of smaller centres inside a town; interaction models are most applicable to a regional or sub-regional scale and are best used for tracing the impact of a new or enlarged centre on nearby competitors. What is perhaps most seriously lacking in the application of these techniques, however, are some strong conceptual guidelines or design strategies to shape the alternative policies that the forecasting exercise is meant to serve. Apart from central place theory, there are simply no logical constructs within which to systematise the allocation of future retail resources. It is in this area of design frameworks rather than the actual theatre of forecasting itself that most planning research is at present needed.

REFERENCES

1. A detailed review of the main types of forecasting techniques is provided in National Economic Development Office, Committee for the Distributive Trades, *Urban Models in Shopping Studies* (NEDO, 1970). This contains a slightly different classification of the techniques to the one employed here, however.
2. For a discussion of the relationship between sales and floorspace, see Cripps, E. L., *Retail Turnover and Floorspace*, Bedfordshire County Planning Department (1967); also McClelland, W. G., *Costs and Competition in Retailing* (Macmillan, 1966).
3. Diamond, D. R. and Gibb, E. B., 'Development of New Shopping Centres: Area Estimation', *Scottish Journal of Political Economy*, 9 (1962), 130–46.
4. See, for example, Coventry Corporation, *Shopping in Coventry* (1964).
5. Manchester University, Department of Town Planning, *Regional Shopping Centres in North West England, Part I* (1964).
6. The method of regression analysis is explained in more detail in Hirst, M., 'Building and Operating a Forecasting Model: the Regression Analysis Approach', *British Journal of Marketing*, 4 (1970), 121–5.
7. Wilson, L. H., *Skelmersdale New Town Planning Proposals* (Skelmersdale Development Corporation, 1964).

8. Berry, B. J. L., 'Commercial Structure and Commercial Blight', *University of Chicago, Department of Geography, Research Paper No. 85* (1963); 'The Retail Component of the Urban Model', *Journal of the American Institute of Planners*, **31** (1965), 150–5.

9. See, for example. Alan Vorhees and Associates, *Baltimore Land Use Study* (1962).

10. Poole, M. A. and O'Farrel, P. N., 'The Assumptions of the Linear Regression Model', *Transactions of the Institute of British Geographers*, **52** (1971), 145–58.

11. See, for example, Bristol City Planning Department, *Cribbs Causeway Out-of-Town Shopping Centre Enquiry: A Report of the Proceedings* (1972); Sunderland Corporation, *The Sunderland Hypermarket Survey* (1971).

12. Cordey-Hayes, M., 'Retail Location Models', Centre for Environmental Studies, Working Paper 16 (1968).

13. Lakshmanan, T. R. and Hansen, W. G., 'A Retail Market Potential Model', *Journal of the American Institute of Planners*, **31** (1965), 134–43.

14. Manchester University, Department of Town Planning, *Regional Shopping Centres in North West England, Part II* (1966).

15. For a discussion about the need for more precise measurements of these variables, see, Lewis, J. P. and Traill, A. L., 'The Assessment of Shopping Potential and the Demand for Shops', *Town Planning Review*, **38** (1968), 317–26; Clarke, B. and Bolwell, L., 'Attractiveness as Part of Retail Potential Models', *Journal of the Royal Town Planning Institute*, **54** (1968), 477–8; Bucklin, L. P., 'Retail Gravity Models and Consumer Choice: A Theoretical and Empirical Critique', *Economic Geography*, **47** (1971), 489–97.

16. This disaggregation has probably been taken furthest by the Planning Research Applications Group of the Centre for Environmental Studies in their various case-studies for different planning authorities. See, for example, Wade, B. F., *Greater Peterborough Shopping Study: Technical Report* (PRAG, 1973).

17. Rhodes, T. and Whitaker, R., 'Forecasting Shopping Demand', *Journal of the Royal Town Planning Institute*, **53** (1967), 188–92.

18. Cripps, E. L. and Foot, D. H. S., 'A Land Use Model for Sub-Regional Planning', *Regional Studies*, **3** (1969), 243–68. See also Lowry, I., *Model of Metropolis* (Rand Corporation, Santa Monica, 1964).

19. Schneider, M., 'Gravity Models and Trip Distribution Theory', *Papers of the Regional Science Association*, **5** (1959), 51–6; Harris, B., 'Models of Locational Equilibrium for Retail Trade', *Journal of Regional Science*, **5** (1964).

20. The approach is summarised in, Cole, H. S. D., 'A Computer Model for the Comparison of Alternative Foodstuffs Shopping Environments', *Socio-Economic Planning Services*, **6** (1972), 329–48.

21. Davies, R. L., 'Variable Relationships in Central Place and Retail Potential Models', *Regional Studies*, **4** (1970), 49–61.

22. Gibson, M. and Pullen, M., *Retail Trade Patterns in the East Midlands 1961–1981* (East Midlands Economic Planning Council, 1971).

23. For some technical discussions about the effects of different zoning systems on the amount of interaction simulated, see, Broadbent, T. A., 'Zone Size and Singly-Constrained Interaction Models', Centre for Environmental Studies, Working Note No. 132 (1969); Batty, M. and Foot, D., *et al.*, 'Spatial System Design and Fast Calibration of Activity Interaction-Allocation Models', *Regional Studies*, **7** (1973), 351–66.

24. For technical discussions of this procedure, see, Black, J. 'Some Retail Sales Models', paper presented at the Urban Studies Conference, University of Oxford; Wilson, A. G., *Entropy in Urban and Regional Modelling* (Pion, 1970).

25. Turner, C. J., 'Severnside Shopping Model: A Discussion of the Calibration Procedure and Results', Nathanial Lichfield and Assoc., Working Paper No. 4 (1970).

26. Cordey-Hayes, M., *op. cit.*

27. Batty, M. and Saether, A., 'A Note on the Design of Shopping Models', *Journal of the Royal Town Planning Institute*, **58** (1972), 303–6.

28. Batty, M., 'Exploratory Calibration of a Retail Location Model Using Search by Golden Section', *Environment and Planning*, **3** (1971), 411–32.

29. Openshaw, S., 'Insoluble Problems in Shopping Model Calibration when the Trip Pattern is Not Known', *Regional Studies*, **7** (1973), 367–71.

30. Davies, R. L., 'Comments on the Calibration of Shopping Models', *Regional Studies*, **8** (1974), 307–9.

9 Store Location and Store Assessment Research

The determination of new locations for individual shops and other business establishments has long been regarded as the corner-stone of marketing geography, particularly in the USA. A wide range of analytical and forecasting techniques have been developed which collectively provide a distinct methodology for store location research. This is mainly attributable to the experience of a group of marketing geographers working in actual business practice. Applebaum[1] has suggested that its origins may be traced back to the turn of the century when a number of chain companies and especially tobacco shops began to conduct detailed surveys of pedestrian flows along streets in order to identify the most desirable sites within the main centres of towns. A second advance came in the 1930s when much more emphasis was given to measuring the broader trade-area characteristics of stores and estimating the likely sales and/or share of the market that could be captured in towns as a whole. A third, and perhaps the most dramatic advance came in the 1950s when attention shifted to conducting both internal and external surveys of the new sub-urban shopping centres that materialised from the massive post-war decentralisation of retail trade throughout the North-American continent.

Although there remains a strong relationship between market-ing geography and the methodology of store location research, too close an equation between them ignores a number of other contributions which geographical concepts and procedures have made to evaluations of existing rather than new forms of shops and related business establishments. Here, attention has been focused on assessments of the relative health or trading efficiency of existing stores, only part of which may be analysed or explained in terms of locational circumstances. Other factors need to be considered, such as the type of customer being served, the images of the stores, the range of merchandise being sold, the age and condition of buildings, and so on. In recent years, a major advance has been made in this kind of work from the application of multi-variate statistical techniques to the large amounts of data which chain companies have amassed about their various branch operations. More objective comparisons can now be made of the relative strengths and weaknesses of individual stores and mathematical models formulated to describe their optimum trading capacities. It is in this area of store assessment rather than store-location research that some significant contributions to the business practices of marketing geography have been made by British researchers.

THE PROCESS OF SELECTING A NEW LOCATION

The fact that relatively more attention has been given to research on store location in the USA than in Britain is mainly due to the greater choice in locations available in that country, as we have indicated in Chapter 1. There is a much greater amount of space to be found, a much more varied retail environment, and much more freedom from planning and other kinds of administrative constraints. An American company essentially has much more direct control over its locational selection process than is the case with a British company. Even so, the actual amount of time and effort which is spent on this process will usually depend on the size and nature of the company involved, for clearly a large chain searching for a number of new supermarket or variety store locations will pursue a greater in-depth research programme than will a small independent firm seeking only its second or third new branch outlet.

The Main Principles Involved

Given that there are sufficient resources within a company to conduct an in-depth research programme, there are three sets of principles that should be adhered to in selecting a new location:[2] the determination of a preferred position within the urban area as a whole; the choice of a particular type of shopping centre or business complex to enter; the identification of the most desirable site within this type of centre or complex. Ideally, these should constitute three sequential steps in the selection process; but in practice, the necessity for making quick decisions often precludes any systematic ordering of the search procedures in this way.

1. General Position Within the City

Every urban area contains a variety of trading opportunities that are continually changing through time. It is clearly in a company's best interest to undertake general surveys at regular intervals to see what parts of the city offer most scope for retail expansion. This overall monitoring exercise may be viewed as preparatory research, enabling a company to screen out the most promising areas for potential locations and within which more specific enquiries may then be conducted. Four main elements have been recognised.[3]

a. Existing Trade Area Capacities.   Various estimates can be made of the present trading capacity of different parts of the city. These range in sophistication from simple map inspections of census and other published information to detailed surveys of the numbers of people to be found and their average expenditure levels.[4] The gross figures that are obtained may then be related to certain threshold standards about population size or sales potential deemed necessary by a company to support a new location. Broad profiles of the socio-economic character of areas may also be derived and considered against the background of those conditions within which a company has hitherto had most trading success. Once certain preferred localities have been earmarked in this way, more specific surveys can then be mounted of the precise amount and character of the trade that is available.

b. Amount of Market Penetration.   Some insight is also

needed on the extent to which available trade in different areas is already commanded by a company's major competitors. A first approximation of this can be obtained by comparing the number of stores that are found with the sizes of the population served. When considered against some general averages for the city as a whole this will indicate whether any particular area is under-provided or over-provided in existing retailing provisions. More precise measurements of the amount of sales generated by individual competitors can then be made from field inventories of the floorspace found and surveys of their customer trade areas.[5] The total extent of the competition to be found may also be treated in terms of an index of saturation[6] calculated as the available expenditure in an area divided by the amount of retail floorspace provided.

c. Differential Growth Prospects. Since most stores have a lifespan of at least twenty years, it is necessary to give some attention not only to the existing trade available in different parts of the city but also to their growth prospects. Some indication of future population sizes can be obtained by extrapolating recent changes reported in the census, supplemented by information about known schemes in the planning pipeline (such as proposals for new housing estates or redevelopment schemes). Future expenditure levels are more difficult to assess but attention can be given to the relative economic stability of an area, measured in terms of trends in land values, housing and business vacancy rates, the employment structure and so on.

d. Relative Accessibility Conditions. The development of new roads and other forms of communication may not only improve accessibility to and within certain parts of a city but may also reduce it and create barriers to movement in other parts. Changes in traffic circulation need careful watching particularly in the case of those businesses, such as auto services, which are heavily dependent on motorised trade. General accessibility maps can be compiled at regular intervals in time for the city as a whole; for more specific localities detailed patterns of movement can be examined that include notification of the position of traffic lights, points of congestion, poor road surfaces, one-way traffic flows and the like.

2. Types of Shopping Centres or Business Complexes

We have already indicated in Chapters Four and Five that different kinds of stores are commonly identified with different types of shopping centres and other forms of business complexes. Most companies will know from experience and the analysis of past sales records in which types of centres they are most likely to achieve success. Careful consideration in the choice of a new location needs to be given not only to the sizes of centres but also to their functional composition, their layout or configuration, and their age.

a. Size Characteristics.   The size of a centre remains important, for most stores still require a certain threshold level of trade area support. Stores with a high threshold level can really only locate in the largest centres; those with a low threshold level usually perform best in the smaller centres. In Britain, the strict hierarchical arrangement of shopping centres in urban areas renders a virtual planning enforcement of those types of centres which particular stores can enter. In the case of companies such as supermarket chains, however, which can operate in a variety of sizes of centres, a much closer relationship between the size of stores and size of centres should be examined.

b. Functional Composition.   The existing functional composition of centres is important from the standpoint that some companies will seek to avoid any close proximity to their competitors while others will find that a close association is desirable. Companies seeking to avoid their competitors should clearly select centres with a minimal amount of competition in the first place; but once a choice of centre has been made, a site should be selected where the new store intercepts the predominant flows of traffic to the competitors. Companies that find that close association with either their competitors (such as shoe shops) or other types of business activities (such as the complementarity between clothes shops and variety stores) tends to lead to increased sales may assess their degree of compatibility more assiduously by applying a formula devised by Nelson:[7]

$$V = I(V_l + V_s) \times \frac{V_s}{V_l} \times \left(\frac{P_l}{V_l} + \frac{P_s}{V_s}\right)$$

where V = the increase in the total volume of business of two
neighbouring stores
V_l = the volume of business of the larger store (total purchases)
P_l = the purposeful purchases made in the larger store
V_s = the volume of business of the smaller store (total purchases)
P_s = the purposeful purchases made in the smaller store
I = the degree of interchange between the two stores

The rule follows that 'if there are two retail stores side by side and one customer in 100 makes a purchase in both, then together they will do one per cent more business than if separated by such a distance as to make this interchange impossible or unlikely.'

c. Configuration and Layout.   Stores may also be classified according to whether they generate their own trade, share in the trade accumulated by a group of stores, or are simply suscipient of the trade derived by others.[8] Generative businesses, such as garages and discount stores, will often prefer to establish themselves in free-standing sites or on the outer edges of ribbon developments. Shared businesses will usually prefer the compact forms of nucleated shopping centres and particularly positions in the most accessible parts of these centres. Suscipient businesses (such as sweet shops or newsagents) will often be found in specialised functional areas of the main centre of a town, such as in entertainment districts, transportation terminals, or office areas.

d. Age Characteristics.   The age of a centre or other business complex is important for a variety of environmental and psychological considerations. Most large companies will want to avoid situations of blight and decay and will prefer the more modern precinct developments that have better amenities and safety conditions. Older centres are usually sought only if they carry a high prestige value and suit a particular image that a company is trying to project. New centres are especially attractive to the major chain companies because they often gain a distinct trading advantage over their competitors by simply being the first company to open up a store in an area.

3. The Precise Site

Once a decision has been made about the general desirability of alternative locations within an urban area, more detailed attention needs to be given to the optimum sites that should be sought within any type of business complex. This involves a number of further field assessments as well as some cost accounting and other administrative considerations.[9]

a. Convenience and Approachability.   Just as most stores require a high degree of accessibility to their potential trade areas within the city as a whole, so also do they require a high degree of accessibility to consumers moving inside a business complex. In this case, the accessibility requirement will be measured in terms such as proximity to car parks and bus-stops, the visibility of a store along a street, its relative position with respect to the volumes of pedestrian flows in different directions (and different sides of a street), the ease of entry into a store, etc. Certain kinds of stores, such as clothes stores, prefer corner sites because of the greater frontage this gives for window shopping; others, such as jewellery and variety stores, prefer close proximity to the geographic centre of a business complex because of the crowd convergence found there; still others, such as the supermarkets and greengrocery stores, prefer sites which are near to the entry and exit points of a business complex so that shoppers have a minimum distance to travel in carrying their goods.

b. Physical Conditions.   Where a retail company is heavily involved in the development of a new shopping centre or redevelopment scheme, attention will need to be given to such factors as the relief and terrain that is found, the availability of utility services such as electricity and telephone supplies, the bearing capabilities of the land for new buildings and so on. These sometimes form actual physical constraints, but more often their significance lies in their economic implications. Though these factors may seem relatively obvious, Kane[10] has reported several embarrassing experiences of being asked to evaluate sites on hair-pin bends, precipitous slopes and plots of land that were completely isolated behind woodland areas!

c. Legal Enactments.   In the development of new shopping centres or redevelopment schemes, clear attention has to be given to the general land-use ordinances of a planning department and the building regulations that govern the erection of new buildings. In the case of individual store sites, further considerations will need to be given to the regulations governing fire precautions, licensing hours, advertising signs and the like. While such regulations are fairly standardised in Britain, there are considerable regional and local variations within the USA.

d. Occupancy Costs.   Besides the initial capital costs that may be involved in acquiring or developing a new site, there are a number of running or operating costs that will need to be carefully evaluated. These include such diverse things as labour costs, rents and rates, insurance premiums, heating and lighting costs, the costs incurred in building up stock, etc. While some companies establish their stores in freehold property, a majority of them lease property, either from a property development company or alternatively a local authority. There are various kinds of lease arrangements,[11] the most common being a flat payment of a fixed amount of rent each month, a percentage agreement where the amount payable will fluctuate according to sales levels or profits realised, and a percentage agreement with a minimum guarantee below which the rent will never fall.

Alternative Research Strategies

The extent to which the above principles will actually be adhered to in the selection of a new location will often depend on a company's organisational structure and the way in which decisions are made. Generally speaking, there are two main approaches to conducting store-location research. In the first and preferred case, a company will establish its own research department or appoint an executive staff member with special responsibility for investigating the company's locational requirements. This will usually lead to a well-defined and co-ordinated research programme in which longer term investment plans can provide a meaningful framework for the day-to-day business of appraising new and existing sites. In the second and more common case, a company will virtually relinquish the research function to a property development company or estate agent who will then simply keep the company informed about new sites as and when these emerge on the market. The wider and future interests of the company will often be obscured or ignored in the pressure to provide a suitable range of short-term proposals.

It is extremely difficult to obtain precise information about the amount of store-location research conducted by individual companies, however. By comparison with industrial firms, retailers tend to be over-sensitive to considerations of confidentiality and many facts are needlessly suppressed which collectively might lead to improved ideas and techniques. A survey by Applebaum[12] of 73 large companies in the USA in the early 1960s showed that on average at that time only $4,075 per annum per store was spent on research, amounting to just over one per cent of the average investment for each location adopted. Such small research outlays are clearly at variance with the potential rewards involved from more intensive work. Nelson[13] has drawn attention to the fact that if improvements in the selection process were to lead to an increase of only $2,000 in weekly sales for a large company, then over a ten-year period this would accumulate to an extra one million dollar's worth of business.

American companies have tended to be more forthright in revealing their research strategies than British companies. Two case histories reported over a decade ago may be mentioned as useful indicators of what can be accomplished. In the first of these, Howard Green[14] reported in 1961 on the initiatives of a new research department in the Montgomery Ward department store company. This undertook a national retail growth programme examining the potential trading characteristics of each region in the USA, the differences between rural and urban areas, metropolitan versus non-metropolitan areas, the suburbs versus central city, and opportunities existing on a country-wide basis. A detailed pilot study was made of Texas to act as a prototype for further studies of the other states throughout the country. Jack Ransome[15] similarly reported about the same time on the efforts of the Kroger supermarket company to establish certain guide-lines about their best areas of penetration. Various threshold criteria were worked out for the sizes of supermarkets most suitable for different sizes of towns (for example, in a town of 5–10,000 population, it was estimated that at least 25–30 per cent of total food sales would need to be captured to support a supermarket of 10–15,000 square feet); various levels of saturation were determined (such as that towns of approximately 40,000 population size would normally support no more than 6–7 supermarkets, and Kroger in any event would not establish more than one branch in towns that were smaller than this); detailed trade area characteristics were worked out, so that the proportions of customers likely to be obtained from different distance bands for different sizes of supermarkets could be estimated; profiles were kept of all existing stores and their relationship to actual and potential food sales assessed; and finally, models were being developed to classify stores into different typologies in order to compare their relative effectiveness.

This type of research effort can often be facilitated by collaboration with university researchers and marketing consultants and has been made easier in recent years by the wealth of census and other data made available in published form. In Britain, there is currently a belated burst of research activity which is partly associated with the pressures being exerted by the business community for more choice in suburban and 'out-of-town' locations. Companies such as Sainsbury's, the Burton tailoring group and the John Lewis Partnership have invested heavily in a more scientific approach to their locational selection process, and happily have recruited increasingly from the ranks of geographers.

FORECASTING AND EVALUATING RETAIL PERFORMANCE

In the same way that the retail planner is primarily interested in the floorspace capacity of new and existing shopping centres, the store-location analyst is ultimately interested in the most appropriate sizes for stores. The key variable affecting this is once again the turnover or sales that can be realised and this has extra significance in a business context from the standpoint that these should be as high as possible. The techniques available for forecasting purposes are similar in kind to those used in planning, although less use tends to be made of gravity models (except in the case of trade-area demarcations) than of the ratio and regression methods. This is mainly because most forecasting is undertaken in a localised urban situation, and interaction theory is more appropriate to a regional scale level of enquiry. However, there is altogether more emphasis put into trade-area assessments and the comparisons that can be drawn with existing stores; and hence we will distinguish here between three main categories of techniques under the headings of: trade-area calculations, the use of analogues, and regression equations.

Trade Area Calculations

The objective in this approach is similar to that adopted in the so-called 'step-by-step' approach in retail planning, namely to calculate the expenditure available in a trade area as a simple guide to the sales level that any store might achieve. Much more attention is usually given to the amount of competition to be found, however, for most stores (unlike many centres) seldom operate in isolation and there is less basis for assuming a pattern of discrete trade areas even in the outer parts of a city. The most common method of application follows a two-stage process. First, an existing potential or actual trade area is demarcated in order to determine what the immediate or short-term level of sales could be. The boundary for a potential trade area can be worked out according to certain rules-of-thumb, such as a three-mile radius for a certain type of supermarket, or an average distance of ten minutes' driving time;[16] the boundary for an actual trade area will usually be determined by undertaking consumer surveys at a focal position inside a shopping centre or an existing store itself.[17] Various kinds of proportional and composite versions of these potential and actual trade areas may then also be defined, as we have indicated in Chapter 7. It is also clearly possible to use the Huff model[18] to calculate a probable trade area, but less attention has been given to this in business applications than in academic research. The amount of trade which may be captured from the resulting trade area by competitors will usually be estimated by conducting further field surveys, ranging in sophistication from detailed home-interviews to simple customer counts (see Figure 9.1) and rules-of-thumb applied to the number of competitors found. The final sales figure expected for a store can then be used as a basis for adjusting its size. The second stage in the process calls for a repetition of this type of exercise for the longer term future, in which case only the more generalised versions of a potential trade area can be realistically defined.[19]

There have been a variety of procedures used in connection with this type of work and two brief examples may be cited for illustration. The first involves a method which has been described as the 'vacuum' technique. This was used by Imus[20] to address the problem of whether there was sufficient sales potential to justify the building of a second department store in a new suburban regional shopping centre that already contained one of 200,000 square feet. The steps that were followed are shown in Table 9.1. The study began with a delimitation of both primary and secondary trade areas for department store goods based on customer surveys in the existing centre. The available expenditure was calculated by relating the trade areas to census tracts and multiplying the population found by an assumed per capita expenditure figure. The share of the available expenditure that could then be expected to be drawn to any suburban centre rather than the CBD was worked out from a general ratio of suburban to CBD sales compiled from the Census of Business. The proportion of this suburban expenditure (or sales) that each competing suburban centre would in fact obtain was calculated on the basis of $40–$70 per-square-foot of floorspace found. This left a residual or unsatisfied expenditure and sales potential—'the vacuum'—from which the new centre in question would likely derive eighty per cent of that amount falling within its primary trade area and forty per cent of that amount in its secondary trade area. This yielded sufficient sales potential both in the short and long term to justify the building of a second department store in the centre at a comparable 200,000 square feet.

The second example involves a method described by Nelson[21] as the 'micro-analysis' technique. This is concerned primarily with deriving more detailed expenditure forecasts for very small areas, and hence is more appropriate for dealing with the size capacities

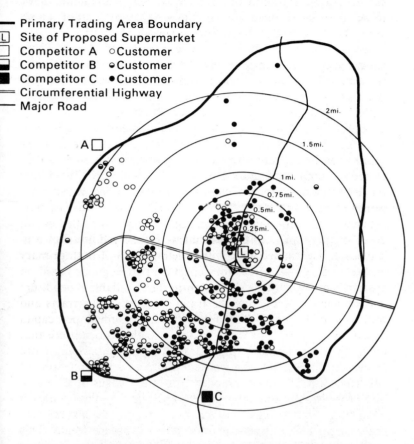

FIG. 9.1 *A customer spotting map to determine the amount of competition within a store's potential trade area.* This type of map will normally require soliciting the precise addresses of customers visiting the competing stores. In North America, it has sometimes been possible to obtain addresses from the licence plate numbers of cars entering the store parking lots. This was the procedure used to construct this example. (After Cohen, S. B. and Applebaum, W., 'Evaluating Store Sites and Determining Store Rents', *Economic Geography*, **36** (1960), 1–35)

of supermarkets or other stores engaged in convenience trade rather than department stores or other types of durable-goods stores. A case-study application is shown in Figure 9.2. The objective here is simply to determine the amount of sales a new supermarket will command given the existing pattern of competitors to be found. Intensive home-interview surveys are conducted throughout a neighbourhood or community with a sufficiently large sample of consumers to be able to describe the average character of shopping on an individual street block basis. The proportion of trade available in each street block which might then be captured by the new supermarket is solely determined by subjective reasoning from the knowledge and insight gained in the field exercise. Nelson's argument is that experienced judgement at this scale level of enquiry will nearly always be more reliable than more objective forecasting from a series of census or other large and arbitrary zones. A similar method has been advocated by Applebaum,[22] but in conjunction with the more

TABLE 9.1

Estimating Potential Department Store Sales by The Trade Area Vacuum Method

	Primary Trade Area		Secondary Trade Area	
	1960	1970	1960	1970
Total Population	373,000	417,000	554,800	637,000
Per Capita Expenditure	$135	$135	$135	$135
TOTAL SALES POTENTIAL*	$50,396	$56,390	$74,898	$85,995
% Suburban Share	70%	70%	70%	70%
SUBURBAN POTENTIAL*	$35,277	$39,473	$52,429	$60,196
Effective Competition*	$15,869	$15,869	$33,467	$33,467
UNSATISFIED POTENTIAL*	$19,408	$23,604	$18,962	$26,729
% Dept. Store Share	80%	80%	40%	40%
DEPT. STORE POTENTIAL*	$15,526	$18,883	$7,585	$10,692

* Figures refer to $000s.

Abbreviated from: Imus, H. R., 'Projecting Sales Potentials for Department Stores in Regional Shopping Centres', *Economic Geography*, **37** (1961), 33–41.

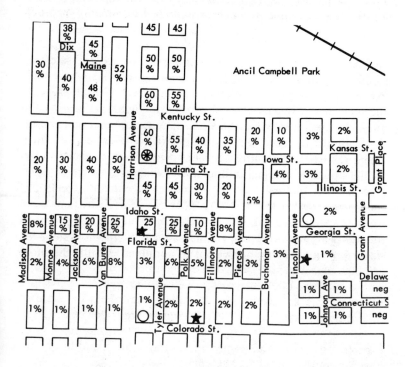

FIG. 9.2   *Nelson's micro-analysis technique for estimating the sales potential of a new store.* The percentage figures shown here represent the amount of the available trade in each street block likely to be captured by the new store. (After Nelson, R. L., *The Selection of Retail Locations*, Dodge (1958))

conventional approach to trade area delimitations and the assessment of market penetration discussed at the beginning of this section.

The Use of Analogues

A second approach to sales forecasting relies more heavily on the guide-lines that can be provided by case histories of other stores in a company's chain. The objective here is to compare a new store with a group of other stores that are alike in locational and competitive circumstances. The simplest yardstick is to measure the average amount of market penetration achieved by the control group. For example, if the existing sample of stores obtain an average per capita expenditure (or sales) of £1·00 from within their primary trade areas, and the average total expenditure (or sales) available is £5·00, their average share of the market is twenty per cent which can then be taken as the amount which a new store may also be expected to command. This can also be used in conjunction with a sales-space ratio,[23] which relates the amount of market penetration expected to the total amount of competing floorspace which will be found in an area. Thus if the new store is expected to command twenty per cent of the market but will have forty per cent of the floorspace its sales-space ratio will be fifty per cent. This can be applied in the following way. Suppose there is a town of 20,000 population size, yielding an average weekly expenditure on certain goods of £50,000, and in which two competing stores are already trading with a combined floorspace of 12,000 square feet. If a new store enters the market with a size of 8,000 square feet, its share of the total floorspace available will then be forty per cent. Given a sales-space ratio of fifty per cent, the new store will be expected to capture twenty per cent of the total expenditure available, or equivalently £10,000 worth of weekly sales.

More detailed analogies can be drawn with existing stores depending on the amount of information that has been gathered and particularly in terms of their trade-area characteristics.[24] An application for determining sales potential of a new supermarket is shown in Table 9.2. In this particular case the sales potential is arrived at by subjectively interpolating between the three models taken rather than utilising some overall averages. A check is made on the estimate using the conventional method of trade-area calculations described in the preceding section. This combination of methods to incorporate a check makes for an extremely effective forecasting procedure and one that is increasingly used both in Britain and the USA.

Such comparative studies can be further extended, however, and especially to include a wide range of data about the stores themselves as well as their trade-area characteristics. The main

Table 9.2

Estimating Potential Supermarket Sales by the Analogue Method

Zone (Miles)	Population of Analogues				Drawing Power of Analogues				Per Capita Sales of Analogues			
	A	B	C	Avg.	A	B	C	Avg.	A	B	C	Avg.
0–¼	6,700	3,400	6,450	5,300	37%	29%	34%	33%	$2·40	$1·79	$1·47	$1·89
¼–½	15,800	8,200	11,450	11,800	29	27	31	29	0·80	0·72	0·75	0·76
½–¾	22,900	12,500	18,350	17,900	11	17	12	13	0·21	0·30	0·19	0·23
¾–1	22,000	10,300	12,000	14,800	6	8	6	7	0·12	0·17	0·13	0·14
Over 1					17	19	17	13				

Application of the Above Analogues to a New Store X

Zone (Miles)	Population at Location X	Estimated Drawing Power	Estimated Per Capita Sales	Estimated Weekly Sales	Computed Drawing Power
0–¼	4,700	30%	$2·00	$9,400	28%
¼–½	12,900	30	0·76	9,804	29
½–¾	23,000	15	0·22	5,060	15
¾–1	36,300	10	0·12	4,356	13
Over 1		15		5,051	15
		100%		$33,671	100%

Source: Applebaum, W., 'The Analogue Method for Estimating Potential Store Sales', in C. Kornblau (ed.), *Guide to Store Location Research* (Addison-Wesley, 1968).

objective here will be less to forecast the sales potential of a new store than to evaluate the existing performances of those already in operation. Several multi-variate statistical techniques can be employed to group the stores into common types and compare them according to their most significant factors. The techniques of factor analysis and grouping analysis have recently been demonstrated in connection with a case-study of seventy-two tailoring stores in a British chain[25] and this may be briefly expounded upon.

The study was based on forty-three variables of retailing characteristics, ranging from the sizes of the stores and their operating costs to the street positions they occupied and the types of customers they served. The way in which these variables were associated or linked together was then first analysed through a computer using a standard factor analysis program. Statistically, this relates the variables together into a series of factors or common dimensions according to the minimum amount of variation that is found between them.[26] Six most important factors were recognised, and the variables most indicative of these are listed in Table 9.3. Factor 1 may be interpreted to reflect on the over-riding importance of trade-area size in any economic assessment of the stores; factor 2 reflects on the importance of a store's own physical and organisational structure; factor 3, the importance of site and situation; factor 4, the character of the town in which a store is found; factor 5, the consumer orientation which the company desires; and factor 6, the selling practices or trading policies that are put into effect. The relative strength or weakness of any individual store in relation to these factors may be gauged by a series of factor scores. Thus, for example, a store in Glasgow recorded 2·4560 on factor 6; 1·9528 on factor 1; 1·2005 on factor 3; −0·5651 on factor 2; 0·4741 on factor 4, and −0·2470 on factor 5. These tend to suggest that the store is very strong in terms of its selling efficiency and sales attainment; it has responded well to the trade potential available; it occupies a generally favourable site and situation; its store size and employment force are rather deficient given the other circumstances found; there is only a weak relationship in customer terms to the prevailing industrial character of the town; and there is little distinct orientation to any one class of the population. Clearly,

this kind of assessment for each of the stores may provide considerable help in guiding the company to undertake corrective
or expansionist action. While there is an overall favourable profile
for the example we have quoted, it may be in the company's
interest to examine the deficiency in store size and employment

TABLE 9.3

*The Highest Variable Loadings on Six Factors
Contributing to a Company's Store Efficiency*

Factor 1		Factor 2	
Urban population size	0·959	Total employees	0·870
Total urb. ret. exp.	0·955	No. of selling staff	0·862
Urb. exp. major product	0·950	Total sales	0·861
Trade area population	0·935	Major product sales	0·815
Trade area ret. exp.	0·912	Gross selling area	0·812
Trade area product exp.	0·896	Shop frontage	0·693
No. of multiples	0·875	Rents and rates	0·438
No. of affiliated stores	0·846	Gross floor area	0·380

Factor 3		Factor 4	
Dis. to nr. multiple	−0·743	% empl. in m'facturing	0·734
Location assessment	−0·725	% males under 15 years	0·669
Shop quality	−0·723	Dis. to nr. car park	−0·617
Dis. to nr. competitor	−0·712	Urban growth rate	0·526
Store accessibility	−0·642	% soc./econ. group A	−0·446
Rent/rates per sq. ft.	0·550	% soc./econ. group B	0·352
Rent and rates	0·425	Urban hierarchy status	0·273
No. of chain branches	−0·237	Rent/rates per sq. ft.	−0·229

Factor 5		Factor 6	
% soc./econ. group C	−0·961	Gross sales per sq. ft.	0·902
% soc./econ. group B	0·783	Sell sales per sq. ft.	0·839
% soc./econ. group A	0·673	Major product sales	0·384
Dis. to nr. car park	0·287	Total sales	0·358
Rent/rates per sq. ft.	0·278	% males 16–64 years	−0·347
Urban growth rate	0·224	No. of selling staff	0·270
Rent and rates	0·196	Shop frontage	−0·269
Dis. to nr. competitor	0·195	Gross selling area	−0·264

Source: Davies, R. L., 'Evaluation of Retail Store Attributes and Sales
Performance', *European Journal of Marketing*, **7** (1973),
89–102.

force in more detail by referring back to the original data inputs and seeing if some remedial improvements can be introduced. It may also be desirable to identify the store more closely with a preferred type of clientele.

The factor scores can also be made the basis of a classification of stores, although more rigorous statistical grouping procedures are available to achieve this.[27] In this study, a grouping technique was used which linked each store with its next most similar store in such a way that a complete set of linkages could be built up, or to a point where six groups of stores were defined and closely associated with the six factors previously recognised. The six groups could then be used either to provide a sampling framework from which to identify some analogue models for new stores or as a means for comparing the relative trading performances of the existing stores. Some average retailing characteristics for each of the groups is shown in Table 9.4. In an evaluation exercise, however, there is usually less significance in comparing the stores of one group with those of another group, than with comparing the internal variations to be found against a group average. A selection of some extreme variations in sales for stores in group II is shown in Table 9.5. These are best interpreted in the context of the factor scores which the same stores registered in the earlier analysis, for the existence of very high or very low sales does not in itself reflect too cogently on the relative economic health of stores. To take an example, store

TABLE 9·4

Average Retail Statistics for Six Groups of Stores

Group	Annual Rent and Rates (£s)	Gross Selling Area (sq. ft.)	Major Product Sales (£s)	Total Employees
I	26,600	7,000	350,000	50
II	8,400	2,400	130,000	17
III	6,300	2,200	78,000	10
IV	11,500	3,200	105,000	14
V	15,500	2,200	100,000	15
VI	18,000	3,700	175,000	23

N.B. These figures are fictitious rather than actual records for the firm.

TABLE 9.5

Extreme Variations in Sales Performance for Stores in Group II

Store	Major Product Sales (£s)	Factor Scores 1	2	3	4	5	6
A	253,059	0·20	2·01	−0·68	−0·13	0·26	0·68
B	232,921	−0·43	1·02	0·57	0·55	0·00	1·47
C	232,217	0·12	0·79	0·82	−0·54	0·25	1·09
D	176,101	−0·23	0·74	−0·15	0·39	0·06	0·44
W	75,091	−1·17	−0·63	−0·44	0·14	−1·86	0·95
X	67,222	0·00	−1·17	−0·61	−0·29	−0·37	0·33
Y	66,811	−0·96	−0·50	0·02	1·87	−0·87	−0·57
Z	66,595	−1·31	−0·78	−0·09	0·24	−1·19	1·19

N.B. These figures are fictitious rather than actual records for the firm.

W shows a very low sales return but this is essentially explained through the high negative scores on factors 1 and 5 as being due to a very limited trade-area size and customer support drawn almost exclusively from the lowest social classes. The relatively high positive score on factor 6 suggests that there is in fact a high level of selling efficiency in the store despite the difficult trading circumstances in which it is trying to operate. In store X, in contrast, the low sales figure is accounted for primarily by the high negative scores on factors 2 and 3 which closer inspection reveals to mean a very small store area, a short frontage, an unsatisfactory location and a poor quality image. Given that this store occurs in a large city with a much greater mixture of socio-economic classes, some improvements in the physical premises and probably the site are clearly desirable.

Regression Equations

The strong relationship that exists between a number of the variables referred to above suggests that another possible approach to forecasting the sales potential of a store, and other characteristics such as its size and employment requirements, is the use of regression analysis. This does not appear to have been widely used in practice, however, until relatively recently. This seems rather curious given the widespread use of ratios between various store characteristics and the subjective comparisons which are frequently drawn. Applebaum,[28] for example, has emphasised the close relationship that exists between store sales and profitability and also such characteristics as the type of centre occupied, the income levels of the population served, the amount of competition faced, the age of a store, and so on. Some of the evidence he cites is indicated in Table 9.6.

TABLE 9.6

*Examples of Supermarket Sales and Profitability
in Relation to Selected Locational Characteristics*

	Store Sales	Store Profitability
	(Company Average $= 1 \cdot 0$)	
Types of Locations		
Planned Regional Centre	2·2	1·3
Planned Neighbourhood Centre	1·7	1·3
Unplanned Regional Centre	1·3	1·2
Unplanned Neighbourhood Centre	1·1	1·0
Main Centre of Small Towns	0·8	0·9
Family Incomes		
Under $3,000	0·5	0·8
$3,000–$4,999	0·9	0·9
$5,000–$7,999	1·2	1·0
Over $8,000	1·6	1·5
Level of Competition		
Inferior to Competitors	0·6	0·7
Equal to Competitors	0·9	0·9
Superior to Competitors	1·3	1·2
Ages of Stores		
Over 20 years	0·3	0·6
10–20 years	0·7	1·0
7–10 years	1·0	1·5
5– 7 years	1·3	1·7
3– 5 years	1·1	1·1
Under 3 years	1·0	0·5

Source: Applebaum, W., 'Store Characteristics and Operating Performance', in Kornblau, C. (ed.), *Guide to Store Location Research* (Addison-Wesley, 1968).

Both simple and multiple regression analysis may be usefully used in conjunction with the factor analytic and classificatory studies referred to in the previous section. Here the main objective will be to discriminate from a vast array of data those particular variables which are most indicative or diagnostic of the relative trading performances of stores. A variant procedure known as step-wise multiple regression analysis is especially helpful in this respect since it shows through a series of successive steps the order in importance of those variables which explain the variation in performance to be found. An example for the case-study into tailoring stores is given in Table 9.7. Three separate models for three samples of stores are shown: initially for the total of stores and then for the sub-groups of stores on corner-sites and those

TABLE 9.7

Examples of a Step-Wise Multiple Regression Analysis

Step Variables Entered	R	R^2	Increase
A. For the Total Stores			
1. Gross Selling Area	0·737	0·544	0·544
2. Rent and Rates	0·797	0·635	0·091
3. Dis. to Nr. Car Park	0·810	0·657	0·021
4. No. of Branches	0·825	0·680	0·024
5. Store Accessibility	0·844	0·712	0·031
B. For Corner Site Stores			
1. Gross Floor Area	0·806	0·650	0·650
2. Store Accessibility	0·832	0·692	0·042
3. No. of Branches	0·850	0·723	0·030
4. Urban Growth Rate	0·873	0·762	0·039
5. Dis. to Nr. Car Park	0·895	0·800	0·038
C. For Intermediate Site Stores			
1. Tot. Urb. Ret. Exp.	0·688	0·473	0·473
2. Store Accessibility	0·805	0·649	0·176
3. Gross Selling Area	0·844	0·712	0·063
4. Gross Floor Area	0·859	0·738	0·026
5. No. of Multiples	0·872	0·761	0·023

Source: Davies, R. L., 'Evaluation of Retail Store Attributes and Sales Performance', *European Journal of Marketing,* **7** (1973), 89–102.

which occupy more intermediate sites. The dependent variable that is explained in each case is the variation in major product sales. In the model for the total stores, the single most important explanatory variable is the gross selling area or size of a store (accounting for over fifty-four per cent of the total variation in sales); next in importance is the rent and rates which are paid (adding a further nine per cent level of explanation); then comes distance to the nearest car park, the number of associated branch stores found in the same centre, and an index reflecting the condition of a store's accessibility.

These types of model may be used for forecasting purposes in two distinct ways.[29] First, it is possible to predict in the short term the sales level that should be achieved in a new store from the coefficients obtained in a best-fit equation for those existing stores that are most analogous to it. This can be undertaken for a variety of assumptions regarding its size and the rents and rates that are likely to be paid, but variables such as the distance to the nearest car park and the number of associated branch stores found are likely to be fixed by the location selected. Secondly, it is possible to predict an improvement or contraction in sales level for an existing store given future changes in the nature of its operating circumstances. This can be illustrated by reference to a hypothetical equation for the five variables described above:

$$Y = 3600 \cdot 0 + 25 \cdot 80(X_1) + 4 \cdot 20(X_2) - 35 \cdot 60(X_3) + 8500 \cdot 05(X_4) - 6600 \cdot 0(X_5).$$

This suggests that an increase of 100 square feet in the gross selling area of a store will lead on average to increased sales of £2,580; an increase in annual rent and rates of £1,000 should be commensurate with increased sales of £4,200; a reduction of 100 yards in the distance to the nearest car park will lead to increased sales of £3,560; the effect of an addition to the number of branch stores found will eventually be beneficial to trade to the extent of £8,500 (because of the compatibility between stores in this chain); and an improvement in the condition of a store's accessibility by a factor of one (in a limited scale of 1 to 5) will lead to increased sales of £6,600.

Regression models can also be usefully employed in a retrospective way for evaluating the relative economic health of existing stores.[30] The main avenue to be followed here is simply to compare a predicted or expected sales level for any individual store against its actual sales record for the current or past year. The difference or residual obtained will then reflect the extent to which the store is performing better or worse than the average for the chain (or some more appropriate sample taken from within it). Most interest will centre on those stores with an extremely high residual. The reasons which explain an excessively good or poor sales performance will be found from a closer inspection of the raw data for such stores. This can also be supplemented by an examination of the factor scores recorded in any preliminary factor analysis.

Considerable care and attention needs to be given to the way in which a regression equation is used and interpreted, however. It is particularly important to ensure that there is a distinct 'cause and effect' relationship between the independent variables and the dependent variable. In the example referred to above, the size of a store is taken to be a significant variable explaining sales, but in many other case-studies (and especially in the context of convenience-goods stores rather than durable-goods stores) it is likely to be less a real 'cause' of sales than an 'effect' of them. Often, simply increasing the size of a store can lead to an initial growth in sales, but then a threshold level is reached beyond which there is no further material benefit. It is the identification of this threshold level or optimum size for a store, in fact, which should normally constitute the end product of store location and store assessment research as we have already indicated.

A number of modifications and refinements can be made to these types of models, nevertheless, and particularly to help alleviate the statistical problems that are frequently encountered from the assortment of data used. In this connection, Heald[31] has suggested a sequence of procedures that involves fitting non-linear equations to the most significant variables and then examining the structural relationships or inter-dependencies between them. This latter step takes the form of an AID (automatic interaction detector) program[32] that works in a reverse order to the grouping techniques that we have mentioned earlier. Briefly, the program disaggregates the most important variables accounting for sales into pairs of sub-samples with differing levels of explanation. In a hypothetical example of this, the first break in the linkage tree occurs over the sizes of the stores. At the second break, the larger stores are found to be particularly influenced by the proximity of key-traders or magnet stores, when the smaller stores are more sensitive to the amount of competition. At the third break, the larger stores are seen to be more dependent on an effective size of population support, when the smaller stores are more susceptible to social class conditions. Further interpretations can be continued in this way but become increasingly more difficult and generally less meaningful as the samples for each variable become progressively reduced.

Heald's own particular case-studies involving the AID program, however, have been severely criticised for demonstrating a mis-use rather than proper application of the potentialities of the technique.[33] The most serious limitation concerns the number of stores that he has dealt with (a total of seventy in the example quoted above). Morgan and Sonquist, the developers of the technique, provide a clear 'warning to potential users of the program —data sets with a thousand cases or more are necessary; otherwise the power of the search processes must be restricted drastically or these processes will carry one into a never-never land of idiosyncratic results.'[34] This virtually rules out the application of the technique to all but the largest chain organisations. The program also operates in such a way that once a given variable has been selected, certain other variables that might be closely associated with it and almost as discriminating, are less likely to be included. The technique therefore does not order the variables in terms of their relative importance in explaining store trading performance in the way Heald claims. Neither is the technique seen to be appropriate, as a sorting procedure, for reducing the overall complexity of those variables affecting store trading performance and identifying the most significant ones. Doyle maintains that 'the correct approach to the dimensionality problem is to explore the correlations among the predictors (independent variables) and either discard some of them as redundant or use principal components analysis'[35] (i.e. factor analysis). He also stresses that the AID program should be used as a basis for the improvement of regression models rather than a logical development or extension from them.

SUMMARY

The literature to be found in the academic journals on the subject of store location and store assessment research is sparse in comparison to the amount of work that is actually conducted by firms. It represents the tip of an iceberg that requires much greater exposure and detailed examination. In this chapter, we have only been able to present the more general locational principles and techniques of analysis that are applicable to retailing businesses as a whole. Clearly, the specific importance or relevance of these to individual companies will vary according to the size of their operations, the particular line of trade they are engaged in, and the types of customers which they seek to serve. There is a pressing need for a much greater reporting through both the academic and business media of case-studies conducted in relation to different kinds of problems. That literature which is available at the present time is heavily focused towards food retailing and particularly the problems experienced by supermarkets. Much more information is required about the locational principles and forecasting and evaluation techniques used by such businesses as shoe firms, television rental firms and petroleum companies. As in the field of retail planning, however, the use of forecasting and evaluation techniques in conjunction with store location and store-assessment research is fraught with difficulties that should not be under-estimated and the adoption of a more scientific approach should not be divorced from the subjective assessments or even 'hunches' of experienced employees. The major benefit of the techniques we have described in fact is probably to confirm or reject the intuitive feelings already held inside a company. They are particularly helpful in elucidating those inter-relationships between the multiplicity of factors which are inevitably involved in any location or assessment decision. The development of an effective research methodology using recent multi-variate statistical procedures, however, requires a much closer collaboration between academics and business personnel than has hitherto been found, especially in Britain. The academic can never really make a practical contribution without embroiling himself in the actual problems encountered by a firm and gaining access to its trading records; at the same time, the businessman is usually too busy or immersed in other requirements to spend time and allocate resources to the necessary experimental work that must usually precede the establishment of some useful techniques.

REFERENCES

1. Applebaum, W., 'Can Store Location Research be a Science?', *Economic Geography*, **41** (1965), 234–7.
2. The most comprehensive study to-date on the principles of the location selection process is Nelson, R. L., *The Selection of Retail Locations* (Dodge, 1958).
3. These elements are considered in more detail and in a more specific context in Applebaum, W. and Cohen, S. B., 'Evaluating Store Sites and Determining Store Rents', *Economic Geography*, **36** (1960), 1–35.
4. Numerous examples of the types of maps useful for this purpose are contained in Applebaum, W. and Schell, E., 'Marketing Maps for Store Location Studies', Chapter 22 in Kornblau, C. (ed.), *Guide to Store Location Research* (Addison-Wesley, 1968). Other chapters in this book deal with the use of census and other published information and also various methods for measuring trade areas.
5. Various methods for measuring the amount of competition found are described in Kornblau, C. and Baker, G. L., 'A Guide to Evaluating Competition', Chapter 20 in Kornblau, C. (ed.), *op. cit.*
6. For a definition and discussion of the meaning of saturation, see Applebaum, W. and Cohen, S. B., 'Trading Area Networks and Problems of Store Saturation', *Journal of Retailing*, **37** (1961), 32–55. See also, Cohen, S. B., 'The Problem of Store Overbuilding' in Cohen, S. B. (ed.), *Store Location Research for the Food Industry* (National-American Wholesale Grocers Association, 1963).
7. Nelson, R. L., *op. cit.*
8. Nelson, R. L., *op. cit.*
9. A more detailed discussion of site factors is contained in Epstein, B., 'Geography and the Business of Retail Site Evaluation and Selection', *Economic Geography*, **47** (1971), 192–9.
10. Kane, B. J., *A Systematic Guide to Supermarket Location Analysis* (Fairchild, 1966).
11. The role of negotiations in determining store rents is discussed in Applebaum, W., 'Toward a Better Understanding of Store Site Evaluation and Rentals', in American Marketing Association, *The Frontiers of Marketing Thought and Science* (New York, 1957).
12. Applebaum, W., 'Store Location Research—A Survey by Retailing Chains', *Journal of Retailing*, **40** (1964), 53–6.

13. Nelson, R. L., *op. cit.*

14. Green, H. L., 'Planning a National Retail Growth Programme', *Economic Geography*, **37** (1961), 22–32.

15. Ransome, J. C., 'The Organisation of Location Research in a Large Supermarket Chain', *Economic Geography*, **37** (1961), 42–7.

16. This may also be determined from a Reilly break-point model. See Converse, P. D., 'New Laws of Retail Gravitation', *Journal of Marketing*, **14** (1949), 379–84.

17. Applebaum, W. and Spears, R. F., 'How to Measure a Store Trade Area', Chapter 23 in Kornblau, C. (ed.), *op. cit.*

18. Huff, D. L., 'Defining and Estimating a Trading Area', *Journal of Marketing*, **28** (1964), 34–8.

19. Applebaum, W. and Cohen, S. B., 'The Dynamics of Store Trading Areas and Market Equilibrium', *Annals of the Association of American Geographers*, **51** (1961), 73–101.

20. Imus, H. R., 'Projecting Sales Potentials for Department Stores in Regional Shopping Centres', *Economic Geography*, **37** (1961), 33–41.

21. Nelson, R. L., *op. cit.*

22. Applebaum, W., 'Advanced Methods for Measuring Store Trade Areas and Market Penetration', Chapter 24 in Kornblau, C. (ed.), *op. cit.*

23. See Kane, B. J., *op. cit.*

24. See Applebaum, W., 'The Analogue Method for Estimating Potential Store Sales', Chapter 27 in Kornblau, C. (ed.), *op. cit.*

25. Davies, R. L., 'Evaluation of Retail Store Attributes and Sales Performance', *European Journal of Marketing*, **7** (1973), 89–102.

26. For detailed, technical descriptions of this technique, see Cattell, R. B., 'Factor Analysis: Introduction to Essentials', *Biometrics*, **21** (1965), 190–405; Rummell, L., *Applied Factor Analysis* (Chicago, 1970).

27. See Frank, R. E. and Green, P. E., 'Numerical Taxonomy in Marketing Research', *Journal of Market Research*, **5** (1968), 83–93.

28. Applebaum, W., 'Store Characteristics and Operating Performance', Chapter 10 in Kornblau, C. (ed.), *op. cit.*

29. Davies, R. L., *op. cit.*

30. Davies, R. L., *op. cit.*

31. Heald, G., 'The Application of AID Programme and Multiple Regression Techniques to the Assessment of Store Performance and Site Selection', *Operational Research Quarterly*, **23** (1972), 445–57.

32. Morgan, J. N. and Sonquist, J. A., 'The Determination of Interaction Effects', *University of Michigan, Survey Research Centre Monograph No. 35* (1964).

33. Doyle, P., 'The Use of Automatic Interaction Detector and Similar Search Procedures', *Operational Research Quarterly*, **24** (1973), 465–7; Robinson, N., 'Application of Automatic Interaction Detector Programme', *Operational Research Quarterly*, **24** (1973), 469.

34. Sonquist, J. A., Baker, E. L. and Morgan, J. N., *Searching for Structure: Alias AID III* (University of Michigan, 1971).

35. Doyle, P., *op. cit.*

10 Conclusion

Inevitably in a book of this kind there will be important aspects of the subject that are given only scant attention or passing reference. The topics selected here are those which have been most fully reported in the geographical rather than marketing literature and which have particular interest or significance from the spatial point of view. Topics which regrettably have had to be neglected include: the patterns of movement in the physical distribution of goods from producers to retail and service outlets; areal differences in the trading policies and organisational structure of firms; the layout of individual business establishments and the circulation of consumers inside them; the special problems involved in the accessibility of shops, particularly in terms of the delivery of goods and consumer use of car parks and bus-stops. The whole field of wholesaling and related commercial service activities has had to be virtually eliminated from the book; and international comparisons in the field of retailing have had to be restricted to North America and Western Europe. There is also the problem in this type of book that much of the statistical data that are presented become changed or outdated by the time of publication. The book pre-empts the final tabulations of the 1971 Census of Distribution which had still not appeared by the end of 1974.

The main objective throughout this book has been to demonstrate that there is a large and distinctive body of geographical work that collectively give credence to a field of study called marketing geography. There are particularly strong relationships between marketing geography and the retail problems encountered in planning and business and hence the subject may be regarded as a key element in Applied Geography. The links in advisory and consultancy work that now exist are likely to be strengthened in the future through the increasing recognition being given by both planners and businessmen to the practical contributions of the subject. Although the methodology of marketing geography originated in the USA there is sufficient similarity in the underlying principles of market behaviour between different countries—despite environmental and societal differences—to give the subject a clear international applicability.

In Britain, there are two major problems which, above all else, will continue to dominate the thinking of academics, planners and businessmen alike. The first concerns the general issue of how far retailing and related service investments should continue to be concentrated in the main centres of towns and what scope exists for permitting a greater degree of suburban expansion. The second concerns the extent to which the existing pattern of business activities in the rest of the city should be preserved or changed from its traditional form. In each of these cases, the marketing geographer's role should be to provide an evaluation of the alternative courses of action available and particularly in terms of what will bring most benefit to the consumer or the community at large. A balanced and imaginative approach is essential for there is an increasing trend towards a polarisation of attitudes and the provision of stereotyped solutions from planners and businessmen alike. The underlying requirements are clear; there must be a considerable improvement in both the conditions and opportunities for shopping for all sections of the population, for minority groups as well as the bulk middle class.

The key to an effective geographical contribution, however, rests in the development of more substantive and flexible theories than are currently available for guiding a future pattern of business activities and understanding the tastes and preferences of the population. Central place theory contains much that is relevant to the domestic shopping system in Britain but it does not illuminate the locational requirements of service activities or even certain specialised retailing activities. Neither does it provide a basis for adjudicating the proportion of retail investment which should be concentrated in the central area rather than other centres given the types of circumstances that already exist. A design framework that allows for the provision of new forms of strip development and specialised functional areas in the outer parts of the city is particularly needed. General interaction theory is similarly limited. While it provides a useful means of fore-casting aggregate demand for future domestic shopping goods it does not accommodate the changing attitudes of the population or the variability in behaviour of different consumer groups. It lacks relevance to the role of leisure and service pursuits within shopping trips and is insensitive to the way in which consumers discriminate between individual shops. A much deeper insight into the complexities of consumer behaviour is needed if the diminishing number of retail facilities are to be kept in harmony with what is actually required.

The main areas of planning responsibility lie in a more comprehensive approach to dealing with problems throughout the distributive trades and establishing in principle, if not in legislation, a determination to control all future major retailing investments on a regional or sub-regional scale. Most current urban development plans (including the new wave of structure plans) make a simplistic distinction between two components only of the distributive trades: the locational requirements and demand to be met for the future domestic shopping system; and the areas that are suitable for allocating to wholesaling, warehousing and like kinds of commerce. No separate recognition is given of the needs of a wide assortment of retail-related service activities, a majority of which are now confined to the inner city and which are steadily being eradicated through redevelopment schemes. This is tantamount to an industrial policy that focuses attention on the needs of the extractive and manufacturing industries but fails to acknowledge the role of the utility services or office employment. Moreover most authorities still act independently to encourage as much retail investment in their own towns as they possibly can. Each town is endeavouring to enhance its overall hierarchical shopping status with the result that there has been a substantial decline in the viability of many small centres and an over-provision of new retail floorspace in the largest ones. The total projected new retail floorspace for the largest centres in North-East England far outweighs the calculated requirement for the region as a whole.

The record of business in terms of its own contribution to the spatial evolution of the distributive trades has been a mixed one. There has been a wide spectrum of different influences at work, some of which have clearly been more irresponsible than others. The North-American retail environment provides a striking example of both the achievements and abuses that may be realised in a relatively free spatial economy. In Britain, businesses have generally been restricted both from playing a creative or innovative locational role and from doing anything substantially detrimental. The pressures exerted from business towards a greater relaxation of the constraints on decentralisation, however, have not been as well co-ordinated or strongly pressed as is commonly supposed. It is primarily the convenience trades which have argued for more suburban expansion and many of their proposals and applications for new sites have not been carefully thought through. A more articulate expression of the logic of their needs would likely bring a much better response in terms of new locational opportunities in the future. An additional area of business responsibility, however, lies in an improvement in the design and layout of individual shops and shopping centres. This extends to such considerations as the architecture and building materials involved, the provision of good amenities and accessibility, and a general air of comfort and attractiveness that comes from a greater attention to detail.

It is extremely difficult to speculate about the future pattern of business activities in Britain. It is much easier to diagnose the problems and suggest the kinds of improvements that ought to be made than it is to actually perceive what the real outcome will be. Inevitably there will be a continuing decline in the numbers of individual business establishments and an increasing growth in the size of chain stores. These will remain predominantly located in the main centres of towns although there will be a proportionately much greater number of supermarkets in the suburbs. Shopping itself is likely to become much more sharply differentiated into two categories of minor and major trips, though the purposes of these will be considerably mixed and much less closely associated with the traditional distinctions between convenience- and durable-goods or specialised trips. While there may be an overall improvement in the ease and enjoyment of shopping, there will also be a much greater uniformity in the types of stores to be found and in the kinds of goods which are sold. The inner city and central area will initially see the most dramatic changes, but in the longer term future there will probably be substantive developments in the middle belts of residential areas (or inner suburbs), particularly in terms of the amalgamation of shops. This may be accomplished through a growth in the size units of the voluntary chains or a stronger penetration by the discount-type stores. Perhaps the overall feature of most significance, however, will be a growth in the imbalance of areal resources and the standards of retail and related service provisions to be found, not only in different parts of the city but also from one type of urban area to another. To end on this somewhat pessimistic note is perhaps an indictment of the current trends in shopping provision. Our hope, of course, is that in some small way the material and discussion provided in this book will help to steer both business and the public away from this course.

Author Index

293

Subject Index